A Thousand Miles of Miracle in China (Annotated)

A. E. Glover

Annotations and Questions to Consider
by Clint Morey

MISSOULA, MONTANA

"Therefore, since we are surrounded by such a great cloud of witnesses, let us throw off everything that hinders and the sin that so easily entangles. And let us run with perseverance the race marked out for us ..."

—HEBREWS 12:1 (NIV)

A NOTE FROM CLINT MOREY

About this Book

Time passes quickly.

Events which once captured the attention of the world's nations quickly fade to short paragraphs in the history books, or tiny footnotes, or even disappear from public consciousness altogether.

The boxer uprising of 1900 is one of those events.

Although secular historians will tell you that it was a battle between the "traditional" Chinese and the "Western interlopers" it was, in fact, a spiritual battle for the very souls of the Chinese people.

European nations had established beachheads within the country and were seeking economic advantage even if that "economic advantage" meant turning many of the Chinese people into opium addicts.

To the secular historians, the western missionaries were little more than extensions of the unwelcome Western governments.

They ignore the work of these missionaries (such as reaching into the opium dens to reclaim lives), the missionaries' condemnation of the actions of their governments, and characterize the misisonaries as people trying to impose their culture upon another people.

The missionaries had come to tell the Chinese people about a God who loved them. They weren't seeking economic advantage or financial gain. Many of those missionaries were willing to give up comfortable and even prosperous lives in Europe and America to share God's love with others. And many Chinese responded to that message and became followers of Christ.

But secular historians don't see that aspect of life. Or at least don't see it as important.

So why bother reading a book over one hundred years old that tells of an event few even know about?

Good question.

The fact is, persecution of Christians is not confined to the distant past.

In today's world many places are decidedly uncomfortable for Christians.

APRIL 2014: In Cairo, Egypt, twenty-five year old Mary Sameh George, a Coptic Christian, was planning to deliver medicine to an elderly woman. A group of Muslim Brotherhood supporters saw her enter her car near a church. They climbed on the car, collapsed the roof, pulled her from the car, beat her, ripped off portions of her scalp, stabbed her multiple times, and slit her throat. Leaving her dead body in the street, they set fire to her car.

MAY 2014: In China, government officials arrested ten leaders of the large Sanjiyang Church, forced others out of the area and proceeded to destroy their church. "Employing such high pressure tactics is not uncommon for Chinese government official attempting to silence outspoken Christian leaders." (International Christian Concern)

JANUARY 2014: A study from the Pew Research Center indicates that restricitions on religion are at a six year high.

Their study also indicated that Christians are persecuted in more countries than any other religious group.

Looking at people who have gone through persecutions for their faith in the past will help us understand, support, and pray for people going through persecutions today. It's important that we don't just glance at a news item about someone being persecuted, feel sorry for them for just a moment, then move on to the sports news or the latest update on some media star.

It is also important for those of us living in "safe" cultures to realize that one day we may actually be called upon to go through hardships and difficulties because of our faith.

I'm not talking about TV comedians making jokes about Christians on a late night show or co-workers making snide comments in the workplace.

The day may come when God calls us to walk through the fire.

If we do have to go through such days, it will be helpful to remember "the great cloud of witnesses" who've gone before us.

We can draw strength from their courage and endurance and comfort from seeing God at work even in seemingly untenable situations.

A Thousand Miles of Miracle by A.E. Glover is one of those stories that should challenge you to grow in your faith and encourage you to trust in God in all circumstances.

As you read through the book, consider how you would have faced situations the Glover's went through. Ask God to increase your faith and trust in Him.

We have been allowed to have a part in this battle for the eternal souls of men.

God has chosen you to live in this time period in your location so that people can come to know Jesus as the Savior of their souls.

> *"From one man he made all the nations, that they should inhabit the whole earth; and he marked out their appointed times in history and the boundaries of their lands. God did this so that they would seek him and perhaps reach out for him and find him, thought he is not far from any one of us." (Acts 17:26-27)*

As you read this one hundred year old story, ask God to show you how He wants to use you today, in the world where He has placed you.

CONTENTS

A Thousand Miles of Miracle in China

A PERSONAL RECORD OF GOD'S DELIVERING POWER
FROM THE HANDS OF THE IMPERIAL
BOXERS OF SHAN-SI.

BY

ARCHIBALD E. GLOVER, M.A. (Oxon.),

of the China Inland Mission

WITH MAP AND THIRTY-SIX SPECIAL ILLUSTRATIONS.

ELEVENTH EDITION
(completing 23,000 copies).
Translated into Swedish, German, and Arabic.

PICKERING & INGLIS
GLASGOW   LONDON   EDINBURGH

INTRODUCTORY

In the spring of the year 1894 I received a clear call from God to the privileged service of the Mission Field in China. Little did I imagine, as I heard His voice saying to me, "Depart ; for I will send thee far hence unto the heathen," that the call was to mean primarily, "I will show him how great things he must suffer for My Name's sake."

Two years later, in the autumn of 1896, I left for my appointed sphere in connection with the China Inland Mission, joining Mr. Stanley Smith (the well-known Cambridge "blue," and leader of the missionary band known as "The Cambridge Seven") at the prefectural city of Lu-an, in the Province of Shansi, North China. In association with him (truly a brother beloved), I passed, with my wife and family, three happy years, preaching among the heathen the unsearchable riches of Christ. In 1899, Mr. and Mrs. Stanley Smith took their fulough, and the charge of the Station thereupon devolved upon me.

Our party at the Mission Station of Lu-an Fu consisted of five Souls — my wife, a son and daughter (Hedley and Hope, aged four and three respectively), Miss Gates, and myself.

CHAPTER ONE

A Cloud Out of the Sea

*"Shall we receive good at the hand
of God, and shall we not receive evil?"*

*"For yourselves know that
we are hereunto appointed."*

"From the year 1661 to the year 1893 there were 130 Protestant Missionaries martyred in all parts of the world, while during 1900, and including the murder of Mr. Stenhouse in 1901, there were 136 Protestant Missionaries and 53 children (altogether 189) martyred in China alone. In Shan-si we had 88 workers in June, 1900. More than half that number were killed (47), only 41 escaping." (1)

It will be readily conceded, therefore, that this narrative touches a period without a parallel in the history of Missions. As I look back upon it in the light of all I have since learned of that hour of darkness, I marvel more and more at the miracle of deliverance God wrought for the 41 (myself amongst them) who came out alive from the bloodstained province of Shan-si. The fact can be explained upon no human method of interpretation. Unique as is the history in regard to the numbers of those who fell, it is scarcely less unique in regard to the numbers of those who escaped the edge of the sword of the " Great Sword Guild." (2)

1. Among natural causes that which should stand first undoubtedly is China's racial antipathy to foreigners and everything foreign. Speaking generally, hatred of the foreigner is in the blood of the Chinaman. This natural hatred has from generation to generation been fostered by a national exclusiveness born of an overweening pride which boasts that the world is a square, China a circle within it touching the four sides, and the four corners outside the circle the domain of the foreign barbarians. And of late years it has been fed by an ever deepening suspicion of the designs of foreign nations founded upon one demand for territory after another, which to the Celestial's mind boded nothing else than the eventual break- up of the Empire.

2. But this innate hatred had received a serious moral aggravation. The opium evil — England's sin and China's sorrow — was virtually forced upon her by the foreigner at the point of the bayonet; and from being merely a " foreigner' he has come to be in her eyes a 'foreign devil.' (3)

Can we wonder? The crying wrong rankles deep in the heart of the Chinese as a race, and it has never been forgiven.

In the province of Shan-si, where the writer was called to labour, the practice of opium eating was all but universal. It is no exaggeration to say that nine out of every ten of the entire population of the province are addicted to the habit more or less. And yet never does he remember meeting a China- man who did not look upon the indulgence as a vice. It is essentially sin (tsui) in his eyes. So much so that, where every other appeal to his moral consciousness seems to fail, you can always bring home to an opium smoker the fact that he is a sinner through the medium of his degrading habit. Not infrequently have we as Englishmen been cursed in the streets while preaching, for having brought in the devastating drug; and the average Chinese mind fails to comprehend how a "devil" who has helped to damn him, soul and body, can be taken up with a concern for his salvation. He argues, Who can bring a clean thing out of an unclean? and how can the Gospel of the love of God come from a land which sent the opium?

The following pregnant passages, furnished by Dr. Arthur H. Smith in his suggestive work *China in Convulsion* (vol. i., pp. 92 to 94), may well be digested by the unprejudiced reader who wishes to arrive at a right understanding of a vexed question from the Chinese point of view. "The use of opium in China is in- dissolubly linked with the foreigner, even in its name ('foreign earth'). While the Chinese have become almost a nation of opium smokers, the national con- science still exists, and vigorously protests against the habit which it is powerless to stop. It is easy to show that many of the most thoughtful of the Chinese in the Empire connect the decay of China and the general use of opium as cause and effect. The following pointed statement upon the subject is taken from the paper written by the Tao-t'ai of Soo Chow, who is in charge of the salt gabelle in that city: 'From ancient times to the present day there has never been such a stream of evil and misery as has come down upon China in her receiving the curse of opium. ... From the time that opium was first introduced into China until now, a period of over 100 years, the number of deaths caused by it must mount up into the millions. Now in China there are many among the upper classes who seem to be in ignorance concerning the true state of affairs, and are not willing to blame the Chinese for their fault in using opium, but ascribe the real cause of the trouble to the avariciousness of foreigners, and thus look upon them with hatred. Also the ignorant masses having even intenser antipathy towards them, we continually see on every hand anti-Missionary outbreaks and riots.'

"This passage is sufficiently explicit as to the Chinese hostility to *the instruments of the national ruin.* That the most intelligent men in China hold the strongest opinion as to the injury done by opium is easily proved; as, for instance, by the widely cir- culated and popular work of the celebrated Governor- General of the two Hu-kuang provinces, Chang Chih Tung, lately translated for English readers under the title of 'China's Only Hope.' In this there is a chapter headed 'Cast out the Poison,' from which the following paragraph is an extract : 'Assuredly it is not foreign intercourse that is ruining China, but this dreadful poison. Oh, the grief and desolation it has wrought to our people! A hundred years ago the curse came upon us, more blasting and deadly in its effects than the Great Flood, or the scourge of the Fierce Beasts; for the waters assuaged after nine years, and the ravages of the man-eaters were confined to one place. Opium has spread with frightful rapidity and heartrending results through the provinces. Millions upon millions have been stricken down by the plague.

To-day it is running like wildfire. In its swift deadly course, it is spreading devastation everywhere, wreck- ing the minds and eating away the strength and wealth of its victims. The ruin of the mind is the most woeful of its many deleterious effects. The poison en- feebles the will, saps the strength of the body, renders the consumer incapable of performing his regular duties, and unfit for travel from one place to another. It consumes his substance, and reduces the miserable wretch to poverty, barrenness and senility. Unless something is soon done to arrest this awful scourge in its devastating march, the Chinese people will be transformed into satyrs and devils. This is the pre- sent condition of our country.'

"When the most respected and most influential Chinese in the Empire addresses to his own countrymen words like these, it is evident that there is behind them a profound conviction. While His Excellency is at great pains to show that the Chinese are them- selves to blame for the ruin wrought by opium, *it is certain that most Chinese connect the misery, degradation, and wreck wrought by this baleful drug directly with the Western lands, through whose agency it became universally known, and that this fact has had an important influence in creating, and, from the Chinese point of view, justifying hostility to foreigners.* While no riot can be said to have had its origin solely through the use of opium, it is doubtful if there has ever been an outbreak in China against the men from beyond the sea which was not either started or promoted by opium smokers, at their places of resort where the worst characters in every Chinese city, market-town, and village are invariably attracted." (The italics are mine.)

3. Another disturbing cause of a local character was at work in Shan-si. The agents of the Peking Syndicate had during the preceding year been pro- specting for coal, iron and petroleum in the province ; and the suspicious fears of the people were more than aroused. To show how real a factor their coming was in the situation, Mr. A. R. Saunders, of the China Inland Mission, subsequently all but lost his life on the supposition that he was one of the obnoxious engineers; and we ourselves were narrowly questioned all along the route of our flight as to whether the busi- ness which had brought us into the interior were not of the same nature. There is no doubt that the memory of the visit of Messrs. Shockley and Sabioni (who repre- sented the Syndicate) to our own station of Lu-an, S. Shan-si, in the early months of the preceding year, contributed in measure to feed the rage of the people against us, when once it was set ablaze by the Boxer agitation.

4. The long prevailing drought and threatened famine was for us another most serious element in the situation. For several years in succession the harvest had been going from bad to worse, and the distress of the people of Lu-an was so great that in the summer of 1899 it all but culminated in a riot. Our premises and even our lives were threatened. The day of destruction was fixed; and we knew that nothing short of God's direct interposition could hinder them from carrying out their purpose. At the time the tumultuous rain-process on, numbering many thousands, was to repass our gates, we were

gathered for prayer. It was a solemn hour, for, humanly speaking, nothing could save us; but prayer was turned to praise as we heard the passing clash of the gongs, and mad beat of the drums, grow faint and die away in the distance. We learned later how God had wrought for us. Unknown to us, the Prefect had sent a detachment of soldiers to guard the gates, and himself, with several of the leading gentry of the city, stood by to hold the rioters in check.

This will suffice to show how desperate the situation might become if the drought continued on into the next year. As indeed it did. The Boxer movement found the people ripe for lawlessness, under the stress of circumstances which were sufficiently appalling. In our district the early wheat harvest was of the lightest, and as the weeks wore on and still no rain fell, the failure of the autumn crop became a certainty. The price of grain was steadily rising in the market, and the seed already sown was rotting in the ground.

April and May passed with nothing more than a bare sprinkling from a shower or two, which only seemed to mock their hopes; and measures must be resorted to. Orders were issued by the Prefect forbidding grain to be sold away from the district, and a city merchant who dared to disobey the order was heavily flogged and fined. But above all, the wrath of the gods who were withholding the rain must be appeased. Arrangements were made so early as the first week in June for a series of rain-processions through the streets and fields, while the Prefect himself made special pilgrimages to the city temple to entreat the favour of Heaven, and to know what he should do to secure it.

In times of public calamity, the superstitious mind of the heathen casts about in every direction for the cause; and, in the case of the Chinese, the scapegoat is invariably to be found in the hated foreigner. For some time wild rumours had been in circulation that we had poisoned all the wells, and this was so generally believed that my Evangelist would not allow me to take a long-looked-for itineration with him into the Tseh-cheo Prefecture, as he said it would be as much as my life was worth to show myself there.

Such a report was as fuel to fire. What with the drought and poisoned wells, we found that the attitude of the people was far from reassuring. From outward friendliness it had passed to indifference, but indiffer- ence was now giving way to unconcealed aversion and open contempt. The hissed "iang kuei-tsi!" ("foreign devil!") as we passed along the road became the rule rather than the exception, and a menace the significance of which was unmistakable. The women shrank from any contact with the lady mis- sionaries, and our services, at the church or on the street, were literally deserted. The rain did not come why? The answer the priests gave back was, "The foreigner has blasphemed our gods in proclaiming them to be no gods; and he has insulted their majesty by bringing in his own gods ; and foreign blood must be spilt before we can have rain."

5. It is a fact to be deeply deplored that one of the leading factors in the disquieted state of the people was the policy pursued by the Roman Catholic Church in China.

Mr. C. H. S. Green (C.I.M.), in telling the marvellous story of his deliverance from the Boxers (4), has not hesitated to affirm, on the universal testimony of the malcontents themselves, that Roman Catholicism alone is responsible for the creation of the Boxer Rising. That it was a powerful lever in setting the Boxer machinery in motion is unquestionable. Other inflammatory elements, however, were in the move- ment, as I have already indicated; and all these together conspired to bring the passions of the people to a head. Invariably the question (usually the first) put to us by the mob was; " What are you? Are you Roman Catholics?" Had we been, it is absolutely certain we should never have got through. If ever murderous hate looked out at the eyes of men, it was when that question was being asked. It is impossible to exaggerate the bitterness of the hatred that the Roman Catholics have brought upon themselves. Their aspiration to temporal power and Spirit of political intrigue; their secret, and withal Unscrupulous methods of work; their arrogant pretensions; their interference in the Law Courts, backed by threats of appeal to the Government of their country; their rule of celibate Living; their despotic exercise of priestly power — all this and more had provoked the natives to the point of exasperation.

A brother missionary working in An-huei once told me that, when itinerating in the north of that province where the Romanists had been labouring, he found that to mention the name of Jesus was to open the floodgates of blasphemy. To use his own words : "The Roman Catholics had made the name of Jesus literally to stink before the people; and the mere fact that the two religions owned the same Jesus for their God was enough in itself to defeat every effort to obtain a hearing for the Gospel."

6. From all this it will be readily seen that the state of popular feeling was ripe for any organized development of lawlessness; and it was taken full advantage of by the initiators of the Imperial Boxer Movement.

Whatever theories may be advanced to account for the origin of this remarkable disturbance, one thing at least may be safely affirmed, viz., that it was a movement "from beneath," immediately Satanic, the result of the necessary antagonism of darkness to light. It was a direct effect of the persistent advance of Gospel effort. Indeed, the victorious ingress of the true light into every part of the Empire could not fail to provoke sooner or later an organized opposition from the power of darkness, begotten of fear not less than of hatred.

The appeal made by this movement to the masses was not merely patriotic, nor was it even only anti- foreign. The writer would humbly venture upon the conviction that it was essentially and before all else religious. Directly recognized by "the Great Religion" — a blend of Buddhism, Taoism and Confucianism — one might almost say it was formally initiated under its auspices. So early as March, 1899, the *Buddhist* Llama Abbot gave it substantial support ; and later on the head of the *Taoist* sect, Pope Chang, in an interview with the Empress Dowager, counselled the slaughter of the foreigner. Close upon this fol- lowed an Imperial Edict of strong *Confucian* type, aimed directly at the Christian Religion, "ordering all civil and military officials to strictly observe the Sixteen Sacred Edicts of K'ang Hsi," and also the "Teachings of the Emperor Yung Cheng " against *heresy and heterodoxy*, and "to set apart certain days every month to explain the same to the masses."[1] On June 25 a proclamation, evidently the substance of the Imperial Decrees of the 21st of that month, was posted up at the telegraph office at T'ai- yuen Fu, the headquarters of Boxerism, which concluded thus: "Foreign religions are reckless and oppressive, disrespectful to the gods and oppressive to the people. The Righteous People (that is the I Ho Ch'uan, or Boxers) will burn and kill. Your judgments from Heaven are about to come. Turn from the heterodox and revert to the true. Is it not benevolence to exhort you people of the Christian Relgion? Therefore early reform. If you do your duty, you are good people. If you do not repent there will be no opportunity for after-regret. For this purpose is this proclamation put forth. Let all comply with it."[2]

Nay more, the style adopted by the Society itself was "The Buddhists' Patriotic League of Boxers." Their banners bore the legend, "*Feng Chi Mieh Kiao*" — "By Imperial command exterminate the Christian Religion." The decrees they issued were given out as the very utterance of the gods them- selves, and flamed with all the fervour of religious fanaticism. They professed themselves to be moving by the command of Heaven, and they claimed to be under the immediate favour, control and protec- tion of Heaven. The qualifying tests to which the recruit was subjected on enlistment were before all else religious. He was required to repeat over and over a certain brief formula, "*until the gods took possession,* and the subject fell backwards to the ground foaming at the mouth and lying for a few minutes as in a trance, then rising to drill or to fight," whereupon he was declared to be invulnerable to foreign sword and bullet. They were for the gods, therefore the gods were for them. In a word, the movement was dominated by the religious idea. True , it was directed against the foreigner as such; but the root of the trouble lay not so much in the innovation of his barbarous civilization and of his Blasphemous religion. That this was so is evidenced beyond Dispute by the Boxer manifestoes.

What, therefore, we were called to face was distinctively a religious persecution. The foreigner was to be dealt with primarily on the ground that he was a religious propagandist, "a setter forth of strange gods." On one occasion during our flight we were sitting by the roadside hemmed in by an armed mob, from whom we were momentarily expecting death. I had spoken a few words on the Gospel message of the love of God, when they began at once to blaspheme, and one cried out, "Away with your Shang-ti (God) ! We will drive him beyond the sea, never to return." At another time, while I was speaking to the soldiers who guarded us in the cart, one of them said, "Stop that talk ! Don't you know that the Emperor has made it a State crime to preach the Jesus doctrine! Your Jesus has brought trouble enough to China, but China will have no more of Him now for ever."

The Boxer rising would have been formidable in any case, but when the movement received the Imperial sanction and support, all hope of our being able to remain was gone. The masses welcomed it as their great opportunity . Yu-hsien, the newly appointed Viceroy of the Province of Shan-si, lost no time in transferring the headquarters of the movement from Shan-tung (the sphere of his former rule) to his new command; and his plans were quickly matured for the extermination of the Christian religion in the destruction of all who believed, natives and foreigners alike. It was soon in the air that he had the Empress Dowager behind him, and ere long it was openly con- firmed by the attitude of the officials themselves. We were informed that they had received instructions to withdraw all protection from us; and from that hour we knew we were at the mercy of the merciless mob.

7. How precious at such a time t be able to "look, not at the things that are seen, but at the things that are not seen"! All

that contributed to this great upheaval was after all subservient to and controlled by a Cause that was far above out of men's sight, revealed to the eye of faith alone. It lay in the determinate counsel and foreknowledge of God. The heathen might rage, and the rulers be gathered together against the Lord and against His Christ ; but they could do no more than "whatsoever Thy hand and Thy counsel determined before to be done." But for this knowledge our hearts would have fainted indeed. That our God was behind the persecution, and would make the wrath of man to praise" Him, was a fact in which we found true rest and comfort. Through all the evil, He was working out His own good and glorifying His own Name. Had He not a gracious purpose in view? For —

(1) Was He not granting us the high privilege of knowing in measure the fellowship of the sufferings of His own beloved Son?

(2) Was not the persecution His call to the pastors and teachers, native and foreign, to fulfil their ministry in filling up that which is behind of the afflictions of Christ, for His Body's sake?

(3) Did He not design by the persecution the purification of His Church in China ?

(4) Was it not the only way known to His wisdom in which the answer could be given to our constant prayers for the opening of "a great door and effectual" to the Word of His grace ?

(5) Was it not His opportunity in us for proving to the native converts the power of the truth we had so often preached, namely, that we should "take pleasure in necessities, in persecutions, in distresses, for Christ's sake," and "rejoice that we are counted worthy to suffer shame for His Name"?

(6) Was it not meant to be, to ourselves individually, an evident token of salvation, and that of God, a seal of our sonship, and a means by which we might become "partakers of His holiness"?

(7) And was it not, after all, only what He told us to expect as the appointed portion of all who will to live godly in Christ Jesus and enter the Kingdom of God?

Yes, there was a needs-be for our sufferings. The silver lining to the cloud out of the sea, was "the eternal purpose of Him Who worketh all things after the counsel of His own will," the Cause behind the causes. And in Him we had peace.

Questions to Consider

*1. Glover points out the terrible actions of the foreign
nations in their treatment of China. Many Chinese
blamed all foreigners. Should the missionaries not
have come to China because their governments did not
deal honorably with the Chinese?*

*2. A theme that will reappear throughout this story is a
dislike (I think hatred might be too strong a word) for
the Roman Catholic Church in China. Do you think
this impacted the ministry of Glover and other
Protestant missionaries?*

*3. Do you think this was a spiritual battle or were the
Boxers just nationalists?*

CHAPTER TWO

The Cloud Upon Our Horizon

"What time I am afraid, I will put my trust in Thee."

The first week in the April of the year 1900 we had the joy of welcoming to our station the veteran missionary, Mr. Alexander Grant (of Singapore and Amoy), who was returning to the coast from the provincial capital, T'ai-yuen Fu, where he had been visiting his married daughter and her husband, Dr. and Mrs. Lovitt, of the Sheo Iang Mission. He was accompanied by Mr. Hoddle, an independent worker in the city of T'ai-yuen. Though they had come from the capital, they had no evil tidings to bring us. Everything was, to all outward appearance, just as usual. How little we dreamed as we met together in happy fellowship what three months hence would have to reveal! Mr. Grant a refugee, barely escaping with his life and only with the loss of all his effects. Mr. Hoddle (together with Dr. and Mrs. Lovitt and some forty other foreign workers) beheaded and in a martyr's grave. Our own station rioted, and ourselves stripped of all and in the hands of the Boxers.

The first intimation I had of the existence of such a movement was through my serving boy, Chu-ri, asking me (I think in February) to let him go home to Shan-tung to look after a small patrimony, which was, he said, being "threatened by the Ta Tao Huei."

"And what may the Ta Tao Hnei be?" I inquired.

"What! hasn't the pastor heard of what is going on in Shan-tung? The 'Guild of the Great Sword' are looting the houses of the Christians, and even putting some to death."

No, I had not heard it. I gave him leave of course to go, though of course also I took his statement with a grain of salt, as one learns involuntarily to do in China, and dismissed it from my mind. Little did I think how that expression "Ta Tao Huei," which fell upon my ears then for the first time, was to be burned in anguish into my very soul.^

Not long after this I received a circular letter from my friend Mr. Horace Houlding, who was pioneering in South Chih-li. It dealt at length and in the most serious strain with the doings of the Boxers and their appearance in the immediate neighbourhood of his own Mission. One sentence went through me: " Who can tell where unto this will grow?" and instinctively I felt the indefinable dread of the certainty that we too would be involved. I tried to put it from me, but the thought remained; and then I took it in secret to God and left it with Him.

Immediately after Mr. Grant and Mr. Hoddle had left us, I accompanied Dr. Julius Hewett (of the neigh- bouring station of Yu-wu) on an itineration to Kao-p'ing Hsien in the Tseh-cheo Prefecture. While preaching on the street of the south suburb of the city on the first evening of our arrival, voices in the crowd called out, "You foreigners won't be here long. The Ta Tao Huei are going to kill you all. Look out!" Everything, however, on the journey was quiet, and a respectful hearing was very generally given to our message; and so we treated the remark as somewhat of an idle tale. But the words rang again in my ears, "Who can tell whereunto this will grow?" and in spite of myself the old forebodings came back upon me in force.

Later on I saw, in these occasional intimations, the mercy of God in preparing us for what was coming.

On May 28, we were visited by our beloved Deputy Director, Mr. William Cooper, in the course of a syste- matic visitation of the Shan-si stations of our Mission. He was accompanied by Mr. David Barratt, of Ioh- iang. The news he brought from the west of the province confirmed the truth of the previous intimations. Yu-hsien had been installed in the Vice-royalty on April 18, and was doing his utmost to foster the movement in Shan-si. His emissaries were everywhere in evidence, recruiting in city, town and village; and the recruits were being drilled in broad daylight. More than this. Shortly before he (Mr. Cooper) reached Hung-tung Hsien (one of our stations) a murderous assault had been made by Boxers on one of the native leaders of the Church, Elder Si, and his house looted. Mr. Cooper felt that the outbreak was to be taken as an earnest of what the Church in every part of Shan-si might at any time now be subjected to. So strongly indeed was this impressed upon him, that his exhortations to the native Christians dealt almost exclusively with the subject of persecution, and were evidently designed to prepare them for the fiery trial that was to try them.

It is interesting to note how the same spirit had been leading us, in the ordinary meetings of the station routine, to follow the same line of teaching. We had been continually dwelling — my wife and Miss Gates with the women, and I with the men — on the possibility of persecution, and the need of readiness to follow the Lamb whithersoever He goeth. And this, when there was nothing specially to call it forth. The Lu-an district was perfectly quiet, and hitherto there had been nothing to indicate the approach of so awful a tempest. Mr. Cooper's visit was the first premoni- tion of the storm. Then it was that the little cloud like a man's hand was, for the first time, clearly distinguishable upon our horizon.

Here I would turn aside for a moment to testify to what I saw and knew of the grace of God in His martyr- servant, Mr. William Cooper. It was my privilege to be present at his ministrations at all three stations Yu-wu, Lu-an and Lu-ch'eng from May 25 to June 4, and those ten days were one continuous exemplification of the words, "We preach not ourselves, but Christ Jesus as Lord, and ourselves as your servants for Jesus' sake." While visiting us as an overseer he yet exercised the oversight, not as lording it over the charge allotted to him, but making himself an ensample to the flock. He was before everything "our servant for Jesus' sake." If ever a disciple washed the feet of his brethren, it was Mr. Cooper. His own need was forgotten in the needs of others; and where he could be of any service to another for Jesus' sake, he was ready at any time and at any personal cost.

If he was wearied out with the last long day's journey of a weary week of travelling, he was still ready in the evening to take a Bible reading or lead a public meeting, as the occasion offered. Fervent in spirit, he was instant in season, out of season, serving the Lord. No one who saw it can forget the joy that would light up the tired face when, in answer to the inquiry, "But aren't you feeling too tired?" he would reply, "Not too tired. Though I tire in the Lord's service, I never tire of it, thank God."

He seemed those last days much occupied with God. He sought to be alone when he could, and his manner generally was quiet and reflective. I was particularly struck with it in the cart journey we had together from Lu-an to Lu-ch'eng the last he ever took in company with a "foreigner." The sun was intensely hot, but he walked by preference, only taking a lift now and again, as he said, "for a change." It was evident that he wished to be alone with God, in the secret of His Presence communing with Him. To be with him was to be conscious that he lived in an atmosphere of prayer, that he literally "drew breath in the fear of the Lord." The intense personal love to the Saviour, that breathed, not only through his addresses, but through his whole conversation, was the outcome, one could not but realize, of a prayer-life, and the evidence of how truly his fellowship was with the Father and with His Son Jesus Christ.

His end was in harmony with the whole spirit of his life, the motto of which might truly be said to be, "And we ought to lay down our lives for the brethren." Certainly he loved not his life unto the death. His ambition was to accomplish his course and the ministry he had received from the Lord Jesus, to testify the Gospel of the grace of God in China; and in the diligent pursuit of it he held not his life of any account as dear unto himself. Doubtless he experienced the same joy in laying down his life for his Lord in death that he had in laying it down for Him in the sacrifice of the daily life. And we are sure that with all boldness Christ was magnified in his body by death when the fatal stroke fell at Pao-ting Fu on July 1, not less than He would have been by life.

On Monday, June 4, Mr. Cooper left Lu-ch'eng for Shuen-teh Fu, en route for Tientsin and Shanghai. With a little company of native brethren we escorted him a short distance on foot. Then the farewell word, "The Lord be with you!" as he mounted his litter, and he was gone. Immediately afterwards I rode back with Mr. Barratt to Lu-an.

The rain-processions had now begun. Such times are always fraught with a peculiar element of danger, and we could not but be conscious that every rainless day served to make our situation more critical. News of the official encouragement given to the Boxer move- ment in the province had found its way to our parts; and the attitude of the people was in consequence becoming bolder in its hostility. All this led us to a definite committal of ourselves and our way to the Lord. But not a thought crossed our minds of leaving the station. He who had interposed on our behalf so marvellously the year before was "the Same to-day," and we rested on His love and faithfulness.

The following night, June 5, we had retired as usual, when between 12 and 1 o'clock a.m. we were roused from sleep by the noise of a rain-procession nearing our premises on the main north street. A sufficiently dreadful sound at any time, but awful in the dead of night. In the semi-consciousness of the awaking it came upon the senses as a hideous nightmare, until one was alive to the truth of it. We held our breath as we heard by the sounding gong and the thump of the drum beating out the mono- tonous measure that they were opposite, and had halted. Then the terror of clamorous cursings; and next, the battering of the gate and a volley of stones and brick-bats flung over the roof of the outer buildings into the courtyard, where our own quarters were. There was no time to be lost. Our hearts went up to God as we hurriedly dressed, expecting each moment would see the gate broken in. Just as we were preparing to take the children from their beds, suddenly the volleying and battering ceased, the procession resumed its march, and the terrifying noise of curses, gongs and drums drew away. Only, however, to pass to the south quarter of the buildings, where our native helpers were sleeping. Here a prolonged and determined attack was delivered, but again the same Hand that had restrained their wrath on our side of the compound held them back, and at length they withdrew, shouting threats of revenge should the drought continue. Again with fervent thanksgiving we committed ourselves to the keeping of our Father, and once more lay down.

It was now about 2 a.m., but for me there was no more sleep. I lay awake, partly to keep watch, in the expectation that the rioters might return, and partly that I might seek the mind of the Lord, as to how to act in the new circumstances. It is not too much to say that I agonized in prayer for the clear knowledge of His will.

A. E. Glover   Flora Glover

For the situation was one of peculiar trial and difficulty, owing to the fact that my wife was within three months of her confinement. If we remained, a period of severe nervous tension was before us, as they were the months, *par excellence*, during which rain was wanted and ardently looked for; and meantime, if the drought continued, the popular excitement would be growing more intense every day. Any hour during those three months we might expect a similar attack, day or night, to the one we had experienced ; and in all probability sooner or later the threats of vengeance would be carried out to the letter. Was I justified in exposing her to such a strain, not of days merely, but of weeks and months? Ought I not to avail myself of the permission already given us by the Mission authorities to go for a needed rest to Che-foo, and take her there without delay until the drought crisis was passed? If so, then no time was to be lost; for the hot season had set in, and it was already full late for taking the road. But then, what about the native church ? And what about our sister

Miss Gates, who would thus be left alone in circumstances of strain and peril?

I need only to mention a few such thoughts to show how my mind was torn with distress and conflict. But in the multitude of my thoughts within me God's comforts delighted my soul. I sought the Lord and He heard me, and delivered me from my fears. As the morning broke the burden was taken off me, and I had the clearest conviction of my duty. I knew that it was right before God that I should take her away to Che-foo without delay.

The thought of leaving was naturally distressing to my dear wife, and the undertaking so serious, from every point of view, that we both felt we should wait unitedly upon God for His definite confirmation of the thought. This we did privately together, and also in union with Miss Gates and Mr. Barratt, who was visiting us that week. These both con- curred in the belief that the thing was of God, and my wife was willing to accept it as His choice for her. When we further found that both our devoted evangelist, Uang Chi-fah, and my wife's trusted helper, Mrs. Chang, at once and without hesitation expressed their readiness to accompany us — a sign we had asked of God — all doubt was for her, as for me, at an end; and we began forthwith to make our preparations.

It was with the greatest shrinking and difficulty that we could bring ourselves to a decision which would leave Miss Gates alone in a precarious situa- tion. Whichever way one looked, the whole position involved a complication which only God could deal with. I could only see one of two courses open to her either to come with us, leaving the station for the time being in the hands of our native overseer Elder Liu; or to join our fellow-workers at the sister station of Lu-ch'eng, only fifteen miles distant. To both of these Miss Gates conscientiously demurred, in the persuasion that there was no sufficient reason in her case for leaving the station at all. She said if further trouble arose she would seek the protection of the Yamen, but more than this she did not feel justified in doing. It was a conspicuous instance of courage, fidelity and self-devotion, possible only perhaps to those who know their God.

To this neither my wife nor I would consent. We said that we felt we could only be free to go forward in the will of God on the understanding that as soon as she saw signs of further trouble she would leave forthwith and take up her residence at Lu-ch'eng, in compliance with Mr. E. J. Cooper's kindly expressed hope. We begged her also to make an interchange of visits with Miss Rice and Miss Huston, to break the sense of loneliness.

The pledge was given, and every serious difficulty in the way of our leaving was thus taken out of the way. Nevertheless, our hearts were very heavy, not so much with presage of evil to befall us by the way, for I had no doubt that the road to Tientsin was safe, and that with Mr. William Cooper just ahead of us on the same road, we, no less than he, would with the help of God get safely through. But to be leaving the little church at all, even though it were only for a few months as we hoped and believed, was a deep trial; and especially so in view of the difficulties created by the prospect of famine, and even it might be of persecution. And then the pain of saying farewell to our sister and valued helper, knowing as we did (and yet we never could know all) the loneliness of the path she was taking in obedience to her Lord. Yes, our hearts were heavy indeed as we put our house in order. It was truly for us the beginning of sorrows. How well I remember my last message to the native brethren, as we met for worship for the last time ere our departure: " Let not your heart be troubled; ye believe in God, believe also in Me."

It was the word of the Lord to my own soul first. The only thing that could sustain pastor or people in such an hour was the knowledge that the Lord of Life was in the midst, that Great Shepherd of the sheep; that God had given Him to be Head over all things to the Church; and that, come what might, living or dying, we were the Lord's.

Questions to Consider

1. When Glover realized the situation at their mission station was becoming untenable, should he have left with his pregnant wife and two young children?

2. When Miss Gates said she was going to stay, should Glover and his family have stayed with her?

3. Should Miss Gates have stayed?

CHAPTER THREE

The Darkness Deepens

*"I have heard the defaming of many,
terror on every side."*

"He knoweth what is in the darkness."

By the morning of Saturday, June 9, everything was ready for the start. In order to keep the fact of our departure as far as possible from the notice of the outside world, we decided to ride our own animals to Lu-ch'eng and hire our mule litters from there. The overhanging cloud of sorrow at leaving our charge was still brightened with the hope that it was but a temporary separation, and our hearts revived under the prospect of the reunion that would, we believed, in the ordering mercy of our God surely and shortly be given us.

We started at ten o'clock, having sent on the baggage to avoid attracting attention. My wife and I rode each a donkey, while our two little ones, Hedley and Hope (aged four and three respectively), in Chinese dress were in the cart with Mrs.

Chang. Mr. Barratt escorted us out some distance beyond the
city wall. Miss Gates was feeling the separation too acutely to
accompany us beyond the doors. She told us after- wards that
the sense of desolation that came upon her as the compound
gates closed behind us was over- whelming. My dear wife felt
it not less acutely. It was the deepest suffering to her to be
leaving her beloved fellow-worker thus, and more than once
on the journey she said that she felt as though she must return,
in the knowledge of her sister's loneliness and need. Indeed, it
was only by reminding ourselves of the various tokens God
had given of His clear leading, and then of Miss Gates'
promise, that we were either of us enabled to go on.

We were just five hours going those fifteen miles, and five
hours in the saddle under a hot sun was trying work to one in
my wife's circumstances. But I recall the calm cheerfulness,
so characteristic, with which she sought to allay any disquiet
that might be felt on her account, and to impart a happy
contentment to those about her. It seemed wiser to go right
through without dismounting, to prevent curiosity and talk; so
that when we arrived about four o'clock she was very, very
weary. What a loving welcome awaited us! It was the first
time Mrs. E. J. Cooper and my wife had met, Mr. Cooper
having only just arrived to take up the station work; and how
thankfully they reviewed the prospect of happy fellowship to
come in the associated work of the district. It was pretty to see
little five-year-old Edith, with her beautiful hair and English
dress, taking Hedley and Hope round the garden, and all three
playing merrily together as though no clouds were lowering
overhead and storms could never be. Shouts of delight told
that their pleasure was at its height when baby Brainerd (two

years old) was put on the donkey's back, and thence, after a judicious walk, transferred to his father's shoulders for a reckless gallop. Everything in that sweet home spoke of peace and love. The moral value of such homes in heathen lands most certainly at any rate in China cannot be over-estimated, or the need of them too earnestly emphasized. Tender memories arise as I think of that Sunday, the last we spent together within the boundaries of our own prefecture and province. To us at least who were taking the road it was "a sabbath of rest" in every sense of the word.

Mr. Cooper had already engaged our litters, and about eight o'clock on Monday morning they came into the compound. We took the precaution of fixing a curtain in front of the opening, that we could let down whenever we deemed it expedient to keep our identity out of sight. By half-past ten they were made as snug as bedding and pillows could make them, and all was ready once more for the road. Dr. Hewett and Mr. Barratt had ridden over from Lu-an to join in bidding us farewell. They had fresh news to bring. Mr. Barratt had just received a note by special messenger from his colleague at Ioh-iang, Mr. Woodroffe, to say that the Boxers had appeared in the neighbourhood and had given out their intention of making havoc of the church there; and he took it as a call to himself to return and stand with his brother in the forefront of the battle.

The news was sufficiently grave to us all. What might not the next word be? Was it not the call to us to be also ready? The situation was becoming critical, and in the light of it the farewell was a solemn one. Well it might be; for of the eight of us four men and four women — who were together that morning in the Lu-ch'eng compound, five were shortly called to martyrdom. Thank God these things were hid from our eyes at the time; else how could our heart have endured? Of those devoted women, the three Lu-ch'eng sisters had laid down their lives for Christ within the next two months, and five months hence not one of the four was living.

One word with regard to our martyred brother, Mr. David Barratt. I count it one of the choice privileges of my missionary life to have been allowed of God to know him. Young as he was in years, he was a ripe Christian. "A man full of faith and of the Holy Ghost," great grace was upon dear David. Short as our acquaintance was, it was long enough for the forging of the bonds of love — the love of Christ — between us. His own soul was alive with divine love. It was his constant theme at all times. He took a tender interest in my two little ones, delighting to play and sing to them and to talk with them about the love of Jesus. To this hour Hedley remembers that the text, "We love Him because He first loved Us," was taught him by "dear Uncle David."

What I once overheard him saying to them "I want you to love Jesus very, very much. Do you know, Hedley, I love Jesus more and more every day," was entirely characteristic. The love of God was the law of his heart and the theme of his lips. During the week he was with us at Lu-an he spent much of his time alone with God, and the sound of his voice would often be heard in the private exercises of praise and prayer. An ardent missionary spirit, he yearned for the salvation of the Chinese. His whole soul went out to them in the compassions of Christ. Every- thing was considered in relation to the great end in view, and whatever was seen to be of the nature of a hindrance was resolutely laid aside.

Mr. William Cooper
Martyered at Pao-ting Chiih-li
July 1, 1900

Mr. David Barratt
Martyered at T'ang-ch'eng
Shan-si, July 1900

The circumstances under which Mr. Barratt met his death at the hands of the Boxers are not fully known; but the subjoined letter, written on the eve of martyrdom, is its own witness to the triumph of his spirit over the terrors of the Power of darkness. I insert it in full by kind permission of Dr. Julius Hewett, to whom it was addressed. It was sent from Yu-wu on July 6, and received at Lu-ch'eng (twenty-seven miles distant), at midnight of the same day :

"After worship this morning, July 6, I saw a copy of the proclamation on the street; Ch'eng and Li do not think it came from the Governor, but only from Tuen-liu Hsien, especially knowing that the official there is a 'Big Knife Society' man. We studied some of the half-hundred 'fear-nots' of God this a.m., and had a blessed time indeed. I send you a few from the Concordance especially helpful to Christians now. I will get some copied out, so that the people can take them home and look into them. Really, it is wonderful ! Isaiah li. 7-16 was honey to me this morning. I pass the comb on to you.

"On Saturday I hope to meditate on some more. At the Sabbath service I thought I would look for your dear mother's photo, as that must not be spoiled. God bless and guide her dear boy! The big framed photo I had taken to the north court.

"'Forget Me not,' then 'fear not' some of Jeho- vah's 'Fear nots'Gen. xv. 1., xxvi. 24 ; Judges vi. 23; Isa. xli. 10, 11, 14; Exod. xiv. 13 'Fear not, stand still and see.' Exod. xx. 20 'To prove you.' Num. xiv. 9 ; 1 Chron. xxviii. 20. Isa. xxxv. 3, 4, 10 'Say to them of fearful mind, fear not.' Isa. xliii. 1, 5, 10, 12, 21; xlvi. 8; li. 7-13, 16. Daniel x. 19. Joel ii. 21 'Great things.' Jer. viii. 13. Matt, x 28-31 'Jesus speaks.' John xiv. 1, 4 Response. Heb. xiii. 5, 6; Psalm xxvii. 3; lvi. 3, 4 ; cxviii. 6 Hallelujah.

"*Later.* — See what I wrote an hour ago on scraps of paper, and now note what follows. An hour ago. Deacon Si, who knew you when at T'ai-yuen with Dr. Edwards he is a man who helped Dr. Edwards, and is now a fugitive fleeing down to Hu-peh (Han- kow) in hope of saving his life, going as a pedlar — came to tell you here of the awful things in T'ai-yuen, and how Mr. Saunders' party had gone to Lu-ch'eng, all the places in P'ing-iao being destroyed. The news nearly made me faint, though His peace filled, and still does fill, my soul.

"The people (missionaries) are all in one place, and may be killed any day, by order of her awful majesty 'The Lord reigneth.' The man did not stay long, but said he wished to warn us. He asked if I could help him with a few cash, and after talking with Ch'eng Chu-ch'eng I gave him 500 cash. He is evidently a true man; we all heard his story breathless. He lived on the premises at T'ai-yuen, and knows not whether his wife and family are gone or not. He flees rather than worship false gods, the only alterna- tive given to the people. He gave Mr. Saunders' and several other names in English, as well as their Chinese names. We got together after he left, and prayed about matters and sang 'Iesu ling o' (He leadeth me). I never knew its full meaning till this hour. A report comes from the street that this place is to be looted and destroyed on or before Sunday. When the news of the fire at P'ing-iao and T'ai-yuen reaches Si-t'ing and around here, there is no telling how things may go. It seems the whole affair comes from the Empress-Dowager. The Empire is evidently upside down. A mighty magazine has been fired in 'The Boxers' and 'Big Knives,' and now 'Mene, mene, tekel, upharsin,' is written on the old Middle Kingdom, and God's Kingdom shall go with increasing power over this land. Extermination is but exalta-tion. God guide and bless us!

"Realizing that Lu-ch'eng is no place for another foreigner, while on my knees (I think) Liang-ma was suggested to my mind as a place of refuge, and I determined to place myself in the three natives' hands to dispose of me as seemed best. While speaking of one or two places to which I might go, saying they would go home and ask God's guidance as to what they should do, they saw the mob coming here, and had to flee. The Governors are against us now, and so we can only trust in God, and do all as He gives wisdom, to 'escape for thy life.' I am quite peaceful in soul, though I feel awfully in body; felt like fainting a bit, since body not strong, truly fragile clay, soon smashed! Well, Ch'eng and Hai-kin said I could not do better than allow Ch'eng Chu-ch'eng to take me to-night to Liang-ma, among the hills, to old Mr. K'oh's house, where I would find a quiet ark of safety for the present. Hard travel! How different to when I came! So we are praying about it now quietly, and if God still points that way, this vigil with God will be all along the road. The old ship sinks, and the lifeboat must be put out, as our Father shows. Ch'eng and others hope you may be led to go there also, but it must be secretly. How I fear you may have gone right into the very fire at Lu-ch'eng, so many people being there; Lu-an is worse, I guess! It is the target of plunder they aim at, and these premises are most unsafe places. I look at these pretty things which may in a few hours be all gone. Ch'eng will carry some of the cash with us which you left him. We hope to take a few of the valuables over to the North Court, as there may be a chance of hiding them. The bank-book and papers Ch'eng thinks of carrying with him to Liang-ma. When I get there he may come back and see how things are. Ah, only our blessed Lord knows! All we have is His, and so we fear not.

'Fear not them which kill.' He says,'Are ye not of much more value than many sparrows ?' 'Peace, perfect peace,' brother, and all at Lu-ch'eng. We may meet in the glory in a few hours or days. A nearer way than to go to Lu-ch'eng. I have been wondering if Ho-nan is troubled; mails to the coast might be got that way before the way is blocked. Sorry the man could not wait for a letter to some Hu-peh place of mission. Now a sleep, no dinner, a quiet time with God, then 'twilight and evening bell, and after that the dark' (moonlight), and I know there will be 'no moaning of the bar, when I put out to sea,' because 'Thou wilt keep him in perfect peace whose mind is stayed on Thee, because he trusteth in Thee.' Lao-san and Hai-kin will stay to k*an-men (keep the door) till it needs it no further . . . they say. They are good men! God preserve them to the coming church, whose baptism is of fire and blood !

"My presence cannot aid in the least now. Let us be true till death. 'Be thou faithful unto death, and I will give thee a crown of life.' They are not strangers to the country as I am, so wish to help me now.' God moves in a mysterious way. His wonders to perform.' There are a few good hiding-places in the Yoh-yang district in which to hide, Brook Cheriths, eh? I do plead for all our West stations, P'ing-yang, etc. Maranatha, Jehovah!"

But to return. The farewells were said and the litters hoisted to the mules' backs, my wife and little girl leading the way in the first litter, followed by Mrs. Chang riding a pack mule. Then my little boy and I in the second litter, with Chi-fah to bring up the rear on a donkey.

And now began a series of journeyings the true nature of which can never be adequately described. Reckon- ing from the day we left our station, the time over which they extended was sixty-seven days (June 9 to August 14); and the total distance covered by them just over one thousand English miles. The dates embrace the hottest period of the Chinese year. Not only so, but the summer of 1900 was the hottest that had been known in China for thirty years. Under ordinary circumstances travelling would be reckoned folly (to say the least) at such a season, even where it was possible to take the usual precautions. What the actual circumstances were under which we travelled will be found in the sequel, to the glory of God.

Our litters had been hired to Shuen-teh Fu. Thence we intended hiring again to Pao-ting Fu. The real difficulties of the journey would then be over, as the rest of the way is by river to Tientsin. This was the route Mr. William Cooper was taking, who was only a week in advance of us. More than once on the road we regretted that we were not travelling with him. But it was the mercy of God to us that we were not.

All was quiet as we passed along to Li-ch'eng, where we slept the first night. We had no occasion to lower our curtains. Probably this was due to the fact that rain sufficient for the present need had fallen in the neighbourhood, and allayed for a time the excitable tendencies of the people. Also it had led them out into their fields, and turned thoughts and hands to something else than mischief. For this we thanked God and took courage. It looked as though we should get well through. The next day the muleteers dis- obeyed my orders and turned off the high road to follow the "small" road, as they always will if they can. The track lay over the roughest, wildest path in the heart of the Tai-hang mountains. More than once the drivers lost their way and took us into track- less, ugly places whose solitude and desolation palled upon one. The mules old, and broken-kneed, unfor- tunately for us were continually stumbling over the rocky steeps and in the torrent-beds, which had the double effect of imparting a distressing pitch to the litter (something akin to the sensation of sea-sick- ness) and of keeping the nerves perpetually on the stretch for fear of a spill. Often in going down or up the rocky passes the only way the animals could keep their feet on the glazed surface of stone was by planting them in holes worn by the immemorial traffic. It was not long before stumbling turned to tumbling. The front animal that was carrying my wife fell, pitching her violently forward, while the hind mule was doing his restive best to work out from under the poles. Then the struggles of the beast to get up under the lash, and the terrible jerk of the last vigorous effort that set him on his feet again what suffering it all was to me by sympathy with her! I tried exchanging litters, hoping that as my animals had not yet been actually down they had something to recommend them over the others; but the fond delusion of superiority was dispelled when ere long we were both down, first one and then the other.

Add to this that the "small" road meant vile inns that catered only for muleteers, not for travellers. For such, no suitable accommodation was provided; hence we had to make shift with food of the coarsest and rooms of the filthiest. How real a trial this was can hardly be understood except by those who have experienced it. After the fatigues of a long day's journey under a hot sun, quiet restful sleep was an absolute essential to my wife, not to mention the little ones. But the tiny, grimy room was too stifling, and the vermin too lively, to indulge even the hope of such a thing. The nights were, for her, torture. The children, too, were bug-bitten about the face till the people asked whether they were not sickening with small-pox !

Thus the mode of travel, which on the high road would have been comparatively restful, was turned to an occasion of peculiar weariness and trial. But this was not all. By the less frequented route we were naturally objects of curiosity, where on the high road we should have been comparatively unnoticed. Thus it came to pass that the halting times, so far from being (what they should have been after hours of pitching and stumbling) seasons of rest, became a real source of added weariness and often of serious appre- hension. In the ordinary way we would think little or nothing of curious crowds, beyond the inconvenience they entailed. Every foreigner has to face this as the inevitable, and endure it as patiently and good- naturedly as he can. But the circumstances under which we were travelling were more than ordinary much more so even than we were aware of at the time. The muleteers gave us a significant hint of this, when. upon my remonstrating with them for disregarding my strict injunctions to keep to the high road, they replied that they had purposely turned aside to avoid publicity. The rumours were so evil about the foreign devil, and the temper of the people so inflammatory by reason of the drought, that it was highly dangerous to take that route. This was not reassuring. It gave room, to say the least, for fears that even these outlandish folk might not be so wholly untouched by the current news of the outside world as we could wish at the present juncture, nor by the prevalent feeling as to the cause of the drought. We could never be sure that there was not something behind their curiosity that would quickly turn it into hostility. It was always a matter of thankfulness if we were back in our litters and on the move again without having encountered an angry demonstration.

The third day we found that these fears were not altogether groundless. At noon we were halted in a village too insignificant to boast an inn. Accordingly the litters were set down in the narrow street, and we were told to make our way to the food shop which had a so-called "guest-room" opening out of it. Here we unlocked our small food box, and began to prepare the children's meal. Before it was ready, the yard was thronged and the room itself packed with a gaping crowd. The heat was very great and the atmosphere of the room soon became overpowering. We answered the questions that were put to us politely and pleasantly as we went on with our meal. But the crowds continued to press in upon us, until my dear wife turned sick and faint. Eating became a difficulty, and as for resting it was out of the question.

Appealing to their better feelings Chi-fah persuaded them to leave us, and then tried to secure the boltless door. But to no purpose, for the door was then lifted from its hinges, and they swarmed in more boister- ously than ever,

Seeing the temper of the crowd, the proprietor now sent us word to go; and Chi-fah told us that we must leave without delay, or the situation might become extremely awkward. This, however, was easier said than done. Our head muleteer was an opium sot, and immovable until he had had his fill of the drug. So we were forced out to our litters in the street; and instead of the quiet meal and sleep we so sorely needed, we had to snatch what food we could as we sat in the broiling sun, confronted by a rude mob whose attitude was rapidly becoming a menace to our very safety. Thus we were for two long hours.

At last the muleteers appeared, leading out the animals; and oh, the relief, as we passed out of that village gate and left the following crowd behind! In view of all we went through afterwards this was a small thing; but I record it, because it marked a distinct period in our experience, and also because it shows how gradually God was training us to endure the hardness of the sterner discipline to come.

From this time our progress was anxious work. We were well into the province of Ho-nan, that northern strip of it which divides between Shan-si and Chih-li; and we knew that the Honanese were no lovers of the foreigner. We found it advisable to stop only when forced to do so; and even then to make short stays and extra early starts.

On Friday, June 15, we reached our last halting- place, fifty li (seventeen English miles) from Shuen- teh Fu. One stage more, and then — ! The prospect of being with dear friends and in the comfort of a home again, always delightful after days of travel, was never so delightful as now. As the litters were set down for the last time, our hearts went up in thanks- giving to God, and we entered the house where we were to take our meal in good spirits. It was a private house, there being no inn in the place; and our hostess received us with courtesy and an unusual show of friendliness. Food was brought in; and we were just praising God for the happier circumstances under which the next meal would be eaten, when a man came in and entered into conversation with Chi- fah. As they sat squatting by the door and talking, food bowl in hand, I became aware that the ordinary voice, in which they had been exchanging the usual generalities of talk, was sunk to a low undertone, and I saw Chi-fah's face change colour. Involuntarily he set the bowl down and listened intently to what the man was saying. I said, "What is it, Chi-fah? Is there anything wrong?" He turned to me as he said, "God help us now. Pastor! Shuen-teh Fu is all on an uproar. The Sub-Prefect's yamen has been burned, the Roman Catholic premises destroyed, and there is not a single foreigner left in the city. All have fled."

I shall never forget that moment. I cannot describe the heart panic of it. It seemed as if I had suddenly stepped out of bright sunshine into dark- ness — blackness of darkness, unrelieved by a solitary ray. My wife had lain down to rest on the k'ang (or dais of hard-baked clay) beside the children; but with a woman's instinct she divined what we were talking about, and begged me to hide nothing from her. I was anxious to keep her from anything that would needlessly agitate, and sought grace to tell quietly the substance of the man's information. It was just the signal for her faith to take fresh hold of God. The darkness was indeed real; but God was there, and that was enough for her. It was such a stay to my own heart at that time to see how in the time of trouble God was literally her refuge and strength. I had seen it often before, but never in such a day of trouble as this.

For now, if ever, it was the swelling of Jordan to us. What could we do? Where could we go? Before us riot and certain destruction; behind us, if we turned back, six days (and who knew how many more?) of such difficulty as we had just experienced, and of exposure to the certain hostility which would now no longer be restrained. In either case we were confronted with peril of the gravest kind. I dared not let myself think of what it might mean to my dear wife. I could only cry out in silence to God for her and the little ones. Then the deep comfort came, "Thou hast beset me behind and before. Thou art about my path." And as she and I knelt with Chi-fah in prayer for strength and guidance, the peace of God flowed like a river.

As we discussed the situation one thing was clear to us to go forward. There was at least the chance that the report might be an exaggerated one, and as the (China Inland) Mission station had not as yet been attacked, it was just possible that our friends might after all be found there. But in any case it was a Prefectural city, and if the worst came to the worst we could put ourselves under the protection of the chief magistrate. We had our Consular passport with us, and to present it was to make him responsible for our safety. The course of action was therefore clear first, to ascertain whether or no any missionaries were still within the city; and if not, then to put our- selves directly under the care of the Prefect. But how to get the information we wanted? Who would be willing to go for us at a time when the popular feeling was running high against us?

Our God had heard and had already provided. It so happened that our informant was a Roman Catholic — a fellow-sufferer, in a sense, who had himself escaped from the riot. He now agreed (not, however, without considerable hesitation), for a thousand cash, to carry a letter to the missionary in charge, Mr. Martin Griffith. We were to pay down half the amount; the other half he was to receive when he had finished his errand. I instructed him to return by a particular road in order that we might not miss each other, since in any case we intended to go on to the city. I then wrote a few lines to Mr. Griffith, idle as it seemed to do so; and the man hid it in his sock and went off. How much hung upon his fidelity to the trust! And how much prayer was made for him in the discharge of it!

It was now about 2 p.m., but we thought it advis- able to delay starting, partly to give the messenger time to do his business, and partly to prevent our reaching the city before dark. We should not have started even when we did but for an untoward event.

A good many people were coming about us, and the small courtyard was full. Whether the actual state of affairs in the city, as reported, was known to them I cannot say. There was no open show of in- civility; but possibly our being where we were had something to do with that. Our hostess had been sitting with my wife and chatting in the kindest way, and we had thankfully noted several little attentions out of the ordinary; indeed, so well disposed did she seem that my wife was encouraged to speak freely to her the Word of Life. What was our distress when this woman suddenly became "uai-li" (as the natives in our part call it) ! I can only describe it as a species of devil possession. We learned that she was a witch or spirit medium, and was in consequence subject to such possession at any time. In the first stage it was a distressing sight to witness; but distress became horror, as the fearful realities of the power of darkness passed before us and penetrated beyond the senses to the inmost parts of our being. There was no violence of any kind. She simply sat on her door-step looking straight before her, with dulled eyes, dead to all expression, and apparently just going off into a swoon. After so much kindness received, my wife and I were much concerned, and, supposing that she had been taken suddenly ill, wanted to assist her as far as we knew how. But Chi-fah warned us to have nothing to do with the matter, as she was under possession. Then the woman straightened herself, and with vacant, stony stare into space began an incantation. As the weird strain rose and fell upon the air it made one's very flesh creep; for the burden of it was our Lord Jesus whom we preached. Higher and higher rose her voice after each pause, and more animated grew her gestures, as she chanted I know not what of blasphemy against the Holy One of God. I cannot describe what it was to be in the presence of such a manifestation of spiritual wickedness. The atmosphere about us seemed suddenly impregnated with a subtle influence of evil unknown before. It was as if the personal Satan stood beside us, and the air we drew in were charged with his very breath. On each one of the four occasions I have been called to witness the horrible sight in China, the impression upon the inner sense has always been the same in a greater or less degree, a consciousness of actual contact with the actual personalities of wicked spirits, indefinably awful and too subtly palpable to be explained on any mere physical or mental hypothesis. A spiritual effect demands a spiritual cause. No one who had stood with us, and seen what we saw or heard what we heard, could have doubted for a moment what (or rather who) that cause was. The incantation was its own evidence that it was an inspiration of the devil, and one of the most devilish of its kind.

The danger we had to fear was that those standing by would lay this devil possession at our door, and say that it was the effect of the "foreign devils" coming to the place. Accordingly Chi-fah told us at once to leave the house, and wait in the litters by the roadside while he went to urge the muleteers to an immediate start. Here again God helped us. For the first time there was a ready response; the mules were led out, and a few minutes later we were hoisted to their backs. As we moved down the street we could still hear the rise and fall of the witch's chant, fainter and fainter, until we were out of earshot. The awful sound followed us as a wail of woe rising from the heart of sin-stricken Christless China as a call therefore to a more earnest devotion than ever to the work of preaching deliverance to the captives, and of praying "Thy kingdom come, Thy will be done on earth as it is in heaven." One could not compare the transformation of that kindly lovable soul into a creature from which one shrank with horror with the transformation that might be hers into the beauty of holiness, without having the longing deepened to be a vessel of God's grace to those "whose debtors we are," or the resolve quickened to spend and be spent for the hopeless millions that know nothing of Him who "was mani- fested that He might destroy the works of the devil."

There was nothing said or done to us as we passed along to the village gate. Doubtless they were thankful to see the last of us, and, had we tarried, would have taken matters into their own hands to get rid of us.

The start was, however, full early for our purpose, and the pace had to be regulated accordingly. I cannot attempt to describe the agony of that ride. Every step was bringing us nearer to — what? Any moment now we might be stopped and our identity discovered; and what then? Our very destination — what was it? A city in full riot. Even if we made straight for the yamen, should we succeed in reaching it, or even in passing the barrier of the city gate? Then, too, it would be pitch dark ere we could expect to meet the messenger. What if in the darkness we missed him? Behind the close-drawn curtain of that windowless litter, as the twilight settled into night, I learnt some- thing of what it meant to be left alone. The darkness seemed to enter from without and wrap itself about my soul. Those eight hours were hours of weakness and fear and much trembling, and of wrestling with God for the mother with the children.

On and on, with nothing to break the silence but the footfall of the mules and the occasional call of the drivers, or their curt response to the salutations of the passers by. I observed that they maintained a rigid reserve in replying to the usual questions, and that the frequent inquiry, "Who have you got inside?" was carefully parried.

On and on, but no sign of the letter bearer. Surely we must by this time have traversed the road along which he was to meet us? Would he never come? Had he, after all, ever meant to come? The suspense was almost unbearable. At last my curtain was pulled aside. It was Chi-fah. "What are the Pastor's instructions now?" he whispered. "We have passed the appointed place, and the man has missed us." There was only one answer "Tell the muleteer to drive us right into the Prefect's yamen."

On and on, until the dark line of the city wall stood out before us. My heart sickened as I peered through the curtain. Fearfulness laid hold upon me as I thought upon what lay behind that wall, and I shrank from the very thought that we had reached our goal. How often had I queried longingly, Would the journey never end? Now it was only. Would that it could be prolonged! The only avenue through which the terrible uncertainty could be relieved had failed us, and we were shut up to the tidings we had heard and which had been more or less confirmed by passers by.

A few minutes more now, and we should know.

****

It was just upon eleven o'clock. As we drew closer to the city, the drivers proceeded even more cautiously.

The bells were removed from the necks of the mules, that our entrance might be as quiet as possible. I could not help wondering at the death-like stillness that reigned. It seemed difficult to believe that we were in the neighbourhood of riot and destruction.

Not a sound was to be heard except the going of the mules. Once more I drew the curtain slightly aside and peeped. There was the great gate right before us, and we were about to cross the bridge. Yes, we were there now; and my cry went up to the God of our salvation.

A moment later and my curtain was drawn aside from without. Again it was Chi-fah.

"What is it? Tell me!"

"Blessed be our God, Mr. Griffith is in the city, and has sent his servant here to await our arrival. He himself has gone out with Mr. Brown by the other gate to meet you, in case you should have been entering the city that way."

It is impossible to express what I felt. The tension of eight hours could only find relief in tears. There was the man standing, lantern in hand, and he appeared in my eyes as an angel of God. I looked up, and there was my dear wife's litter standing close beside my own. "Oh, Archie!" she said, "isn't it too wonderful! He has heard our cry."

Though it was eleven o'clock, strange to say the gate was open and we could enter unnoticed. Over the bridge and through the gate; and now we were inside the walls. As I sat behind the curtains and listened, not a sound broke the stillness. The city was wrapped in sleep. Almost before we were aware of it the litters had stopped and the curtains were drawn. Lanterns were lifted to the opening; and the faces of the dear friends we had longed but scarcely hoped to see were looking in upon us, with words of loving greeting in whispers on their lips.

The "few minutes more" were gone, and now we "knew." What did we know? Not riot and destruction not even the Prefect's yamen; but a home of love, and the tender mercies and compassions of our God.

Questions to Consider

1. I think it's important to note that one of the people who helped Glover during the incidents described in this chapter was Catholic. Do you think Glover dealt with this individual as a fellow Christian?

2. Glover describes one woman in this chapter as possessed by an evil spirit. This brings us to a question we considered at the beginning. Was this a spiritual battle? Do you believe in actual demons or evil spirits?

CHAPTER FOUR

The Breaking of the Storm

"In the day when I cried Thou
answeredst me, and strengthenedst
me with strength in my soul."

It was not long before we were in possession of the real facts. The messenger had fulfilled his trust, and duly delivered the letter to Mr. Griffith. Why he failed to meet us on the road was never made quite clear to me. But the main end was secured. Our friends had not fled and were aware of our approach, and the lesser trial was forgotten in the greater mercy.

The report that we had heard was to a very large extent exaggerated. Certain incidents had occurred both in connection with the Roman Catholics and with the Sub-Prefect's yamen,which formed a good basis for the story; but there had been no actual riot, nor had the foreigners fled. None the less, the state of popular feeling was highly inflammatory, and it was generally believed in the city that not a foreigner remained in it. It was a remarkable providence of God that we entered the city at the precise hour we did. A large idolatrous fair was in full swing; and had we entered earlier we must have encountered trouble. Mr. Griffith also remarked upon the fact that the streets should have been deserted as they were, for the night before the revelry had been kept up till past midnight. In this, too, we could not but see the hand of our God. As it was, our coming was a dead secret to the city. How little they thought that instead of there being "no foreigners left within the walls" there were more than had been known there for some time!

As, however, such a rumour was abroad, Mr. Griffith felt it advisable to let it stand so, and not allow the general ignorance to be enlightened. So he begged us to keep altogether out of sight and not attempt to show ourselves even at the compound gate. Thus for the eleven days of our happy, though hazardous, sojourn there (June 15 to 26) we never once went beyond the walls of the mission premises. This precaution proved to be only too necessary, as I shall presently show.

We now learned for the first time something of the extent of the Boxer rising and the direction it was taking. News was forwarded us by Mr. C. H. S. Green from Huai-luh by special courier, from which we saw that the hope of our being able to continue our journey would have at least to be deferred. It was evident we were to "tarry the Lord's leisure" and not to make haste. Though we were anxious to press on to the journey's end, yet we were sure that the restraint was of Him, and the event proved it to be His care for us in His purpose to deliver.

We could not but feel considerable anxiety for the safety of Mr. William Cooper, who had left Shuen-teh Fu for Pao-ting Fu that very week. A telegram from Shanghai urging his return by way of Ho-nan arrived just too late to alter his route, as he was then too far on the road to be overtaken. This telegram was used of God to show me, later on, the possibility of escape in that direction. But for that, so far as I know, I should have been in ignorance of such a possibility and probably have made no attempt to leave the station beyond flight to the hills. As it was I studied the route while at Shuen-teh, and knew how to act when the emergency arose. The telegram was too late to save Mr. Cooper, but I have a conviction that it turned to the salvation of myself and my house.

Those days at Shuen-teh were unspeakably precious to us. Looking back upon them now I cannot sufficiently thank God for all that He gave us in the loving ministrations of Mr. and Mrs. Griffith and Mr. R. Brown. They did not allow us to know, until events revealed the fact, how they were risking their own lives to shelter us; for when once the secret of our arrival was out, the peril to themselves was extreme. As a matter of fact, our coming brought on the riot which lost them their all and compelled them to face what seemed to be certain death in flight. The privilege as well as the consolation of being with them at such a time was very great. I shall neverknow in this life how much of the grace to endure in the hour of trial, then so close upon us, was imparted in those days of waiting together upon God and of learning really to say, "Therefore will not we fear though the earth be removed." It was one thing to say it in the day of our prosperity; but we found together all of us, I doubt not that it was another thing to say it truly when "the heathen" all round us actually were "raging" and "the kingdoms" were, in a very real sense, being "moved." Community of suffering drew us very closely together; for though we were not exposed as yet to physical hardships, we never knew what an hour, day or night, might bring forth. Once discovered, riot was inevitable; and this of course, if only in the apprehension of it, meant suffering of a very tangible kind.

My dear wife and Mrs. Griffith were specially drawn to each other in the peculiar circumstances by the common bond of motherhood; and I know that the sweet fellowship in the Lord my wife enjoyed with Mrs. Griffith was signally used of God to the inward renewing of her strength and preparing her for the great fight of sufferings yet to come.

The first thing we did was to send on a message to our district superintendent, Mr. Bagnall, at Pao-ting Fu to report our arrival and to ask advice as to our taking the next stage to that city. We waited and waited, but no return message ever came. We also wrote to our home people, as the mail communica- tion had not to our knowledge been stopped. These postcards were received fifteen months later, September 11, 1901!

Meantime Mr. Cooper's servant, a member of the Hung-tung Church who had attended him through from Hung-tung, returned from Pao-ting Fu. He reported that they had had the narrowest escape of being taken, and that it was only by forcing the stages in the concealment of a closed cart that they had got through at all. Mr. Cooper sent no letter by him in case he might be searched, for the penalty of anything foreign being found upon the person of a native was death. This lad was now returning home and suggested that we should return with him. We felt, however, that having come so far we ought not to think of returning unless we were absolutely compelled, and as yet the hope of getting through was not wholly shut out. I thought, too, that I ought to await my superintendent's instructions until the latest moment.

Influenced by the boy's report, Chi-fah now came to me and said that the risk of going on was too great, and that whatever I might choose to do, both he and Mrs. Chang felt that they must discourage the thought and refuse to accompany us. This was of course simply cutting the ground from under our feet. Our only chance of getting through (humanly speaking) was to be covered by trusty natives as Mr. Cooper had been. Failing that, it would be madness to go on.

Tidings, however, of the gravest nature shortly reached us from Haui-luh. The Boxers had torn up the rails at Tientsin, cut the wires, and occupied the road between Tientsin and Cheng-ting Fu. Mr. Green also reported the murder of a large party, including several ladies, who had tried to escape by river boat from Pao-ting Fu to Tientsin. All hope of reaching our destination by that route was therefore now abandoned. The only other possible route was that to the East, via Lin-ts'in Cheo and the Grand Canal; but armed bands, rendered desperate by hunger, were scouring the road in that direction. These things taken together showed us that the only path now open to us was to return to Lu-an.

This conclusion was, however, settled out of hand by another circumstance. The secret of our presence in the city was out, and we could no longer be hid. In a heedless moment Mrs. Chang had gone out on the street one afternoon in company with Chi-fah. The impropriety of a woman on the city street at once attracted notice, and while the shape of her garments marked her as a stranger to those parts, her opened feet branded her as a " foreign devil." From that time suspicion was excited and daily grew in intensity. The premises were visited by spies, and sullen groups hung all day about the doors. At length the rumours became so ugly that the landlord insisted on our leaving the house one and all, or the mob would pull it down about our ears.

Litters were accordingly engaged for the return journey to Lu-an. Not a moment too soon. Even as we were making ready the crowd were battering at the doors, and were only restrained from an actual outbreak by the tangible assurance afforded them by the litters that we were clearing out.

I think there is no doubt that another case of devil possession had not a little to do with precipitating our departure. The subject of these attacks was a young woman, the daughter of respectable parents close by, who when under possession would sit in the middle of the road, heedless of traffic and everything else, pouring out torrents of vile talk. The foreign devil and his religion naturally came in for a full share. Such a nuisance had it become that her parents had sent her from home. But it so happened that a few days before we left she unexpectedly returned and the devil with her. I can hear the uncanny cries even now as she sat cursing in the road outside the mission gate; and one could not help shuddering to think how materially such cries would help at such a time to feed the fears of superstition and fan the fires of hate.

It may or may not be true that coming events cast their shadows before. Certain it is, however, that a nameless dread took hold both of my wife and myself in the thought of that journey. I cannot explain it. I only know that I shrank inexpressibly from it, and would have given my right hand to have remained where we were. But it was all part of the lesson of obedience to the Father's will which can only be learned through suffering (Heb. v. 8). Our leaving was a deep distress to our friends; but we had waited much upon God for the clear unfolding of His mind and none of us doubted that the step was of Him. The sorrow of the farewell, as we parted from our beloved brethren and sister and the little band of native Christians, was mutual. But it was inevitable, and the word was with us, "Let not your heart be troubled; ye believe in God, believe also in Me."

Somewhat to our surprise and greatly to our relief, the crowd made no demonstration as we passed out into the street and on towards the city gate. Mr. Griffith kindly accompanied us on foot for about a mile, and then once more we were alone.

The muleteers had the strictest orders to take the high road, and to ensure this I had it inserted in the written agreement. The first stage was to their own home, for the purpose of completing their preparations (so they said) for the journey; and here we slept the first night. Whether this was a ruse of theirs to furnish an excuse for escaping the high road I cannot say. I only know it was a deviation, and a deviation that cost us dear.

Early the next morning, June 27, we were off again. It was not long before I saw to my indignation that they were taking the "small" road. Their excuse was ready enough. Having come thus far out of the way, they would have to take it for a short distance in order to strike the high road at the most convenient point. This was a deeper trial than any words can express. I could only see in it the old duplicity, and yet we were powerless to do anything. At the mercy of unprincipled men (as I believed), and with such a journey as the last to look forward to, my heart sank. But we were in our Father's hand. He knew there were depths to be gone through deeper than we could conceive, and in view of this He was gently leading us on in the lesson of helplessness and trust.

We made the usual stage (about fifteen miles Eng- lish) without annoyance, and halted for the midday meal and rest at a village town called I-ch'eng. All was quiet as we entered the inn yard, and we began to prepare the children's food. The meal was not ready before the yard was filled with a pushing, curious crowd. It was no use to plead the heat of the day and the fatigue of travel. Every view point was occupied. The rice paper was torn from the window of the small guest-room and every aperture framed a face.

This in itself would not have troubled us much. But with riot in the air we knew not what might lie behind. We had scarcely swallowed a bowl of food when Chi-fah came in and said, "We must be off at once, or I cannot answer for the consequences." As quickly as might be, but without betraying undue haste, we settled ourselves once more in our litters, almost unfed and wholly unrested. The crowd had now grown to immense proportions. The whole of that large village town seemed to be there thronging about us, following behind as we moved out of the inn yard and closely pressing us to the gate with an ominous silence. Suddenly, as we cleared the gate, a yell went up, "Foreign devils ! kill them !" and a storm of stones and hard clay clods rained about the litters. A large stone caught my little boy full in the chest and knocked him flat. The dear little fellow cried bitterly, but he soon recovered, as I prayed with him and told him not to be afraid because God was with us. Several stones entered the litter, but I parried them with a pillow. The mules were hit and became very restive, so that I thought we should be turned over; but by shifting now to one side now to the other, I contrived to maintain the balance of the litter.

The framework now began to show signs of giving way under the shower of missiles. It would have been broken up ere this but for the unusual fact that the covering was formed of new straw mats over which, as a protection against the intense heat, we had thrown a thick cotton wool coverlet. The coverlets were torn off and the stones showered against the yielding straw.

Just as the mats were parting the litters were surrounded and the stoning all but ceased. A big, powerful man seized the mule's head, and looking in at me ordered me to get out. I asked him what he wanted with me, and he said, "I have something to say to you; get down at once." Knowing well enough that once down I should never get up again I refused, and said, "If my respected elder brother wishes to say anything, I can listen to him just as well inside as out."

"You are Roman Catholics," he said ; "get down, I tell you."

"We are nothing of the sort; we abhor the Roman Catholic religion."

"Not Roman Catholics! what are you then?"

"Our religion is the true religion of Jesus, and our doctrine the pure doctrine of God."

The man turned to the crowd and said, "They are not T'ien Chu Kiao" (Roman Catholics), "they are Ie-su Kiao" (Protestants). "Let them go on." Upon this there was a great outcry, and the greater part were for taking us back to the village. But the big strong man got hold of the mule's bit and forced the litter on saying, "Off with you out of this place as fast as you can! We do not want you here."

Only too thankful for this turn in events, I was just shouting in the man's own words to the muleteers to hurry on with all speed, when Chi-fah rushed up, caught the animal's head, and like one desperate forced him round.

"Is the Pastor talking madness?" he said. "At all costs we must return to the village." Return? Why, we had only just been stoned out of it. Surely this was only to court certain death. Again the feel- ing of utter helplessness, as we swung round in the very teeth of the raging mob ; and again the consciousness that the Lord was there.

I had had no chance, of course, of communicating with my dear wife. How it had fared with her I could not tell, as she was behind. It was only when we turned round that I saw her litter in the midst of the surging crowd, battered and torn and all but a wreck. How I longed to say one word to her, and to know how the matter had gone with her and little Hope! In this way we were led back (quietly, to my surprise), just within the gate, and lodged within a small dark room behind a food shop. The litters were brought in and the doors shut on the crowd.

Here, at any rate, was silence after storm. It seemed wonderful to see that such a lull was possible. Now we could spread our bedding on the k'ang and speak one with the other in comparative quietness and rest. As we compared experiences we saw continual cause for thanksgiving. My dear wife had been kept in perfect peace all through. The stoning had been severe, and had bruised her about the arms as she was pitched, first to this side, then to that, against the bulging framework. But a song of praise was in her mouth as she told me that she saw a man load a pistol in a field close by, and that he was in the act of taking aim at her when he was hustled by those about him and the weapon knocked out of his hand. Whether this was accidental or otherwise it was impossible to say, but it was a signal deliverance from death, and together we gave God the glory.

For several hours we were left in comparative quiet. Food was brought, and my wife then took her opportunity of rest with the children, who were soon fast asleep. We heard the hubbub of the crowd outside, and the loud, suggestive battering at the street door; but no one was allowed in except a handful of men. As evening closed in, however, a side door was opened, and a continuous stream of men, women and children filled our tiny room until a late hour. The heat was stifling, and we were well-nigh exhausted with the strain of keeping up after such an anxious day. At last the room was cleared, and we could lie down in peace. Only, however, to find that we were being pelted at through the window just over the k'ang. The curtain I fixed up was almost immediately torn down, and I then blocked the window with a bundle of clothing.

All that night Chi-fah and Mrs. Chang sat in conclave with some four or five of the people's representatives while I kept watch by the window. It was a night of alarms and fears. Every now and again Chi-fah came to tell me the result of the negotiations. They were demanding ransom money, and had fixed an impossible sum. The alternative was that we were to be handed over to the Boxers, two of whom were that night sleeping in the house. Five times at intervals during the night a gun was fired at the street door, to show us what we had to expect. Hands outside the window were trying to push the bundle back, and I thought it quite likely that they would shoot us as we lay on the k'ang. So I set my back against the bundle and gave myself to prayer. Thank God my wife was sleeping quietly with the children. What a long, long, weary night ! And yet I dreaded inexpressibly the return of day.

In the small hours, while it was yet dark, Chi-fah came to me, his haggard face looking years older, and whispered, "The negotiations have failed. Our hope is in God alone." Just at that moment my dear wife was rousing to wakefulness, and instantly divining the drift of things, asked, "What is Chi-fah saying to you? Tell me all." Never shall I forget the perfect calmness with which she received the news, and then said, "Let us ask him and Mrs. Chang to join us in prayer while we can," or the strength I received through the quiet utterance of her unfaltering faith as she herself prayed, "Father, glorify Thy name." We then quietly discussed the situation, and the possibilities of escape suggested by our muleteers under cover of the darkness. The risk of leaving was, however, felt to be greater than that of staying; and with sinking hearts we abandoned our last hope. It was well we did so; for we learnt in the course of the day that, in expectation of our making the attempt, liers in wait watched all night outside the village to kill us. Doubtless there was a plot to get rid of us, but characteristically in such a way that the crime should not be brought home to any responsible person. So we decided, if we had to die, we would die where we were, that the authorities might be compelled to take cognizance of the crime.

Very early, almost as soon as it was light, the crowds began to pour in upon us again. They even pressed on to the k'ang, pulling our things about and examining carefully all we had. Very few remarks were directly addressed to us; but we heard and saw enough to show us that we were more the objects of contempt than of curiosity. At length the proprietor appeared with one or two others, and in peremptory tones ordered every person out. No sooner was the room cleared than some dozen evil-looking men were admitted, who at once began a close and most offensive scrutiny. Chi-fah was not amongst them, to my dismay, and I could not imagine what had become of him. I was thankful to feel, however, that my wife was covered by Mrs. Chang, who sat by her on the k'ang, and answered for her. We were not troubled with many questions, but we were freely discussed and closely examined to see whether we had the marks which would identify us as devils.

A Boxer song of good literary style was having a great run at this time, in which the people were given to understand that foreigners were devils and not men, and that they might know it by certain marks, chief among which was the "blue eye." A translation of this song was given in a copy of the *Pekin and Tientsin Times* early in the year (1900), where I first saw it. I here append the translation given by Mr. A. H. Savage-Landor in his work, *China and the Allies* (vol. 1, p. 15).

"God assist the I Ho Ch'uan (Volunteer Unionists), The I Ho Tuan (Volunteer United Trained Bands). It is because the foreign devils disturb the Middle Kingdom,
    Urging the people to join their religion,

To turn their backs to Heaven,
Venerate not the gods and forget the ancestors.
Men violate the human obligations.
Women commit adultery.
Foreign devils are not 'produced by mankind.
If you doubt this.
Look at them carefully.
The eyes of all foreign devils are bluish.
No rain falls.
The earth is getting dry.
This is because the Christian religion stops the heavens.
The gods are angry.
The genii are vexed.
Both are come down from the mountains
To deliver the doctrine.
This is not hearsay.
The practice will not be in vain.
To recite incantations and pronounce magic words.
Bum up the yellow written prayers.
Light the incense sticks.
To invite the gods and genii of all the grottoes (halls).
The gods will come out of the grottoes.
The genii will come down from the mountains,
And support the human bodies to practise the I Ho Ch'xian.
When all the military accomplishments or tactics
Are fully learned.
It will not be difficult to exterminate the foreign devils
then.
Push aside the railway track.
Pull out the telegraph poles;
Immediately after this destroy the steamers.

The great France
Will fall cold and down-hearted (be vanquished).
The English and Russians will certainly disperse.
Let the various foreign devils
All be killed.
May the whole elegant
Empire of the great
Ching dynasty be ever prosperous!"

As they put their sinister faces close to ours and examined the colour of our eyes, my heart sickened with fear and I trembled as they drew the children forward and said, "Look at these 'siao kuei-tsi'" (little devils); "their eyes are as blue as the big ones'." I cannot honestly say that I was, either now or at other times, exempt from the pain, whether mental or physical, that always attaches to the idea of suffering. To be innocent of the sensation of suffering is one thing, to be divinely sustained and strengthened under the felt power of it is another. Speaking for myself, I learned to the full what it meant to be in " weakness and in fear, and in much trembling." These pages must, if they are to be a faithful reflection of real experience, reveal it again and again. But I trust they will also reveal that we learned with it and by it the meaning of the Word, "When I am weak, then am I strong."

It now seemed evident to me that the room had been cleared, and these men introduced, for one pur- pose only. The ransom demanded was not forth- coming, and the alternative was death. I saw in these men our executioners. Their awful faces were enough to discourage any other thought; but when one of them produced from behind his back two steel stabbers, bayonet shaped, and began toying with them before our eyes, all doubt was gone; and I could only pray God that He would now give us, each one, the special grace for such an hour. The suspense of this terrible moment was possibly the more agonizing that it was the first of many similar situations, and that the terrors of a violent death were at this time fresh to me.

The strain was relieved by the sudden appearance of Chi-fah. How I thanked God at seeing him again! But his face showed no sign of hope. "We are ordered to leave," he said; "the proprietor refuses to keep us here any longer." Without further ado the proprietor himself pushed in, snatched the coverlets from the k'ang, and, cursing us as he went, carried them outside. There was nothing for it. Without a word of remonstrance we made haste to follow.

A long narrow passage led from our room to the street front; and in single file we walked, as we be- lieved, to our death. I placed my dear wife between Mrs. Chang and myself, bringing up the rear of our small band with little Hope in my arms, while Chi-fah led the way carrying Hedley. I observed that the evil gang kept with us, and that the man with the stabbers waited to fall in immediately behind me. I cannot give any idea of that short walk down the dark narrow passage from our prison house. If ever a man walked through the valley of the shadow of death, I did, in those five minutes. Many times were we called to pass that way within the next few weeks, but never was the anguish keener than now. I be-lieved that the man meant to stab me from behind, and every moment I expected to feel the steel. My relief when we reached the street door, great as it was, was certainly not greater than my surprise. I could only suppose that, the proprietor having refused to stain his hands with our blood, we were to meet our end outside at the hands of the mob.

When we came to the street, however, the spectacle that met our gaze was one for which we were certainly not prepared. Dense masses of people lined the roadway on either side, but our appearance was greeted, not as yesterday by the sudden outcry of a riotous rabble, but by a silence so profound as to be awful to the sense. Not a sound escaped them. Surely this was but the calm before the storm; it seemed im- possible that it could be otherwise than ominous of ill, A narrow pathway through the middle of the crowd showed our litters set down in the road, repaired and ready packed, the mules beside them, while just beyond, on a grassy knoll high above the crowd, stood a com- manding figure in a white silk gown, motionless save for the slow flutter of his fan. It was the Ti-fang, or local magnate. I can see him now, standing like a statue with calm and dignified bearing, the centre of the whole scene. The proprietor led us straight to our litters, where several men, the headmen of the village, were standing, who directed us to get in.

Almost before we could settle ourselves on the bedding, we were hoisted to the mules' backs, when to my amazement the Ti-fang came down from his vantage ground, and without a word himself took the leader's bridle and led my wife's litter to the village gate. Close behind him followed the headmen, one of whom led my litter in the same way. Not a soul of all that huge multitude moved from his place as we passed down the narrow lane they left for us. I thought of yesterday and how they had waited till we had cleared the gate before they set on us, and I fully expected that the reigning silence and restraint would give way to an increase of tumult and violence, the fiercer that they were baulked of their ransom money. Now we were outside the gate. Not a sound. The Ti-fang and village elders were still leading the animals, and the road behind us was deserted! In this way we were escorted to the boundary, when the Ti-fang made us a courteous bow and returned. The headmen remained with the professed intention of getting us a proper escort from the yamen, but not long after their chief's withdrawal they also took their departure.

It is impossible to describe the state of our feelings when we found ourselves once more free and un- molested. The unexpectedness of the situation, after being face to face with death for some eighteen hours, and no hope of escape, was almost bewildering. It seemed too good to be true. We were both conscious that it was nothing else than a direct intervention of God on our behalf; and the joy of the deliverance swallowed up the sorrow of the affliction. A song of thanksgiving was in our mouth as we spoke with one another from our litters. It was only later, however, that we learnt from Chi-fah how really miraculous our escape had been. There was nothing to account for the Ti-fang's espousal of our cause. And that the people should have been held in as they were, unable to lift a finger against us it was nothing but the work of God, His fear upon them. Again and again in our after experience we were permitted to see the same supernatural phenomenon; but this first manifestation of it, though by no means the most remarkable, left an impression peculiarly its own.

Questions to Consider

1. According to Glover, the timing of entering the city was evidence of the direct hand of God. Do you believe God gets involved in life at that level? Do you believe God intervenes in your life in "small" things?

2. Chinese families took the Glover's in at their own peril. Would you have taken them in if you knew it would put your entire family at risk?

3. It is one thing to say you will not fear when everything is going well. Do you think you would be able to say you will not fear if torture and death were before you?

4. What causes you to fear now? How do those "causes" compare with the situations the Glovers faced?

5. The Glovers had to decide if they would face the Boxers or armed bandits. Some choice. How do you make a choice like that when all the options appear bad?

6. Again Glover describes a person who he feels is possessed by the devil. Do you think people are possessed by the devil today or do they just suffer from psychiatric problem?

CHAPTER FIVE

Into the Valley of the Shadow

*"Even there shall Thy hand lead me, and
Thy right hand shall hold me"*

Our muleteers now resumed charge of the litters, and we journeyed quietly on with praiseful hearts. I longed, however, for the time when we should strike the highway, as my fears about the "small" road had not proved so groundless as the men would have had me suppose, after all. We had gone perhaps a mile and a half (some five li), when I saw a band of about twenty men spring from the roadside, where they had been squatting, and make for my wife's litter, which was now about one hundred yards in advance of mine. At the same time others came running over the fields to join them. My heart sank: mischief was yet before us. I called aloud upon God as I saw my wife and little girl surrounded, unprotected, and I helplessly apart from them. Instinctively I shouted for Chi-fah, who should have been riding close behind me, but there was no voice in reply. I turned in the litter, and with difficulty forced a hole with my finger through the rush matting at my back, when I was troubled to see a crowd in full pursuit, and our attendants nowhere to be seen.

My own litter was now quickly surrounded and taken forcible possession of by the pursuers. It was evident we were prisoners once more, and completely at their mercy. They made us know it too. With rude violence they began to rob as we went, snatching at the loose articles that lay nearest to hand. My distress can be imagined when I saw the crew that held my wife's litter slash the cords of the light framework, and tear the matting from the poles. The back was shorn clean away, and I could see her supporting little Hope with one hand, and with the other beating off the hands that clutched the goods. To this hour it is a mystery to me how ever she contrived to maintain her balance, for the litter was tilted to a seemingly impossible angle as the men dragged at the very bedding beneath her. Every moment I expected to see her roll heavily to the ground, under the feet of the desperadoes; and I cannot describe what I felt as they turned a bend in the road and were lost to view.

The distance between us had been rapidly increasing, and it seemed as if I should never get to the place where they had disappeared. I covered my face at the thought of what the next sight might reveal, and prayed for grace to bear it; for apart from God's direct interference I could not reasonably hope to see them alive. The bend was reached at last, and from that point the path led by a steep incline to a dry torrent bed. I looked anxiously forward, but there was no sign of my loved ones. In the meantime the plundering of my litter went on, and the wrecking of the framework, just as in the case of my wife's. But this was as nothing now. All was swallowed up in the one thought, "Are they yet alive?" Now we were at the foot of the pass. The mules' heads were turned towards the village at the head of it, when there before me I saw my dear wife's litter set down on the ground in the middle of the torrent bed. Once more the painfulness of the situation was forgotten in the thanksgiving that went up to God, as I saw that both she and my little girl were still sitting within it. A few more paces, and then my own litter was set down in the same way beside hers, and the animals led away. To my amazement she was as calm and free from agitation as though she were in her own home.

It was now about 9 a.m., and the sun was getting hot in a cloudless sky. From the time we left I-ch'eng we had seen nothing of our attendants, and had no idea of what had become of them. Hundreds of people hemmed us in, squatting on the slopes of the ravine or pressing around us with something more than the usual curiosity. In the ordinary way they should have been in the fields at work; but it was a prime element of danger to us all along the route, seriously complicating the situation, that the continued drought had brought all agricultural work to a standstill, and turned quiet, inoffensive labourers into a band of idle, mischievous loafers. Again our hearts went up to God in praise as we saw first Chi-fah and then Mrs. Chang making their way towards us. Their animals had been taken, and they were on foot. They told us that we were again to be detained until ransom money was forthcoming, and that we were not to leave the torrent bed until an earnest of it had been paid down. But both price and earnest had to be fixed; and that meant for us six weary hours under a scorching sun, from whose fierce rays our shattered litters afforded us no protection. The gully, indeed, proved a very furnace, all chance of air being excluded first by its natural position, and then by the suffocating pressure of the hundreds that ringed us round. It was indeed a time of proving, and we found our God again to be a very present help as our shield and strength. Grace sufficient for fainting heat and the cravings of hunger and thirst was richly supplied, as well as for a forbearing spirit and courteous manner towards those who thrust themselves rudely upon us, or plied us with a round of contemptuous questions. Nor was our behaviour wholly lost upon them. The heart of one old woman was so far touched that, unknown to us, she sent her son home for a kettle of "k'ai shui" (boiling water) for us to drink, repeating this kindness until our need was satisfied; and a draught of cold water was also sent us from a neighbouring well.

At length it was decided to require the payment of one hundred ounces of silver. This we absolutely refused, and hours more had to be passed in our painful circumstances as the penalty of refusal. The amount was (to our surprise, I must say) brought down to fifty, and finally thirty ounces, ten of which were to be paid down before we moved from the spot. There was nothing for it but to agree to this; but how to get at the silver without the crowd knowing what I was about? In the providence of God I had weighed out a number of small ingots before leaving Lu-an, to avoid the difficulty of changing on the road, and had taken the precaution to mark each nugget with the exact weight. These I kept in a small packet under my bedding, ready to hand in time of need.

Covered now by Chi-fah I felt for it, and managed somehow quickly to open it from beneath. The few nuggets that came up first amounted to just a trifle over the sum needed! Had it not been so, the longer delay within the litter would have aroused a suspicious curiosity, which would doubtless have ended in our being robbed of all.

The earnest money was no sooner paid than the leading headman of the village ordered the mules to be put in, and himself took charge of my litter. We were led up the stony steep of the straggling street, till we came to a large doorway. The folded leaves parted, and we entered a spacious courtyard from which we saw at a glance that it was the house of no ordinary man. Here our litters were set down, and we were directed to pass on within the next enclosure, the door of which was promptly closed behind us. An old lady, who afterwards proved to be the headman's mother, together with his wife, received us with a show of cordiality which was as cheering as it was surprising. Meantime we were shown into one of the dwelling-rooms — small enough, but comfortable — and told to rest ourselves and not be afraid. Bowls of millet and a kettle of boiling water were quickly at our disposal, and also a hand-basin for washing purposes.

In all this we found abundant cause for thanksgiving. The mere fact of privacy and quiet was a blessing of no mean order. For we were worn out with long fasting and watching, and with the strain of a situa- tion which had brought us into the continuous appre- hension of a violent death. The long hours of detention under the noontide heat of a scorching day, never certain for a moment of the attitude of those who watched us by hundreds, had told upon us. And now we had at last found a shelter from the heat, a refuge (however temporary) from the storm that had beaten so fiercely upon us, and the supply of our present needs. The unexpected kindness, too, of our hostess quite overcame us, and we saw in it all the tender compassions of our Father in heaven.

The situation was, however, sufficiently critical. There was no disguising the fact that in, spite of the outward show of kindness, we were prisoners, and more or less objects of contempt. Moreover, as the hours went by, and Chi-fah had had an opportunity of gauging the temper and purpose of our captors, it became evident that we were in an evil case. Two courses only were possible to us either to acquaint Mr. Griffith by letter of our peril, and through him secure the interference of the Prefect of Shuen-teh; or to apply to the Hsien at Wu-an for the help he was bound by Treaty rights to give us as the magis- trate immediately responsible for our safety. But who would venture to take a letter to the foreigner for us? Or who was there that could be trusted to inform the Hsien at Wu-an? For Chi-fah was himself a marked man; and all else were against us.

How often we were brought to the cry, "We have no might, neither know we what to do; but our eyes are upon Thee!" We had no paper at hand to write on, and besides, if we had, no one must suspect that we were writing, or it would bring us into even greater peril. In the mercy of God, I found a tiny bit of crumpled rice paper in my pocket; and, dividing it between us, we watched our opportunity. Not long after we learned that an extra muleteer, who had for some reason come with us thus far, was returning to his home near the city that night, and was willing for a consideration to take the letter in. About midnight, when all was quiet, he started off with the precious missive hidden in his sock.

The note I sent to Mr. Griffith was, as nearly as I can remember, to the following effect:

Dear Martin,

The day after we left you we were stoned, imprisoned and held to ransom at I-ch'eng. We were let go by the miraculous intervention of God; but have again been seized, and are detained in this place, a village about ten li away.

We are in sore straits. Our only hope of escape seems to lie in your being able to get us help from the Prefect.

The situation is most critical and urgent; but our hearts are being kept in the peace of God. May He guide you and us.

Yours affectionately in Christ,

Archie Glover.

What the message my dear wife sent to Mrs. Griffith said I do not know. But a year later, when in England, I learned that God had used it in a remarkable way. Mrs. Griffith told me herself that all through their subsequent flight and long confinement at Cheng-ting Fu, she kept the tiny fragment — the only writing she had in her possession until the pencil marks were faded out and the paper worn to tatters. She said that she could never thank God enough for having sent her that little word to lighten the darkness of her weary night of suffering, and to revive her fainting spirit in distress.

The next day (Friday, June 29) passed quietly, a grateful contrast to what had been, even though our way out was hidden from us. Chi-fah was scarcely visible all day. He was anxious above everything to let the Wu-an mandarin know how we were situated, and he was watching for any opportunity that might offer. None, however, presented itself. Every thought was baffled, and we were brought to our wits' end. As we waited upon our God, we learned how good it is to trust in Him at all times, and to pour out our heart before Him.

It must have been about ten that night when Chi-fah came to us with the exclamation, "Kan-sie Chu tih ngen" "Thanks be to the Lord's grace!" The headman in whose house we were was, he said, con- nected with the yamen. An opium sot and a thoroughly bad man, he wanted to make something for himself out of the situation, and so had agreed to let Chi-fah go to Wu-an in company with his old mother at daybreak, provided we paid him fifteen ounces of silver down. It seemed almost incredible. Even Chi-fah had hardly dared to believe that such a thing could be, and even up to the last feared that some excuse would be found for its not being carried through. More than once threats to this effect were thrown out. But the money was paid down (how thankfully!), and the bargain struck; and, furnished with my passport and visiting card, they stole out ere it was yet light, and were gone. Thus both the plans which had seemed so hopeless were fulfilled. Our letter had been dispatched to Shuen-teh, and our attendant to Wu-an.

All Saturday we watched in prayer, and waited for God's answer. The tiny courtyard where we were lodged was kept very quiet; save for one or two relatives no one was allowed in, and we, for our part, were strictly forbidden to show ourselves at the court- yard gate. Several opportunities were given of speaking the Word of life to the members of the household, including the headman himself. I recall particularly the deep interest which the young woman who first received us evinced, as my wife sat by her side in the doorway, and, holding her hand, told her tenderly the story of the Saviour's love for her, even unto death. It is one of the pictures of that time that has engraved itself with peculiar distinctness upon my heart. Who shall say that our captivity there was not of God, in His design to set another captive free?

Hour after hour went by, and no message from Shuen-teh. We had expected Chi-fah, too, not later than the early afternoon; for the distance to and from Wu-an would easily admit of that. But the afternoon wore on into evening, and evening into night; and neither the one nor the other appeared.

Just upon midnight there was a noise in the outer courtyard of loud and angry voices. The inner door was flung open, and by the light of lanterns we saw the old mother being led in, supported on either side. She was in a state of devil possession, and chanting the weird incantation peculiar to such condition. They took her to her room; and there, through the remaining hours of the night, we heard the unearthly voice above all the rest, as it rose and fell in cursing cadence.

It was an untold relief to see Chi-fah safely back; for, circumstanced as we were, it was not difficult to believe that he might have fallen a victim to foul play. He told us that after considerable difficulty he had been allowed to see the Hsien, and had been given an escort of ten soldiers, who were accompanied by a petty official and several gentlemen of the yamen; and we were to be ready to start at morning light. The noise in the outer courtyard meantime increased, and Chi- fah came back to say that the soldiers were wrangling over the question of pay, and were on the point of making off. The headman, moreover, had suddenly relented of the contract he had entered into, and was now raging against us in a fit of uncontrollable passion (seng ch'i), and swearing that he would not let us go. A moment later, and the man plunged into the room, quivering with blind rage, and cursing us all at the top of his voice. The resonant wail of the mother's chant blended with the loud tempest of the son's abuse, in a unison that only devils could create. It made one tremble — the presence of the power of darkness was brought so near.

But now see how marvellously God was working for us. Just when matters were at their worst, and we at our weakest, a messenger from Shuen-teh Fu appeared. I recognized him as a well-to-do business man of that city, of good standing and repute, and one in whom Mr. Griffith placed much confidence. Addressing himself immediately to the headman, he asked him how it was he dared to molest us, and told him that the news of his conduct had come to the ears of the

Prefect, who had forthwith dispatched a band of fifty soldiers to look into matters, and that Mr. Griffith was with them. He had himself been sent on before to tell him that if a hair of our head was touched or one single cash taken from us, he (the headman) would have to answer for it in person to the Prefect himself. Never shall I forget the extra- ordinary effect produced by his sudden appearance and speech. The terrifying bully, all cursing and bitterness, was instantly transformed into the fawning sycophant, all flattery and consideration. He was in terror at the thought of the fifteen ounces of silver he had demanded, and implored us not to expose him.

We told him that he had treated us kindly while we were under his roof, and that as the silver was promised on our part in return for the service he rendered in securing us an escort from Wu-an, we should certainly not regard it in any other light. His gratitude was profound and genuine enough, I have no doubt; and from that moment he was kindness itself to us. He quickly adjusted the difficulty with the Wu-an escort, and soon all was quiet. The only thing that broke the silence of the last two hours of that troubled night was the haunting cadence of the old witch mother's chant.

When all were asleep the Shuen-teh messenger returned and handed me a pencil note from Mr. Griffith. It was dated "Friday, 5 a.m.," and ran much as follows :

"Your letter just received does not come to reassure us. We are preparing for flight ourselves, and have been up all night packing, every moment expecting to be rioted.

We deeply grieve to hear of the peril you are in, but are powerless to help you, as we are practically in the same plight as yourselves. The Fu (Prefect) will do nothing for us. Our eyes are upon God alone. We shall sleep to-night at the muleteer's home, and take cart thence to Lu-ch'eng, if possible."

I turned to the messenger. "This is a very different story to what you have given out. There is not a word about the Fu giving help, and so far from Mr. Griffith being on his way here with fifty soldiers, you must be aware that he is himself in need of help and about to flee."

"Hush!" he said, "not a word! It is a ruse of my own to get you out of this net. Mischief is brewing, and if you do not get out now, you never will. All you have to do is to keep quiet and leave matters with me." We lay down, but we could not sleep. Our heart was filled with wonder. God, even our God, was with us, mighty in working. He had verily broken gates of brass, and cut bars of iron in sunder; and in the night His song was with us, and our prayer unto the God of our life. We thought much of the dear Griffiths and their kindred peril, and our hope was that we might yet meet them at Lu-ch'eng, only one stage distant from our own destination of Lu-an; but we never even heard of them again, until our two months' wanderings were over; and we could not but conclude of them (as they were led to conclude of us) that a violent death had overtaken them.

Questions to Consider

1. Mrs. Glover was allowed to share about Jesus with a young woman in the leader's house. Glover sees this as the hand of God. "Who shall say that our captivity there was not of God, in His design to set another captive free?" Do you think God would allow Christians to suffer persecution in order that others might come to know Him?

2. Do you think God will place you in situations that might be uncomfortable for you so that someone else might come to know Jesus?

3. Again we are presented with devil possession. Is it real?

4. The Chinese messenger lied to the ruler and frightened him into letting the Glover's go. Should the messenger have lied? Would you have lied?

CHAPTER SIX

Out of the Depths

"In all their affliction He was afflicted, and the
Angel of His Presence saved them"

Our litters were once more rigged up, and eight o'clock that Sunday morning saw us released from captivity and again starting out with thankful hearts. July 1 the first day of a week and the first of a month of unimaginable terrors and undreamt of sufferings. Thank God they were hidden from our eyes; and there was given us instead the sight of the Lord lifted up above all, and the promise, "Fear not, for I am with thee; look not around thee, I am thy God." The day of slaughter at Pao-ting Fu, (1) it was destined to be to us also very memorably the day of darkness and of the shadow of death.

It was not easy to face the mob again after nearly three days of privacy, and with the knowledge (now more than ever certainty) of what it was sure to mean.

But then we were under official protection, and this went far to allay anxiety. Expectant crowds had gathered as usual, and now we were fairly launched In the thick of it once more.

The headman led my litter, accompanied by the Shuen-teh messenger, who wore an air of authority that seemed to carry everything before it. The latter accompanied us beyond the village boundary, and at the parting of the roads took courteous leave of us and returned to the city. The Lord render to him again the kindness he showed us, our true friend and benefactor! The yamen gentlemen and soldiers kept close beside us; and their presence undoubtedly made itself felt. At any rate, it was an untold comfort to us; for as yet we knew nothing of the widespread conspiracy under Imperial auspices which converted our passports into mere paper and our rightful protectors into our persecutors and very murderers. (2)

Our reception all along the road to Wu-an was of such a kind as to show us what our fate would have been but for the escort. The word had gone on that we had paid out money for our release, and it was clear that each town and village we passed through was eager for a share of the spoils. The men were generally armed with some implement or other, and our appearance was greeted with an outcry of "lang kuei-tsi! Shah iang kuei-tsi!" ("Kill the foreign devils!") Our curtains, kept closely drawn, were quickly torn away. From the evil look and malicious gestures of the crowds, as they hooted and cursed us out of their place, I am sure it would have gone very hard with us, had not God's mercy provided official help. Even as it was, the people were hardly restrained from assault- ing us, and one could only be conscious that it was again God's fear holding them back at the very crisis of their rage.

Arrived at Wu-an we were driven into the yamen, where word was speedily brought us that the Mandarin was willing to give us audience. I confess I followed the "runner" with some trepidation, as I had never interviewed a Ta Ren (great man) before, nor seen the awful majesty of a yamen judgment hall. Besides, my vocabulary was not of the largest, and my knowledge of yamen etiquette by no means of the pro- foundest. However, Chi-fah was with me, and I took courage. We passed through two small, mean-looking courtyards it surprised me to see how mean they looked into a third equally small, but with a display of tinsel and dingy finery which marked it out as the Mandarin's own quarters. At the doorway was the Ta Ren himself in full ofiicial dress waiting to receive me with a small retinue of gentlemen. As soon as he saw me he reached out his hand in the most fatherly way, and with a genial smile led me to the guest's seat on his left. Two cups of tea were brought immediately for himself and for me, and the reassuring manner of the kindly-seeming old man (however hollow) sent all my fears to the winds. He conversed most affably with me, examining my passport, and assuring me he would do all in his power to get me through to my station without further annoyance. While we were thus talking a small crowd stood by, dirty underlings rubbing shoulders with the upper ten, and one and all, the higher with the lower, innocent of even the smallest semblance of decorum in the presence of their chief. In due course a "uen-shu" (or passport letter to the next magistrate) was made out, and an escort to Shae Hsien provided.

On returning I was surprised to find my wife seated, not in the litter as I had left her, but on the ground, the little ones by her crying bitterly, and she herself looking as if she had received some shock. The mules had become restive and refused to stand, with the result that just before I appeared the litter had been overturned, and they thrown to the ground. Thank God, they sustained no serious injuries albeit my dear wife, in trying to save the children, had fallen heavily enough to be badly bruised. But she made light of the misadventure, and her brave spirit soon brought smiles into the little ones' eyes in place of tears.

We lost no time in getting off, as delay meant in- creasing crowds, synonym at such a time for increasing danger. The escort given us consisted of six sorry-looking underlings, who shortly after starting dropped to four. These men, who should have been for our help, proved to be our worst enemies.

We must have been travelling about four hours in the mountains for a distance of some thirty-five li (twelve English miles), when we struck a broad, dry river bed, along which the mule track lay. I had noticed that an hour or so previously the escort had again dropped to two, which made me not a little uneasy. However, I persuaded myself that the remaining two represented officialdom; and after all, what more did we need? — no one would attempt to touch us where Government authority was in evidence. How little I knew! At a bend in the river track we came upon a large straggling village town; and ere we were well abreast of it the torrent bed was swarming with excited men and lads, and the air rent with shouts and yells of "Shah iang kuei-tsi! Shah, shah! "We saw they were preparing to stone us. Any number of missiles lay around them ready to hand, and already the greater number had armed themselves. Several stones had actually been hurled, when Chi-fah stopped the litters and asked the escort the meaning of it all.

Upon this they stepped forward, and in a very casual, half apologetic way produced our papers for the head- man to see, who forthwith took possession of our litters and led us to a large newly-built inn, standing by itself at the head of the way. As we entered the courtyard the gates were closed behind us, no one being allowed admission but the village elders. The guest-room ran the whole length of the north side of the courtyard, and was only partially finished. There was a good k'ang, however, at one end, and a good roof was over our heads, affording substantial shelter from the intense heat; for both of which we thanked God. In this room we passed through a time of agony such as was not surpassed at any period of our sufferings, before or since.

It was the old story of a ransom price with the alternative of death. The matter was discussed in cold blood before the very officers who were pledged to protect us and with their connivance. Nay, more, at their instigation. For on arrival at the inn the two who had been left with us were rejoined by their comrades who had so mysteriously disappeared. With the knowledge of the previous attempts (not wholly unsuccessful) to levy blackmail, they had hastened on before to inform the townsmen of our approach and to arrange the plot for our arrest. They were not such fools as to let slip a golden opportunity of making a handsome squeeze for themselves; while the blame, if it fell upon anybody, would fall upon the townsmen; for what could they do against a riotous multitude?

I never saw Chi-fah in such distress of mind. We were strictly guarded. The escort withdrew themselves sullenly to the opposite end of the room with their opium and tobacco, and made not even a pretence of doing their duty by us. Our one hope (humanly speaking) lay in our being able to inform the Kuan at Shae Hsien of our plight, and secure his prompt intervention. But the distance was long (from 80 to 100 li there and back), and who could go? The muleteers utterly refused; and when Chi-fah planned under cover of darkness to slip out on mule-back, they be- came so nasty that the thought had to be abandoned. So the afternoon wore on, the plotters plotting at the one end, and we making our prayer to God at the other.

At nightfall a small lamp was brought in, the feeble light of the raw cotton twist only serving to make darkness visible and to reveal the shadowy forms of the evil men at the other end as they sat in conclave. Partly to hide them from our view, and partly to provide ourselves some privacy, we contrived to stretch a cord from wall to wall and hung it with our coverlets. We had just put the children to bed when Chi-fah told me that there was now no hope of getting out alive. It was not merely a money question, he said, but we were held responsible for the prolonged drought; and it was the common belief that nothing but foreign blood would bring the rain. Unless God Himself directly intervened by a miracle, nothing could save us.

"But," said I," we are under official protection, and when the Government has undertaken to safeguard us, what have we to fear ?"

"That goes for nothing in the circumstances," he replied; "the escort itself has betrayed us, and they can easily excuse themselves to their superiors by saying that they were overpowered by numbers."

Then indeed sore anguish came upon me and soul distress. The news must be kept at any cost from my dear wife, and I charged both Chi-fah and Mrs. Chang to tell her nothing that would unduly alarm her. I sought grace so to control my feelings that I should not betray them by look or manner; but not- withstanding, she guessed the truth, and begged me never to keep anything, however painful, from her. She would not be denied her wifely privilege of fellowship with me in prayer, nor therefore of partnership in all the suffering; and from that time on I kept nothing back. We had all things in common, the worse as well as the better.

Thus it came to pass that we had been pouring out our heart before God, and seeking grace to endure even unto death, if His will were so, when a truly marvellous thing happened. The door was pushed open, and a soldier in full uniform entered, and quietly hung his coat and cudgel on the latchet. His hand- some face and commanding manner were something out of the common, and could not fail to arrest attention. But this was not enough to account for the effect his sudden appearance produced upon all. I cannot describe it. It was simply startling. He was only a non-commissioned officer sent on special service to Li-ch'eng ; and he was merely putting up at the inn for the night in the ordinary course of his journey that was all. No, not all. Our eyes were opened to see in him none other than God's deliverer. Even as he entered the door, he stood before us as the very angel of God. I might almost say "a light shined in the prison" there was something so supernatural about his presence. It was the most remarkable experience of its kind that I ever had, or my wife either; for we were both conscious of it at the same time. Not only so; but his coming produced a cor- responding fear in the hearts of our enemies. We learned afterwards that the escort were in dismay, believing that his business was in some way connected with them. In any case, the general impression produced on all was that he was charged with some important commission concerning us and in our behalf. In keeping with our conviction was the remarkable fact that from the first he identified himself with us and espoused our cause. Chi-fah invited him to eat his food within the privacy of our curtained space and talk with him there an invitation to which he at once responded. How vividly the picture stands out before me the two figures dark against the coverlet in the dim flicker of the lamp flame talking earnestly in whispers inaudible to all beside! As yet we knew nothing of the stranger and his errand, and could know nothing of the tenour of his conversation; and yet we seemed to know intuitively that he was God's mes- senger, and that his words were of peace and not of evil.

After the soldier had finished his meal he withdrew, and with a heart almost too full to speak, Chi-fah came to tell us all. It was believed by our captors that the man was officially sent to look after us; and on the strength of this belief he undertook to pass us out at dawn the next morning, and himself accompany us to Li-ch'eng. What this news meant to us cannot even be imagined. It was literally the turning of the shadow of death into the morning.

There was still, however, the difficulty to face of the people's temper towards us on account of the drought. Continually throughout the day they had been battering at the gate and threatening to break it in with repeated cries to bring us out to them; and we gave ourselves earnestly to prayer on this account. It being the Lord's day, we determined to hold Divine service before lying down to rest, and with our Chinese Bibles and hymn-books we took our seat on the ground by the curtain under the lamp. As we prayed and sang praise to God, a deep hush fell upon all in the room, and ere long we were joined by the soldier and the two muleteers. As he would be better understood, I asked Chi-fah to read and expound the Scriptures; and then we sang again and each prayed in turn. The soldier listened with the deepest interest. There was something beautiful about that young man's face and manner that drew the heart out peculiarly towards him. I see the earnest eyes still fixed on the preacher as he preached unto him Jesus; and I cannot but believe that, in answer to much prayer, the seed of eternal life was sown in the fruitful soil of a heart prepared by the Spirit of God to receive it.

"Whoso offereth me the sacrifice of thanksgiving, glorifieth me; and prepareth a way whereby I may show him the salvation of God." The second miracle of that memorable day followed almost immediately upon the conclusion of our worship. We had pleaded with our God to have mercy upon the people, not only in their deep spiritual need, but also in their temporal distress. And we asked very definitely in the hearing of all that, for the glory of His great name, He would be pleased to send the rain in abundance that night, that they might know that He was the merciful God, and that we His servants were not the cause of the drought. Scarcely had we laid ourselves down on the k'ang, ere His voice answered from heaven in a thunder crash that shook the prison, and the rain fell in a deluge that ceased not all the night through. When morning broke it was clear shining after rain; and the song of the Lord was in our mouths. The gate of our prison-inn opened to us, as it were, of its own accord. Our heaven-sent soldier rode beside us and never left us all the way. No one molested us as we passed out into the road and along the highway to Shae Hsien. Indeed, we scarcely saw a soul, for at daybreak all hands had hurried to the fields to take early advantage of the long-looked-for opportunity for putting in the Seed.

Arrived at Shae Hsien, I had to leave my wife and children at the inn under the soldier's care, while I accompanied Chi-fah to the yamen. I was determined to guard as far as possible against a repetition of the last experience; and an official interview was an urgent necessity. We found that we had to walk from one end of the city to the other — to me an interminable walk in the thought of my loved ones alone in the inn and at such a time. In spite of pigtail and gown I was recognized as an alien, and the inevitable crowd began to haunt my heels. By the time we reached the yamen it was uncomfortably large, and from the expressions which repeatedly saluted my ear it was by no means certain that we should get out without trouble.

The "Men-shang " (or Mandarin's deputy) received us coldly enough, and said it was impossible for us to see the Lao-ie. I presented my card, and insisted that he should take it in my business was imperative. He returned with the excuse that his Excellency was too unwell to see me. Upon this I said that, that being so, I had no alternative but to appeal to his superior, the Prefect of Chang-teh. The gentle hint had the desired effect, and in a few minutes we were ushered into the "great man's" presence. I told him briefly of all we had suffered on the way from Wu-an, of the inadequacy of our escort to protect us, and of the current report that our passport was a forgery. I begged him to endorse it with his seal, and to give us a guarantee of safe conduct to the next Hsien of Li-ch'eng. Glad to get rid of us at any price, he readily agreed; and thanking him for his kindness in receiving me, I made the customary bow and withdrew.

In the mercy of God, the curiosity of the people, either on the street with us or with my dear ones at the inn, did not break bounds, although it was clear that their feeling towards us was not what it was in the near past. We did well to be moving, and as soon as our escort arrived with our official papers we were off. The non-commissioned officer accompanied us still. His presence at the inn had been of the utmost service and comfort to my wife; and together with a runner from the Wu-an yamen a lad who had followed us um-officially and attached himself voluntarily to us he had kept the crowd away from the door of the guest room, thus enabling them all to get their meal without molestation.

There was no demonstration as we filed down the high street to the south gate, and from that time on our journey was pursued in peace. At Li-ch'eng we changed escorts without the formality of a visit to the Lao-ie; and here we took farewell of our soldier deliverer. My wife's eyes moistened, I know, as we commended him at parting to the mercy and love of God in Christ; and I am not ashamed to confess that my own did, too.

In addition to several books we made him a present of five hundred cash a sum utterly inadequate to his services as it seemed to me; but CJi-fah knew his own people best, and cautioned me not to give beyond that amount. Unworthy as I thought the gift, the recipient acknowledged it graciously and with every appearance of unaffected gratitude.

The abundant rain had tranquillized the hearts of the people, at least for the time being; and they were now too busy in the fields to notice us much. As we neared our sister station of Lu-ch'eng, the familiar road seemed to parable our inner experience and to sing aloud of the loving kindness of our God. For the parched ground had become a pool, and the thirsty land springs of water; and we, since last we passed this way, had seen the glory of the Lord and the excellency of our God.

Questions to Consider

1. Chi-fah said there was no hope of getting out alive. At that point, Glover said they were resigned to death and asked God for grace to endure. What would you have done?

2. A soldier "happened" to appear in a tense situation. Do you think this was accidental or do you think God arranged for it to happen?

3. The soldier not only saved the family but also heard the gospel message. Do you think this was God ordained?

4. If you face persecutions or difficult situations will you try to share the message of Jesus with the people you come in contact with?

CHAPTER SEVEN

Flee! Flee!

"Though the Lord give you the bread of adversity and the water of affliction, yet . . . thine eyes shall see thy teachers; and thine ears shall hear a word behind thee, saying, This is the way, walk ye in it; when ye turn to the right hand and when ye turn to the left "

We reached Lu-ch'eng about 10 a.m. Tuesday, July 3. Our friends were not wholly surprised at seeing us back; and deeply thankful, when they heard our story, at seeing us at all. With themselves, the rumours on the street had been getting worse and worse so much so that they had necessitated Mr. Cooper's communicating with the Hsien. At our own station of Lu-an, it seemed that the situation was very precarious. Miss Gates had kept Mr. Cooper informed as to the state of things there, and was evidently feeling the strain of a position which at any moment might become critical.

We determined to make no halt, but to push on the remaining fifteen miles with what speed we might. The lad from Wu-an had undertaken at Li-ch'eng to go on before with a letter to Miss Gates and prepare her for our coming a gracious provision of God's providence, as Chi-fah could not possibly be spared for the service.

It was desirable to keep our return as quiet as possible, and to this end we reduced our luggage, leaving our more foreign-looking boxes at Lu-ch'eng. We also dispensed with an escort, as their appearance in the city would, we thought, create talk, and suggest a situation in connection with our return which it was well to keep out of sight as far as possible. As we once more bade each other farewell, we were all conscious that it had a deeper significance for each one than usual. Ere we were destined to meet again, four weeks hence, we were one and all to know, as never before, what it meant to drink of His cup, and to be baptized with His baptism.

The muleteers urged the animals, and we travelled well. The road was perfectly quiet, but we took the precaution of keeping our curtains down. Half way lay a large village called Lan-shui, which had always been more or less hostile to us. Only quite recently they had attempted to drag Mrs. Dugald Lawson from her cart as she was passing through. Before coming in sight we made a detour, and so avoided them, happily without being discovered. Ten li from Lu-an we passed through the village of Kuan-ts'uen, an outstation of ours, where we had a chapel and a bright little band of Church members and inquirers. As we peeped through the curtain we saw several of the dear familiar faces on the street, and could not forbear revealing ourselves to exchange the Christian salutation of " P'ing-an!" ("Peace!"), and to commend them to the grace of God. (1)

We dared not stay, however, for more than a passing word. An hour later we were entering (for the last time) the north gate of the city. All was quiet. It was intensely hot, and no one was about. So far as I could hear behind the curtain, the drivers were not once challenged by a passer-by. Yes, we had entered unobserved. And now we were alongside our mission buildings. Oh, the goodness and mercy of our God! We turned the corner into the "keh-lang " (or side street) where our more private entrance was, and a minute later our litters were standing within our own compound, and we within our own sweet home!

The reunion with our sister, Miss Gates, in view of the events that had happened since we parted, was an intense relief to us all. We learned that her path, not less than ours, had been an increasingly difficult and perilous one. The Boxer movement in the province had grown apace, and had spread to our own immediate neighbourhood. Corps were being rapidly organized in every city; and in towns and villages recruiting was brisk. At T'uen-Hu Hsien, sixty li off (twenty miles) a corps of 200 men had already been formed, and the Boxer chief entrusted with the work at Lu-an was daily expected in the city.

Not long after we left, rain processions had begun again to parade the streets. Owing to the Boxer rumours which were now circulating freely, together with the inflammatory placards they were posting up wholesale, these processions became a more than ordinary source of anxiety. Miss Gates decided that, should an emergency arise, it would be wiser for her to go into the Prefect's yamen, as a removal to Lu-ch'eng would almost certainly be construed into flight a construction which would result in swift disaster, not only to herself, but to the Lu-ch'eng community as well. Meantime, she took counsel with Mr. E. J. Cooper, and was in almost daily communication with him.

The Sunday before our arrival that eventful July 1 these processions culminated in a grand func- tion, which was attended in person by the Fu, the Hsien, and all the city notables. There was a legend to the effect that somewhere in the remote past a devotee of the village of Su-tien (about a mile south of the city) had at a time of excessive drought been divinely guided to a fountain in the neighbourhood of Li-ch'eng, the water of which had the virtue of drawing down rain from heaven upon the locality to which it was brought. From thenceforth the discoverer and his family became famous in Su-tien. Whenever the season was unusually dry the fountain was resorted to by the head of the clan, a local deputation accompanying him with the village idol. The function in question was the reception of the sacred water outside the city, and the bringing it within the walls to the temple of the God of War, where with befitting ceremony it was laid up until it had proved its miraculous power.

As the procession would have to pass our premises to meet the returning deputation outside the north gate, the native Christians were apprehensive of evil. Not without reason; for the Su-tien folk bore us a special hatred from of old, and more than once had threatened us. They now gave it out openly that on returning from their pilgrimage they intended to attack the "Je-su fang," and wreck it as they passed. The continued drought had been so definitely attributed to us by the Buddhist priests, that the thought had only to be suggested, they knew well, to find acceptance with the processionist mob. Moreover, the rumour of our having poisoned all the wells had been revived; so that, with such inflammatory material to work upon, the threat was simply as spark to tinder.

Miss Gates considerately sent the native helpers and servants to their homes, retaining two only, who refused to leave her — Chong Sheng-min, and Chang P'ao-ri. Several of these, however, together with one or two inquirers, came in on the preceding Saturday purposely to share the time of trial with her, and to protect her, if need be, to the last. One of the latter, Li Tong-chii, a recent convert who had already given striking evidence of his fidelity to Christ, walked 120 li (forty miles) over the mountains as soon as he heard that "Chiang kiao-si's" life was in danger. Such devotion had been a wonderful cheer to our sister. These dear brethren greatly strengthened her hands in God, continuing instant in prayer, both in fellowship with her and by themselves.

At the hour appointed when the procession was expected to pass our doors, the little company gathered in the chapel. The meeting took the form as much of praise as of prayer; and while 10,000 were giving glory to their idol, the handful within, whose lives they sought, were praising the beauty of holiness and ascribing honour and strength to His name. Li

Tong-chii's prayer specially impressed itself on Miss Gates' heart, his petition being that if it were not the will of God at this time to call them to lay down their lives. He would so put His fear upon their enemies that they might have no power at all against them.

Whilst thus engaged the roar of the huge procession was heard gathering in volume as it drew nearer. Without a pause it swept on, thundered past the gate, and died away in the distance. How marvellously had God answered! It transpired that, all unknown to Miss Gates and those with her, the news of the intended riot had come to the officials, both of whom, in company with many of the most prominent gentry, took up their position opposite our premises, the Fu and the Hsien themselves standing in the very door- way until all had gone by. The incident is interesting in another connection, viz., as affording a suggestive contrast to the attitude adopted towards us by the same men within the same week.

I may here add that the heavy rainfall that night (July 1), which had been instrumental in securing our own deliverance from the inn, was at Lu-an attributed to the virtues of the miraculous water, and construed into a sign from heaven that the gods were pleased with the devotion manifested in the Boxer movement towards the "Great Religion."

The following day (July 2) it was rumoured that the Empress Dowager had issued secret orders for the extermination of the foreigner. Thereupon Miss Gates insisted on the native helpers and servants returning to their homes, and began to make preparation for possible flight to the hills.

The faithful Sheng-min refused to leave her, but knew of a cave whither he undertook to pilot her, pledging himself to care for her through every vicissitude.

Such was the situation we found on our return.

It was now clear to us all that we were face to face with a crisis the nature and extent of which it was impossible fully to gauge, but whose gravity was sufficiently apparent. We could not but feel sure that the recent action of the officials in showing themselves our friends and protectors was something of a guarantee of security. Moreover, we knew that in general a heavy discount must be allowed on all street rumour; and so we hoped, and encouraged one another to believe, that things were not as black as they looked. Still, though we were in ignorance of the provincial Governor Yu-hsien's violent antipathy to the foreigner and of the active measures he had already taken in hurrying on his bloody purpose, we knew that the Boxer movement was spreading to our parts, and had now become a fact that we must definitely reckon with.

Yu-tsien, the Butcher of Shan-si

The day following our return (July 4) I sent our cart out to Lu-ch'eng for the boxes we had left behind. We united in the earnest prayer for the clear knowledge of the will of God; and it seemed to us then that unless we had something more definite to go on than street rumours, we ought not to think of leaving the station.

At dinner time, while sitting at table, Elder Liu came in to say that the Hsien had sent to ask "whether we were going South." The inquiry surprised us, as being so altogether out of the ordinary, and so apparently uncalled for; but we concluded that possibly he was at a loss to account for our having returned, and wished in this way to get at the reason. In the light of later events, I now think it may have been intended as a hint to us to make good our escape while we might, consequent on his knowledge of the edict communicated to him that day, the requirements of which he was told to carry out. However that might be, we thanked his Excellency for his kind inquiry, and assured him that we had no intention of leaving the city.

At dusk the boy returned from Lu-ch'eng with our boxes. He brought also a note from Mr. Cooper, with a pencil message enclosed (hastily written on a scrap of paper) from the Rev. A. R. Saunders, of P'ing-iao. The latter was to the effect that they had been rioted at their station, and had only just escaped being taken and put to death. They were making for Lu-ch'eng, in the hope that matters were still peaceful there, and might be expected within the next few hours, the party consisting of four adults and four children. (2)

Mr. Cooper drew the inevitable conclusion of im- pending trouble for our own stations also, and the need of our all being prepared for a similar experience, while he asked our prayers that special grace might be given him to know how to act in circumstances OF added responsibility.

It was clear that matters were heading to a definite issue, and we began to ask ourselves seriously: Ought we not at least to be ready for flight in case of sudden emergency? The climax, however, was reached when positive news was brought in later that the edict which it was rumoured the Empress Dowager had issued for our destruction might be seen posted up outside the yamen; and that our death was now the topic of the hour. Not only so, but the actual day had been fixed for our execution the tenth day of the sixth moon.

On the north side of the Mission compound there was a small door in the wall opening on to fields remote from the main thoroughfare. This we hardly ever used. But during the morning the thought had occurred to us that a time might come when we should be glad to avail ourselves of it for purposes of escape, and that it would be well to have the key at hand. Accordingly I went to take it from the place where it usually hung; but it was gone. High and low we searched for that key, but it was nowhere to be found. And now the time had come when I needed it. To slip out to the yamen by the back way of the fields was my only chance of getting through; for I was warned that it was not safe to show myself on the street. Again we betook ourselves to prayer, when another long search unearthed a few disused keys, one of which fitted the lock. Fervently thanking God, I took Sheng-min with me and slipped out at dark by way of the fields to the Hsien yamen. The Men-shang received me with the usual show of courtesy, but was evidently primed with his answer in view of an expected visit. Upon my urgently requesting to see the Ta Ren himself, I was told that it was utterly out of the question the Lao-ie was indisposed, and must not be disturbed. He would himself hear my business, if I wished, and report it to his chief. He invited us into an inner room, and bade me be seated. I then told him of the report I had heard, that an edict was out, purporting to come from the throne, for our destruction; and I wished to acquaint his Excellency with the fact, and to beg him, if the rumour was an idle one, to take immediate steps to suppress it. The Deputy's manner was of the blandest. He too had heard that a little small talk of the kind was about, but he could assure me there was nothing in it, positively nothing. And with a reassuring " Puh p'a, puh p'a" ("You have really nothing to fear"), he promptly dismissed me. I went back with the burden considerably lightened, though not wholly removed. In the light of the Men-shang's assurance, we felt there was nothing to indicate that it was God's will for us to leave the station. Indeed, the friendly action of the officials so recently as Sunday last led us to believe that we were far safer within the city walls than exposed to irresponsible hostility without. And then, how often had these rumours proved to be mere idle tales, and these threats but a breath!

However, when I awoke next morning (July 5), the shadow of the cloud was over me. I felt it parti- cularly as I went to my private devotions, and opened my Bible at the portion for the day, in the regular course of reading. It was the eighth chapter of Joshua. I came to the fifth verse, "It shall come to pass that when they come out against us we will flee before them." My thought was arrested, and as I prayed over the passage, I heard but one voice, "Flee before them, flee before them!" The word "flee" seemed to stand out from all the rest. I shrank from the call the memory of the road we had just passed over was too bitter. Was it possible God was calling us to pass that way again the mother as she was and the little ones? Then the words in verses 1 and 8 lighted up, "Fear not, neither be thou dismayed. See, I have commanded you." The call was so clear and emphatic that, in spite of our resolve the previous day and the assurance given by the Mandarin, I felt convinced that flight was now for us a God-appointed duty. After breakfast we gathered according to our regular custom, for family prayer, Miss Gates uniting, as usual, with us. We were reading consecutively through the books of Samuel; and the chapter for that particular morning was 2 Samuel xv. Imagine what I felt when I opened to the chapter and read on to verse 14, "And David said unto all his servants that were with him at Jerusalem, Arise and let us flee; for we shall not else escape from Absalom: make speed to depart." Again I heard the authoritative "Flee! Make speed to depart, for we shall not else escape." It was enough. Closing the book, I said, "This is the Lord's word to us. The path is clear beyond the shadow of a doubt. We have nothing now to do but to obey and 'flee.' "I then related to my wife and Miss Gates the incident connected with my private reading before breakfast, and the striking confirmation of the word then given so impressed them that they no less than I recognized it as the declaration of God's will for us, and we began forth- with to set our house in order and to prepare for flight.

Not long after a message arrived from the Hsien asking me to send my servant round to the yamen, as he had something important to communicate, but on no account to come myself. An hour later Sheng-min returned with the dreaded confirmation from the Mandarin's own lips of the rumour we feared. The Hsien told him that the substance of it was perfectly true. Secret orders had been received from Peking directing that official protection was to be entirely withdrawn from us. He wished to say that we could do as we chose, stay or go; but that in either case he was powerless to help us.

We now saw the reason, as well as the mercy, of the clear guidance just given us from God. To stay was to be left absolutely in the hands of the people, who but four days before had vowed our destruction, and who would now recognize, in the withdrawal of official protection, the official sanction of the deed. To go had at least an element of uncertainty about it, that was wholly wanting in the alternative choice an element the very faintest, but still there. In staying, all hope that we should be saved was taken away. In going, there was just a ray of all but hopeless hope to which we clung; for who could tell if God would be gracious and bring us through?

It was now that God used the telegram, addressed from Shanghai to poor Mr. William Cooper at Shuen-teh, to guide me in the decision. If only we could get clear of the district and work down towards the coast in a southerly direction, we should be always getting farther away from the disaffected zone, and might yet outdistance the trouble. The thing to do, therefore, was to hire mule litters to Chau-kia-k'eo, in Ho-nan, where we had a mission station, and thence by native boat, if necessary, to Shanghai. If our money supply ran short, our brethren at Chau-kia-k'eo would make up the deficiency until a fresh supply was received from headquarters. For it must be understood that at this time we had no idea that the trouble was other than local. We had to learn piecemeal, by bitter experience, that it had affected Ho-nan not less than Shan-si, and that the Chau-kia-k'eo scheme, even if it could have been carried through, was a thing of naught. As it was, however, God used it to foster hope and to accomplish His purpose in our escape from the city.

Sheng-min was accordingly sent off to secure three litters.

Quietly, busily, prayerfully, the day was spent in packing, settling the affairs of the Church, and making the necessary dispositions of property. Our flight would, we knew, be followed inevitably by the looting of the premises. To attempt to save any articles at all seemed lost labour. But a friend of Sheng-min's volunteered to take two of our boxes and hold them in safe keeping for us; and we trustfully gave them into his care. We also gave permission to the personal staff on the place to take whatever they found that might be of use to them, feeling that we would rather they had the benefit of our goods than the lawless rabble. One of the last things I did was to send our dining-room clock as a present to the Hsien, in the hope that it might move his heart to some degree of pity for us.

Not the least trying part of the sad offices of that sad day was the taking farewell of the few members of the Church who came in to see us in the course of the day, believing as we all did that we should see each other's face no more. Elder Liu entreated us with tears to lose no time, but make the best of our escape while we might. "It is your only chance of life," he said, "poor as that chance is; but to remain within the city walls till the morrow's light is certain death." The last prayers were breathed, the last exhortations and promises from the Word of God given, the last affectionate assurances exchanged, and they were scattered every man to his own.

How many times our hearts went back to the ever recurring question. Should such a man as I flee Are we right in leaving the flock in the cloudy and dark day? It was only after a conflict too great for words that the peace of God reigned in the knowledge that our flight was of Him and really for the sake of the Church we were so loth to leave. For if we remained, their destruction was sure, so closely were they identified with us; whereas, if we left, they could escape to the hills or wheresoever else, and preserve their lives in the will of God, to His glory and the furtherance of the Gospel.

While eating our midday meal, Sheng-min returned from his long quest to say that he had been to every hiring place known to him in the city for carts and litters, but that no one would take the "foreign devils." What was to be done now? We were beginning to realize that in very deed we were as the filth of the world. Had it really come to this, that we were so hated of all men that no man cared for our souls? The announcement was as the knell of approaching doom, for it revealed a state of feeling towards us which foreboded nothing but death.

I saw that, as the road to the south was our only hope, no effort must be spared to secure conveyances of some kind, and I again sent the boy out to search while we prayed. Oh, how earnestly we prayed! Everything hung upon the success or failure of the errand. Yet had not God said to me, "Flee, fear not; see, I have commanded you"? Surely He would provide us the means of flight. At sunset the boy came back to say that, after hours of wearying search, and just as he was giving it up as hopeless, he lighted upon two muleteers in the west suburb Roman Catholics who secretly agreed to carry us to Chau-kia-k'eo for 80,000 cash. The bargain was struck (although the sum was exorbitant) and the agreement written out.

In the course of the evening a former servant of ours, Man-ch'eng, came in, in a state of deep concern for us. An order had been issued to close the city gates. He entreated us, therefore, to hazard flight on foot, taking with us nothing more than a small packet of necessaries for our immediate need. Our only hope now was to be lowered by a rope over the city wall an offence punishable at any time by death if detected; but he would undertake to do it for us if we for our part would go out with him at midnight to a place on the north wall not far distant.

Here was a new problem. The city gate closed of what use were the litters to us now? Escape by the wall the thing looked a sheer impossibility. The risks, even physically, were many and great; and since detection was almost certain, it would be better to die for well-doing than for apparent evil-doing. It might be that God, who had given us the litters, would work for us to open the gate. At any rate, we would abide by the hope of the litters, and if it failed in the will of God, it failed.

That night, while we were packing in the bedroom, Sheng-min came in, exclaiming with an unwonted degree of excitement :

"Come, all of you, do, and look at the moon; it is a strange eight! I never saw anything like it. Every- body is talking about it." I saw from his manner that he read in it some fateful omen; and partly to allay any alarm to my wife which his manner tended to excite, and partly to rebuke his superstitious fear, I said, "We who believe in God trust only in Him. We put no faith in the things the heathen look at. They are nothing to us, and have no power to make our hearts afraid." After he was gone, however. Miss Gates thought it might be as well to see what the phenomenon was. When she came back she could only say, "Oh! you really ought to see this moon; it is too extraordinary." So we went.

Never shall I forget the horror of the sight. I use the word advisedly. As we looked up, my wife and I involuntarily exclaimed, "How really awful! " There, staining a clear sky, it stood among the stars a mass of blood! I could only repeat the word that came immediately to my lips so singularly in keeping with the dark judgment hour now close upon us "The moon shall be turned into blood before the great and terrible day of the Lord come."

It certainly seemed to be literally fulfilled before our very eyes. God only knows why it was thus, and His own purpose in permitting it on *this* night, of all nights. From the human point of view, nothing could have been more untoward. It practically sealed our doom, and cut off the last hope of escape. The final aggrava- tion of a condition of things already sufficiently fearful, it could convey to the superstitious mind but one meaning and one determination. Certain it is that one word only was on the lips of all: "See! blood written in heaven! T'ien Lao-ie himself confirms the Emperor's decree for the destruction of the foreign devil; and, look you to-morrow is the tenth day of the sixth moon!"

Questions to Consider

1. How do you handle lies and rumors told about you? How should you handle them?

2. There were several Chinese Christians willing to stand up to violent mobs in order to protect Miss Gates. Are you willing to stand up to "mobs" that attack individuals in your world (the workplace, school, groups, etc.)?

3. Should the missionaries have left the church members behind?

4. Note that once again some Roman Catholics came to the rescue of the Glover family.

CHAPTER EIGHT

The Tenth Day of the Sixth Moon

"Remember the word that I said unto you,
A servant is not greater than his lord "

It was not far from midnight when the litters appeared. By special arrangement, they were to put up for the night in our own stables, so that the early start might be made with the utmost possible secrecy. We had expected them earlier in the evening; and as the time wore on, and still they did not come, we felt some uneasiness, in the fear that, with the omen of the blood-red moon to daunt them, the men had thought better of the bargain. It was with no small relief, therefore, that we heard the clatter of hoofs upon the stones; and our hearts went up in praise to God that He had put the means of escape actually under our hand.

Those last moments that closed our happy station life at Lu-an I cannot dwell upon them. The sorrow upon our hearts was, in a very real and solemn sense, even unto death; and yet behind it all was the peace of God, and beyond it, we knew well, was the glory of God. My precious wife was borne up by Divine strength for the physical fatigues of that laborious night: so indeed were we all. In sweet unconsciousness, our two little darlings lay asleep, side by side, on the bare bed-frame, ready dressed for the moment of flight. My wife and Miss Gates packed as calmly and methodically as if they were leaving for an ordinary visit or itineration. There was haste, but no hurry.

All was carried through in the quietness and confidence of God's strength, and with a conscientiousness which left every room and every cupboard as neat and orderly as if the expected absence were but for a few days.

By lantern light we packed the three litters. It seemed like a dream. Only just off the road, and now, could it be that we were really taking the road again? After weary weeks of peril, we were at the home so often longed for: could it be that we were really leaving it again, to face peril certainly not less grave than that we had already passed through? For myself, I know I put the things in with a heartache that often groaned itself out to God.

And now the muleteers were here to give the finishing touches to the litters, and to warn us that the hour had come. For the last time we knelt together in our loved home beside the sleeping children, and commended ourselves and the little flock we were leaving into the hands of our Father and theirs. Then, lifting the dear little ones in our arms, and locking the doors behind us, we took our seats and were hoisted once more to the mules' backs.

The first streaks of light were breaking over the hills as the little cavalcade stole across the wide compound; and, like light from heaven, the promise was flashed into my dear wife's heart, "I shall not die, but live, and declare the works of the Lord." Precious promise! How many a time it carried her over the power of death in the awful "valley of the shadow" she was just entering, the sequel will show.

Silently we passed out by the big gate into the main north street. Sheng-min accompanied us, leading the donkey our own animal. P'ao-ri remained to close the gate behind us and shoot the bar, that our flight might not be perceived. He then scaled the wall, and rejoined us farther down the street. One other elected to follow us~-our faithful dog, "Bobe." With an almost human instinct, he seemed to divine that there was trouble before us, and that he should never see us again; and nothing would turn him back, though never before had he attempted to leave the premises when we were going away.

The dead stillness of the sleeping city palled upon the sense and intensified the nerve-strain. The road- bells upon the mules' necks had been dispensed with; but even so, the ring of their hoofs upon the stones had, to my anxious ears, a sound about it so loud and penetrating that one felt it could hardly fail to call the curious from their beds. So far as I could judge, as I sat behind the close-drawn curtain, not a soul was met with. In absolute silence we pressed on, down the north street, across the east and west streets, into the by-road running parallel to the south street. The moments seemed minutes, the minutes hours. At length we struck across into the main street, close down by the great south gate. A few moments more and we were halted before the massive barrier, fast closed against us.

Loud and long the drivers knocked at the gate- keeper's door. In vain; not a sound from within, nor any that answered. The light was broadening in the east, and ere long men would be astir, and the precious moments upon which our hope of getting outside the city hung, were swiftly passing. "Be still, and know that I am God": the Spirit breathed the word into my heart, and there was perfect peace.

Then a loud, uncouth voice, demanding who we were and what we wanted at that time of day; and an insolent refusal to open the gate. What happened upon this I could not tell. There was silence for a time; then voices in hot debate, and then were my ears deceived? the creaking of the huge iron-plated leaves as they swung slowly, slowly open! Then the drivers' call to the animals; and a moment later we were without the city.

God had wrought for us very signally, as He that openeth and no man shutteth; for while we had to pay a certain sum, not only was the amount demanded a comparatively trifling one (10,000 cash) (1) but it was nothing short of a miracle that the man should agree to receive money at all in the circumstances; and we gave Him the praise, as we hurried on through the narrow suburb out into the open.

It was broad daylight now; but as yet we had met no one to challenge us. I began to breathe freely as the distance from the city increased, and a sweet sense of freedom seemed borne in upon the fresh morning air. At the pace we were travelling, we might even hope to reach Kao-p'ing Hsien (forty miles distant) before we halted for the night and before our flight was discovered. So I thought, and so I prayed.

We had gone about ten "li" between three and four miles when I found that Miss Gates' litter, which should have been close behind mine, was nowhere to be seen. Thinking that our two litters had out-paced hers, I called a halt to give her time to come up with us. The enforced delay troubled me sorely, as every moment was of consequence. We waited some minutes, but there was no sign of her coming. Just as I was giving the muleteer orders to turn and go back for her, P'ao-ri came running up to say that, shortly after clearing the suburb, a small band of men had given chase, held up the litter, and demanded so much money before they would let her go on. She was free now, and would be up with us directly. I saw at once that, with the discovery of our flight, our chance of escape was, humanly speaking, gone.

As soon as she came up with us. Miss Gates urged us to hurry on with what speed we might. There was no question but that, as soon as the world was astir, we should be hard pressed by other robbing bands from the city; and not a moment was to be lost. Oh the heart-cry that was going up to God from the concealment of those litters! The dear children were awake, and it was hard to silence the gleeful laugh and prattle that might betray us. They could not understand why they might not "draw the blinds" now it was morning, nor why they must "sit all in the dark and keep so quiet, as though it were bedtime." But their absolute obedience in a situation that, to a child, would be trying to a degree cooped up and cramped as they were within the narrow space of a darkened litter, with every object of interest shut out from view was beyond praise. Indeed, so far from being a trouble, the presence of our little ones was the greatest cheer and comfort to us. Except for the sorrow that they should be exposed to such suffering, we could not be sufficiently thankful for their company.

We must have been pushing on steadily for close upon another hour, when we found ourselves suddenly pulled up. The noise of men pursuing told its own story. The fact of our flight was out, and the issue was in the hands of God.

From that time on, until we reached our first halting place — a distance of some fifteen "li" farther — we were dropping cash at intervals in varying sums to satisfy the insolent demands of these robbers. If there was any demur, we were stopped and detained until the demand was complied with. No actual violence was offered us at this time. Sheng-min and P'ao-ri succeeded in so holding them, that they were taken up for the time being with the contents of the cash bag. Not until this store was exhausted did they turn their thoughts to other things.

It was just at the crisis when the cash bag had nothing more to offer them, that we reached the market town of Han-tien, somewhere about nine o'clock.

To our surprise, instead of passing through and on we were driven into the inn, the mules stabled, and ourselves shown to a room on the east side of the quad- rangle. Not long afterwards, we discovered that our muleteers had played us false, and that we were the victims of designed treachery. They had been in collusion with the robbers by the way, and it was they who had betrayed us now into the hands of our enemies. From that hour for forty days to come we were to know no rest day or night, under the ever present sense of storm and tempest and the shadow of death.

We took from our litters only such of our things as we needed for an ordinary halt, in confident ex- pectation of resuming the journey an hour or so later. But any such hope was soon dispelled. The court- yard was fast filling with men; and from the tenour of their talk and general demeanour, the boys gathered at once that mischief was determined. Under pretext, therefore, of fetching out pillows and coverlets for a siesta, they contrived to bring in all the silver we had with us one hundred and forty-eight ounces. Dividing the ingots amongst us, we succeeded in secreting them upon our persons without being observed.

Meantime, the news that the "iang-kuei-tsi" ("foreign devils") were in the town had spread far and wide, and the inn was soon besieged. All day long they poured in from the surrounding hamlets, until one wondered how the streets could hold them. Foremost amongst them all, in the bitterness of hate, were the people of Su-tien; and with their advent, in the early afternoon, the situation began to take on a darker hue. Up till then I had been able to show myself in the courtyard without being molested, but now this was no longer possible. We realized that, to all intents and purposes, we were no longer the occupants of a guest-room, but the inmates of a prison.

From the first the landlord treated us with marked incivility and neglect so much so, that we had the greatest difficulty in getting food. Though we had been travelling since dawn we were allowed to taste nothing till noon, and absolutely nothing after. From that hour until the following Sunday afternoon two days and nights not a morsel of food passed our lips.

As the day wore on the noise outside increased. Sheng-min and P'ao-ri mingled with the crowd to glean all they could of their intentions; and every now and then the one or other of them would slip in to let us know the result. The drift of it all was revenge for the drought, and compensation for the loss of their harvest.

The Su-tien folk were not long in getting to business. We knew it by the agonizing cries of our faithful "Bobs," as they stoned him to death just outside the door. Our donkey, too, was led away and put to a cruel death, though, I am thankful to say, we were spared the knowledge of it at the time.

Attention was now turned to our litters, and a search for silver began. As soon as we were made aware of it, I saw that it was no longer safe to conceal the money in our clothing. If they could not find it elsewhere, they would without doubt search our persons; and this would mean violence, to say the least if not death. So, while they were engrossed outside, we divested ourselves of our small hoard, and hid it among the stuff on the "k'ang." The fact that they dared to violate their traditions so far as to lay hands openly on travellers' property secured within the walls of an inn, proved how far they were under the impulse of hatred and rage.

Meanwhile, a detachment of Boxers arrived at the inn and proceeded to discuss the situation with the leading men of the villages represented. Baffled in the search for silver, and burning with the spirit of revenge, they unanimously resolved to put us to death. Sufficient justification for the crime, if any were needed, would be found in making it the alternative of an impossible sum, which they would demand as legitimate compensation for losses sustained through the drought, of which we were the cause. The amount agreed upon was 200 ounces of silver.

When Sheng-min came in to break the news, we saw that he was much agitated. Seating himself on the k'ang, he said, "The Boxers are here, and we are all to be killed"; then, burying his face in his hands, he leaned his head on Miss Gates' shoulder and wept bitterly. We were all much affected the more, that the little ones had caught up the words as they fell from his lips, and began to cry bitterly too, as they clung about us, questioning, "Oh, father! Mother! what are they going to do to us? Are they going to till us? really kill us?" What else should we do at such a time than draw nigh to God? Humbly and trustfully we lifted our eyes to Him from Whom alone our help could come; and as we looked at the things not seen, and yielded ourselves into His hand for life or death in the prayer that He alone might be glorified, the peace of God took possession of our hearts and stilled every fear. Even the darling children's terror was hushed to rest as they repeated after their mother, while she kissed away their tears, "I will trust, and not be afraid"; and soon after they were wrapped in a calm, untroubled sleep.

We now urged Sheng-min and P'ao-ri to leave us to our inevitable doom, and to save their own lives while they might. They both refused, and that with the full knowledge that their identification with us would involve them in the same certain destruction. I cannot speak as I would of such self-sacrifice. When the story of the Boxer persecution is fully told, it will be known that despised China can furnish instances of devotion that would adorn the records of any country in any age. Those dear lads literally laid down their lives for our sakes, in a surrender as disinterested as it was voluntary and deliberate.

They had scarcely gone out to resume their watch in the courtyard, when suddenly the air was filled with a tumult of shouts, yells, blows, and groans. We looked at one another, but dared not give audible expression to the conviction in all our minds that this was the beginning of the end for us the murder of our boys. To judge from the sounds, they were being beaten to death there could be no doubt of it; and my heart stood still as the horrid thud of blow after blow fell upon the ear. It was a time of mute crying to God in speechless anguish. A few minutes more, and it was over; the tumult ceased as suddenly as it had arisen. The door was flung open, and a "small" mandarin named Ma, from the Lu-an yamen, entered, lit his pipe and sat down. Others followed, with whom he conversed in low tones, completely ignoring us the while. At length he rose, and addressing us said that as we foreign devils had caused great suffering to the good people of the neighbourhood, we were to be fined in a sum of 200 ounces of silver; that we should be detained until the money was forthcoming, and that therefore it was to our interest to pay up. To remonstrate, of course, was useless, though remonstrate we did. We respectfully reminded him that, as we had resided several years in the city, he must be aware that our teaching and our whole manner of life was against evil-doing, and that to take our money upon a false pretext was grossly unjust. Whereupon he sneeringly turned on his heel and went out, with his following.

The afternoon of that long and bitter day was closing in, and the twilight fast fading into darkness. What thoughts were ours in the gloom of our prison room! Betrayed, in the hands of the Boxers, and given over to certain death; our animals killed already; and, for aught we knew to the contrary, our two boys also the situation could hardly be darker. But "the darkness hideth not from Thee"; nor could "the power of darkness " rob us of the light of God's countenance.

Just at the moment when the outlook was darkest, the door opened, and in walked Sheng-min! His appearance, just when we were mourning him as dead, was truly "light in the darkness" the earnest of our Father's care for us, the promise of His mercy for dark days yet before us. It was not he and P'ao-ri, after all, that had been attacked, but some three men who had spoken up for us when we were condemned to die, and had declared that the Boxers should not touch us, a sentiment for which they had been set upon and severely beaten, but not actually killed. Later on, these poor fellows came in, and, showing us some of their ugly bruises, appealed to our compassions, as having suffered in our behalf; and we gave them some 8,000 cash (or about six ounces of silver) a piece.

A lamp was now brought in and set in a niche of the wall above the table. Ma Lao-ie followed, and others with him, until the room was full of men. Whether these men were the local representatives or just the Lao-ie's own creatures I could not say. They were his for the business in hand — willing instruments, of one heart and of one mind.

Forms were fetched and ranged round the table, at the head of which the Lao-ie had seated himself with magisterial dignity, and the mock formality of a trial began. We were not required to leave our place on the k'ang, nor was any word directly addressed to us. The proceedings consisted apparently of a general indictment, which was supported by specific charges, sworn to by false witnesses. Truly "they laid to our charge things that we knew not" things too vile to put on paper. Among the more innocent were old hackneyed stories of cutting out children's eyes and hearts for purposes of alchemy, of bewitching the ground, spoiling the "feng-shui," and what not; reeled off in company with those of a more recent type, such as poisoning the wells, disturbing the repose of the Earth Dragon (by the introduction of railways), shutting up the heavens, frustrating the prayers of the needy, and blaspheming the gods. The dim flicker from the single strand of cotton twist, doing duty for a lamp above the Lao-ie's chair, fell with uncertain light upon the livid faces of our accusers, revealing in part the passion that worked in every feature a picture revolting enough at any time, but horrible in the distortions of semi-darkness. As charge after charge was brought forward and proved to the satisfaction of all, the excitement grew in intensity, until it reached the vehemence of fury. We were unanimously declared unfit to live, and sentence of death was passed.

Interior of the room at the Han-tien Inn where the sentence of death was passed upon us.

Forthwith they fell to discussing the mode and time of execution. The suggestions selected for consideration were to poison us with opium there and then; to behead us with the sword in the inn yard; to shoot us with a foreign gun they had in their possession; or to carry us outside on the street, and fall upon us en masse.

The last proposal found the most general acceptance, and was accordingly adopted. Its great recommendation, apparently, was that it would give an opportunity to all who had a grudge against us to gratify their feelings of revenge. It would, above all, shift the responsibility of the crime from the shoulders of any known individuals to those of the intangible many always a consideration of moment with a Chinaman, and probably the one that settled the matter now.

The time chosen as most suitable for carrying the sentence into effect was daylight the following morning.

And with that the dark conclave broke up. And with it was ended the tenth day of the sixth moon.

Little did they think that there was One standing amongst them, Whom they knew not, but against Whom they were imagining vain things. One, in Whose sight the souls of the helpless little ones before them were precious, and Who was even now their light and their salvation. Of a truth, we realized what it was to be "accounted as sheep for the slaughter"; but we also tasted in that solemn hour the triumph of the word

"Neither death . . . nor any other creature shall be able to separate us from the love of God, which is in Christ Jesus our Lord."

Questions to Consider

1. All of the "foreign devils" (missionaries) left the mission. The local church members, who were also in danger, were left behind. Should the missionaries have left them or stayed and shown their willingness to die with them?

2. The Glover's seem to be paying bandits all along the road. Should they have done that?

3. Shen-min and P'ao-ri not only were their guides but continually put their lives at risk to help the Glover's. Would you have been willing to do that?

4. When they learn they are to be killed and the only matter for discussion was the method of killing, the Glover's children asked why they were to be killed. How would you have answered the children?

5. Would you have been able to pray for the salvation of the people who were deciding whether to poison you with opium or behead you?

CHAPTER NINE

Condemned

The few remaining hours that were left to us before the death-sentence was to be executed were, so far as our outward circumstances went, nothing but unrest. Ma Lao-ie took up his quarters in our room, and with another an evil man, his close companion spread his bedding on our k'ang. Far into the night, many were coming and going, all insolence and mockery as the event of the morrow was freely and jestingly discussed before us. Among them all, none was more offensively ribald than Ma himself.

Our persons and effects were now subjected to close scrutiny and search. The Lao-ie mounted the k'ang, and with his own hands overhauled each article in turn. At last he came upon what he wanted silver. With the exultant greed of a miser he clutched the packet and said, "You foreign devils will have to make this up to two hundred taels before we have done with you. Where's the rest?" Seeing that nothing was to be gained by remonstrance, and knowing that resistance (even had it been possible) was not after the meekness of our Master

Christ, Who, when He suffered, threatened not, we quietly surrendered our little store, at the same time rebuking the sin.

When all was in his hands, scales were called for and the weight verified. I see him now — how vividly — seated at the table, surrounded by some half-dozen sycophants, intent on the adjustment of the weight to the beam. The lamp had been lifted from its niche to the table, that the figures might be accurately read; and as the taper lit up the sordid features of the bending group, the dirt-begrimed and cobwebbed room looked, what in fact it was, a veritable den of thieves. It was as impressive a spectacle of human depravity as could well be seen. I understood then, as never before, how the love of money can be said to be "the root of all evil." Every unholy passion lurked in the lust depicted in their faces. There was no sin those men would not commit to possess the coveted thing. They were possessed by it; it was their life. Their soul was in it, and they would sell their soul to have it.

When the weight was told, it was declared at so much. Turning to us. Ma said, "There is such and such a deficiency. Come, bring out the rest of your money, or it will be the worse for you." We replied that he had our all; that he had already made a thorough search himself, but that if he doubted our word, he was free to look again. Upon this he and his companions searched our persons; but finding nothing more in the way of sycee, he significantly said, "Very well, if you can't make it up in money you will have to make it up in kind"; and forthwith they hilariously fell to appropriating whatever their heart coveted amongst our goods on the k'ang. That done. Ma turned to us again: "This is not enough; it will not nearly meet the deficiency. What else have you got? Quick, give it up!" His manner was insolent and abusive; and seeing that he was about to search our persons again, we gave up the last possessions we had our watches, which were secreted in an inner pocket. These, and my pocket-knife, were evidently considered a great find, and were turned over and over with every mark of satisfaction. But all to no purpose. "Still not enough," he said; "what we have here will not even bring the amount up to a hundred and fifty ounces. In default of payment, your effects in the litters are forfeit also." No need to be told that. We guessed it long before. It was only a Chinese-y attempt at "saving their face" over a shameless piece of wholesale robbery, determined upon from the beginning.

Having thus justified themselves in their wickedness, they lay down beside us, not to sleep, but to regale themselves with opium, and to gloat over their spoil. I see the Lao-ie still, in the haze of the smoke, fondUng the large fifty-ounce "shoe" of silver, as ever and anon he turned it to the light of his opium lamp and examined the marks of its purity. And so with each article in turn.

I suppose it must have been about three o'clock a.m., when a man with a large yamen lantern came in, evidently to receive instructions. Almost immediately after he had withdrawn the deep boom of a gong broke out upon the stillness, and continued at intervals until it was light.

For all this the grace of God sufficed us. Not withstanding the intense heat, the vermin, and the opium fumes, my dear wife was given a spell of quiet sleep, for which I could not sufficiently thank the gracious Giver. For the rest we spoke but little, and that only in whispers, that we might not rouse the suspicions of our captors. But as we communed with our own heart upon our bed, in the near prospect of a violent death, we each experienced the deep peace of the words, "I know Whom I have believed, and am persuaded that He is able to keep that which I have committed unto Him."

And now, with the summons of the gong, though it was yet dark, the stir of rousing life began to make itself heard without. Every now and again the door would open and two or three would look in, leer at us, exchange a few words with the Lao-ie, and go out. These, doubtless, had to do with the business in hand. Then, as the grey of early dawn appeared, the inn yard began to fill; and with the broadening daylight the whole place was alive with thronging crowds.

For some two hours longer we were kept in durance vile, awaiting the end. By the help of God, we were enabled courteously to answer the many questions with which we were plied, and patiently to take the cruel revilings of the many who watched us. Among the deep consolations of those bitter hours, not least was the joy of being allowed, in the compassions of Christ, to bless those that cursed us, and to pray for them that despitefully used us. The fact that we did so was remarked upon by our enemies not once nor twice in the course of our many weeks' captivity; and the contrast with what they themselves were accus- tomed to under similar circumstances made its own impression. They would be heard to remark aside, "These people cannot be so bad, after all; for while our mouths are full of cursing and bitterness, their's are only full of kindness and good words. They never revile us back again: truly, they heap to them- selves great merit against the life to come."

Meanwhile, Ma Lao-ie was busily occupied without. The turbulent hubbub seemed to subside in presence of an expected end: and the significant hush told us that the last preparations were being made. With no audible word or outward sign to indicate it, my wife and I took the secret last farewell of each other. The glory of which she whispered to me was even now in her face; and the tender firmness of her hand's pres- sure told me how completely she was lifted above the fear of death. Only her eyes moistened when she kissed her little son good-bye that was all.

We now engaged unitedly in prayer, in which I commended each one into the hands of our Father, in prospect of the death we were about to die. But even as I prayed, the petition seemed forced to my lips, "If it is not Thy will that we should die at this time, then, our God, for the glory of Thy great Name bring their counsel to nought and weaken their arm."

Almost immediately afterwards the Lao-ie entered with his following, and in peremptory tones ordered us out to the litters. I led the way with my little boy, followed immediately by my dear wife, leading baby Hope. But Ma's impatience could no longer brook restraint, and brutally broke bounds. Seizing Miss Gates by the hair, he dragged her from the k'ang, and thrust her to the door with a blow from his clenched fist.

We were scarcely allowed time to seat ourselves before the signal to move on was given. Our boys were dragged back and not permitted to accompany us. So far as I was able to see the three litters started together, that occupied by my dear wife and little girl following close behind mine: for which I thanked God, as the thought that possibly we should be divided in the article of death was the one thing that had burdened me.

As we passed out of the courtyard into the street, what a sight met our gaze! The roadway for the first hundred yards was held by Boxer guards, armed with sword and spear, and brave in Boxer red: while on either side, as far as the eye could see, was massed in dense formation a countless multitude, eagerlv expectant, and armed (apparently, to a man) with some rude implement or other.

No sooner had we cleared the inn gate than the mob closed in upon us. Then we were halted, and they formed themselves into a procession, headed by Ma Lao-ie. A young man with a large gong stationed himself beside my litter. When all was ready marshalled, at a signal from the Lao-ie the procession moved forward to the measured beat of the gong.

I could only attach one meaning to all this. It was a sacrificial procession: and our murder was to be viewed in the light of an offering to the gods. The appeal, therefore (very subtly), was to the strongest of human passions — the religious — in order to make the issue doubly sure.

As we swung on in the midst of the surging mob to the place of sacrifice, it was only to prove afresh the power of Him, on Whom our mind was stayed, to keep in perfect peace. To the natural man, the situation was one calculated to inspire the utmost terror; but I bear record that the only dread I felt, so far as my own lot was concerned, was that suggested by the barbarous implements carried by the mob. I am telling the simple truth when I say that at the sight of the keen blades and pointed spearheads of the Boxer soldiery, I fervently thanked God; for they argued at least a speedy despatch. A desperate set of men hung on to the poles of the litter. I can see the man who was next me even now, stripped to the waist, his queue lashed round his head ready for action, a great stone in his right hand, and a bowie knife in his left.

I longed to know how it fared with my loved ones behind, and also with Miss Gates; and with a great effort, amid the lurchings of the litter, I contrived to turn and tear a tiny hole with my fingers in the straw matting at my back, just large enough to peep through. Oh, the sight! The way behind was a billowing sea of heads and weapons; and the frail litters, oscillating dangerously from the pressure, looked like two cockle- shells tossing on the crest of foaming waves.

I was thankful to see that their occupants were still within; though Miss Gates was so far behind that I could only make out the bare fact that she was there. My precious wife, with wee darling Hope, was sitting well forward, so that I could see every feature per- fectly. Her arm encircled the shrinking little one, and she was talking gently to her; and as she talked, it was wonderful to see how her face reflected its own restful calm in the pale features of her baby girl. Ever and again she would gaze out upon the wild scene before her, as seeing not that, but Him Who is invisible; for a heavenly smile was on her lips, and her countenance shone with a light that was not of this world. I saw her face, literally, as it had been the face of an angel. It was, for me, a vision the beauty of which will never fade — a glimpse of heaven open, amid the sights and sounds of hell. My soul could only magnify the Lord as I saw how absolutely, in His weak handmaiden, death was swallowed up in victory, through the power of the indwelling Christ, Who was her Life.

We had traversed about two-thirds of the long main street when an extraordinary commotion ensued. The Lao-ie dashed at my leader's head, and tearing at his mouth forced a halt. Then, in orthodox Chinese style, he raged and cursed, and denounced the people of the place for their "peaceableness," and for having "ruined the whole business." What this could mean I was at a loss to understand at the time: but evidently the preconcerted signal for attack had not been re- sponded to. In all probability the Lao-ie's orders were that, at a given spot, and when the gong ceased to sound, they were to fall upon us. The spot had been reached; the gong had ceased to sound that, at least, was certain; and the people had failed to answer the call! Yes had we not definitely prayed before leaving the inn, that God would bring their counsel to nought? It was a remarkable incident the very last that one would have thought could occur in such circumstances; and I who witnessed it and realized, as no one else can, the absolute hopelessness of the situation from the human standpoint, testify that it was nothing else than the work of Him Who had heard that prayer, and taken the wise in their own craftiness.

Tho Lao-ie's rage yielded at last to the persuasive vehemence of those about him — the men who had witnessed against us as they urged him to have us taken to the boundary of the town, where they would themselves finish the matter to his satisfaction. Where-upon the procession moved forward, and we were borne rapidly on without the gate.

We were well outside, when Ma thrust his head into my litter, and said, "Throw out your bed-bag quick!" This was easier said than done: for not merely was it a heavy and awkward article in itself, but it formed our seat, and how to dislodge it while on it was a problem. However, the Lao-ie appreciated the difficulty as much as I did, and without further ado set to work to solve it with his own hands. My co-operation saved him a good deal of trouble and us, too; for, under God, it doubtless saved our lives. Heavily the unwieldy bulk lumped over the side, almost dragging both us and the whole structure with it; but the litter righted like a boat relieved of ballast, and I found myself, with my little boy, lurched on to the sharp edges of the boxes in the ropework below.

The disappearance of the bed-bag and its contents was followed forthwith by the temporary disappearance of those immediately about us. It was as a sop to ravenous wolves; and while they tarried to fight over the spoil, we were hurried on to the boundary. Their place, however, was quickly taken by others, as I knew from the wild scrimmage going on underneath, and from the fact that we were sinking uncomfortably lower into the netting. With an effort I hoisted myself on to the cross-pole, taking Hedley on my knee; but our proximity to his hind-quarters was too upleasantly close to be relished by the "seng-k'eo," who began kicking and plunging in a most unsettling way.

It was now clear to me that the end had come. To remain longer in the litter was an impossibility, unless we committed ourselves to the ropework; and to do this only meant eventual death in the entanglement of its meshes. So, infinitely preferring to die outside rather than in, I took Hedley under my arm, and lifting my heart to God jumped to the ground.

The scene that now passed before my eyes baffles description. Shut in as one had been in a vehicle closed on three sides, it had been impossible until now to take in the whole situation. It would seem that the Lao-ie's demand for my bed-bag had been the signal for a general melee. The mob that had flocked out after us set upon the three litters simultaneously, and was soon broken up into squads of fighting demons, mad for plunder. Amid fiendish shouts they fought for the spoil. I had not been a moment too soon in leaving the litter; for scarcely had my feet touched the ground before it was overborne, crumpled up, and demolished.

A light mule litter of northern China.

And now I looked anxiously for the other two litters. Not that I expected to see any one of their occupants alive, any more than I expected to be left alive myself. This was death, certain death, for us all: it was only a question of moments. But it was the natural and the uppermost thought in my heart Where are they? Are we still together? Is it possible for me to know whether they have been already called home

Miss Gates' litter was nowhere to be seen, and I concluded that she was dead. But there, parallel with mine, about twenty yards away, was my wife's; and between her and me the howling, fighting mob, surrounding and besetting her on every side. Looking back over the whole period of my sufferings, deep as were the waters of anguish that I passed through before and since, I can think of nothing that touched the agony of those moments. If ever a sword pierced through my soul, it did then. I had to be a helpless spectator of what I knew could only be the taking of the life of my nearest and dearest. I saw the litter heave over and fall heavily to the ground, the mules stampeding. I saw it buried the next moment under a seething, struggling mass of devilish humanity. I saw the knives with which they slashed at the cordage and framework; and I called aloud upon God to have mercy upon my precious wife and child, and to shorten their sufferings. Death was easy to me now, and I was even thanking God that it was as near as it was — when, as I looked, out from the midst of that murderous mass crept the form of my beloved Flora, and sweet Hope was with her! I looked upon them both as one might have looked upon Lazarus coming forth from the grave. The miracle was not less astounding now than then. It was nothing else than resurrection. As Abraham received his beloved from the dead, so also (I speak with deepest reverence) did I receive mine. Oh, how I sprang forward to meet her! Her hair was dishevelled, and her face ashy white: but she was as calm as when I saw her through the hole in the litter. Both mother and child had come out unscathed. There were bruises and torn clothing, but not a wound, not a scratch; and baby Hope was as calm as her mother. Not only so, but to complete the marvel. Miss Gates was with them, unhurt and calm as they!

It is impossible to convey to the reader's mind any adequate idea of the miraculous nature of their deliverance (for Miss Gates' experience was, I believe, the counterpart of my wife's). How it came to pass that the frail structure did not collapse under the impact of that great human mass hurling itself upon it; how it was that the occupants were not crushed by the weight under which they lay buried; how it happened that not a knife-blade came near them as their assailants struck at the single mat of straw which formed their only protection; or how it was possible for them to break free from the narrow confines of their prison, and to find a way of escape, uninjured, through the murderous mob about them these are questions the answer to which can be found alone in the Word of God, "The Angel of His presence saved them."

I cannot pretend to describe the feelings with which we stood once more together. We drew aside to a clear spot just off the roadway, and lifted our hearts in praise and thanksgiving to Him Who alone doeth great wonders. It seemed to me the earnest of deliver- ance even to the end; and together we rejoiced over so signal a fulfilment of the promise given when we started, "I shall not die, but live, and declare the works of the Lord."

There was nothing, however, in our actual circumstances to suggest that we had escaped, or could eventually escape, the death to which we had been definitely sentenced. "We walk by faith, not by sight;" and faith means looking at the things that are not seen God's promise, power and faithfulness — and giving glory to God, just at the very time when the things that are seen present to the eye of the natural man only an outlook of sheer impossibility. Thus we learned that the next thing before us needed a fresh act of faith. There was never a moment during those dark weeks when we did not need to be looking away from the hopeless circumstances of ever threatening death to Christ, the Resurrection and the Life; and to account that "God is able to raise up, even from the dead." There were times when my feet had well-nigh slipped, and when, as I let my eye rest on the absolute desperateness of the situation, I almost found myself limiting the Holy One. and asking the dishonouring question, "Can God?" But I praise the mercy which lifted me up, and enabled me to repel the blasphemy, looking away unto Jesus, the Author and Finisher of faith. So now we stood quietly waiting to see what God would do next in His hand, for death or life.

When once the litters were cut up, it did not take long to dispose of their contents. As soon as one and another possessed themselves of what they wanted or could lay hands on, they made off with their ill-gotten gains. To our amazement, they were presently hurrying in all directions, as if in flight; and we were left standing alone! Was it the breath of God scattering them? Or had they, like one of old, seen the form of Another, like unto the Son of God, standing with us? In a few minutes, there was nothing left of the great throng that had carried us out to death, save a few scattered groups in threes and fours watching us at a distance.

Among those who made off was the redoubtable Ma. Just at the time that I was standing with my little boy, expecting to be cut down every moment, he dashed suddenly upon me from amongst the crowd, his face livid with passion, and, dealing me a staggering blow, ordered me to show him whether I had yet any secret possessions upon my person. I quietly opened my tunic, when he caught sight of a small pocket attached to my girdle, in which I carried my Consular passport. Thrusting in his hand, he drew forth the document. One glance at the heading sufficed to show him its purport, and with a malicious gleam he tore it to pieces before my eyes. Then, ordering me to give up the pouch as it was, he took it and its emptiness and was gone. And that was the last I saw of Ma Lao-ie.

Thus miraculously ended one of the most critical episodes of that critical period. Not the least remarkable fact about it was that the Boxer soldiery never came near us. I saw nothing to indicate that they even followed us beyond the gate. They may or may not have done so; but I have no recollection of seeing one of them among the rabble that set on us. When one considers that the extermination of the foreign devil was the express object of their organization, and that not only were we actually in their hands, but that they were there avowedly to do the work of death in common with the rest the fact is inexplicable on any other supposition than that of Divine interference and restraint. We who were the individuals concerned, and knew all that the situation meant of the terrors of death and the hopelessness of escape as none other can know, testify that, from first to last, it was a series of miracles. And we read in it the completed answer to the prayer we offered unitedly before leaving the inn, "If it is not Thy will that we should die at this time, then, our God, for the glory of Thy great Name bring their counsel to nought and weaken their arm!" Had He not done both these things? "Associate yourselves, ye people, and ye shall be broken in pieces; take counsel together, and it shall come to nought; for God is with us."

Questions to Consider

1. Given the sentence of death, how would you spend the final few hours of life with your family and friends?

2. How would you deal with the men who were joking about what they were going to do with you?

3. Several times in this narrative we see people willing to do things for money. We recognize the "love of money" is a powerful force. What are you willing to do for money?

4. Several of the Chinese were incredibly wicked toward the "foreign devils" yet they justified their actions. What justifications did the Chinese give? What justifications do you give when you do bad things?

5. What impact did prayer and kindness have on the men who were about to kill them?

6. When they were led into the mob, why did Glover thank God when he saw the Boxers with their keen blades?

7. What did Glover consider to be the "dishounoring question"?

CHAPTER TEN

The Sorrows of Death

"And who is sufficient for these things?"
"But our sufficiency is of God."

The position in which we were now placed called indeed for a fresh committing of ourselves and our way to God. Here we were, with our life yet whole in us, it is true, but robbed of every earthly possession, without so much as a "cash" to buy food with, and in the midst of enemies whose resent- ment towards us burned as fiercely as ever. What should we do now? Whither should we turn our steps? If we went forward, there was a band of cut-throats awaiting us. If we went back towards Han-tien, it seemed only to be courting the very destruction we had just escaped at their hands. In real perplexity, we looked up and asked Him very simply to lead us as He led His people of old, according to the word, "He led them on safely, so that they feared not." Our helplessness was such now that we were consciously shut up to God even for the literal putting of one foot before the other.

After praying thus, it became very clear to us that we should return to Han-tien. We knew that it was their "peaceableness" which had upset Ma's calculations; and we concluded that, whatever that might mean, we should be safer in their vicinity than out on the open road, where lawlessness could work unabashed. Again, if our boys were alive, they would find us more readily there than elsewhere. And then, too, we were hungry and thirsty, having tasted nothing for twenty hours since noon of the preceding day; and we hoped that we might look for some to take pity, even amongst enemies, and give the dear children at least a morsel of food. So we turned and went back.

Wearily we re-passed the "via crucis" of an hour ago, and entering the gate sat down, some twenty yards from it, on a stone block by the roadside. The long street was almost deserted — strange contrast to the scene of which but now it had been the theatre! But for the too palpable fact of our destitution, one could have imagined that it had been only a dream. Here and there one saw little knots of men talking together; and at the doorway immediately opposite was a small group of women curiously eyeing us. We waited a little while to see what the effect of our reappearance would be; but finding that we were left unmolested, and almost daring to hope that our forlorn condition might have touched the chord of pity in the women's hearts. Miss Gates spoke to them from her seat, entreating their compassion and asking them for no more than a drink of water. At the sound of her voice they looked at one another, and then, in a half scared way, shook their heads and retreated into the safe seclusion of the doorway.

With no protection from the scorching sun we sat on, fearing to leave, and wondering what the end would be. Anxiously we watched for the coming of our boys; but as the time went by and still they did not appear, our heart sickened with hope deferred. For, at this period of our sorrows, it seemed to us that their presence was indispensable to our safety. Where none would dare to give us food, for instance, a native could procure it for us. And so, in many other ways, they could do for us what we could not do for ourselves.

Meantime, the situation was becoming awkward again. The riff-raff, who had been hanging about the outskirts of the town in expectation that we should turn our steps away from it and toward the country, began to collect and gather round us. They seemed almost superstitiously fearful of us, coming nearer by degrees, until, emboldened by one or two who ventured close up, they gradually ringed us round. They were all armed, and were evidently the scum of the place a low looking, evil set, who would stick at nothing. They stood looking at us in an ominous silence that shivered its dread secret through our hearts. At length the exchange of a few asides amongst those on the inner edge of the ring led us to conclude that it was time to be making a move. And yet what move could we make? Whither should we flee?

Once more the gracious answer of our God met us at the threshold of our need. As we were preparing to go, who should push his way through the ring but Sheng-min. I shall never forget that moment the comfort and the joy of seeing the dear lad again, and just in the nick of time, when we needed him most. He took in the situation at a glance, and said in a low tone, "It seems as if the Lord means to save you, since He has protected you so far. But come quickly: we must be going."

The effect upon the bystanders was apparently one of bewilderment. They fell back sullenly as we rose; and not a soul attempted to touch us, or even to follow us as we passed by and out through the gate into the open. Keeping close to the boy, we walked on until we came to a place where it became a choice of roads. The main road bore to the left; while in front, a kind of bridle-path led through a gully. As it seemed to afford greater facilities for eluding observation, we elected to take the latter for awhile, with the intention then of striking the high road at a point where in all likelihood they would not be looking for us. Shortly after entering the gully, however, we passed two tramps, the elder of whom eyed us in a way that boded no good, and then turned to follow us. It was a lonely spot; and so strong was the presentiment of ill upon me that I preferred even to take the risk of the public road. So, somewhat prematurely, we climbed the bank and struck across the fields.

The Han-tien scum had by this time so far recovered themselves as to regret that they had let us go so quietly, and as we reappeared over the top of the bank, an armed group caught sight of us and gave the alarm. Accordingly, upon Sheng-min's advice, we retreated once more to the gully.

The two tramps now pressed us hard, but, not wishing to give the impression of fear, we slackened our steps to a leisurely pace, even to sitting down now and again as if for rest. But when we sat, they sat; when we rose, they rose. There could be no question that they had an object in view. However, the fact that we were covered by the presence of a native evidently acted as a deterrent, and was, I am sure, in the ordering mercy of God, our salvation at this juncture.

It was in this gully that the utter forlornness of our condition came over me as it had not done hitherto. Stripped of all means of support, seven hundred miles (English) from the nearest place of refuge, without a conveyance or the means of providing one; beset on all sides by hostile crowds literally, we were wandering in the wilderness in a solitary way ; we found no city to dwell in. Hungry and thirsty, our soul fainted in us. But a few days more and we should be entering the hottest period of the year the "fu-t'ien " or dog days; and as I looked at the two weak women and the two tiny children before me, the question forced itself upon me, "Can thy heart endure? Who is sufficient for these things?"

I was greatly upheld and comforted by the marvellous calmness and cheerfulness given to the ladies. The necessity, too, of drawing the dear children's thoughts away from past and present distress, and of keeping them from asking undesirable questions, was doubtless helpful in holding the mind from self-occupation. We would tell them little stories, or together look out for flowers, and climb the banks to gather them. In this way we came at length to a marshy spot where, to our joy, amid the rank grass we discerned the gleam of water; and there, at the stagnant pool, we thanked God, as we drank the first draught for twenty-two hours, and cooled hands and face. Presently the elder tramp called to Sheng-min, who after exchanging the greetings of ordinary civility, and feeling that possibly he might be open to friendly advances, sat down by him and conversed for awhile a little distance from us, on the opposite bank. The gist of their talk was that he (the tramp) had a cave not far off, where he would hide us for a few days if we wished, taking upon himself the supply of all our needs. This was too evidently a plot, and we refused to entertain the idea for a moment.

From that time Sheng-min's manner towards us changed very markedly. He answered roughly when spoken to, and simply indicated by a gesture the direction we were to take. Meantime, he kept company with the men, following on behind with them. Whether this was merely a blind on his part, seeing how completely we were in their power, or whether he had really turned against us (a thought well-nigh unthinkable after the proofs of devotion he had already given) we could not determine. It occasioned us much distress, and even fear, for he pointed us on in the direction of the tramp's cave.

When we emerged from the gully a small village was before us, about half a mile distant, called Sha-ho-k'eo. Our appearance was evidently anticipated, for a crowd of men and lads were in waiting, and, as soon as they sighted us, made towards us. Every one of them carried some weapon or other, mostly of an agricultural sort — hoes, prongs, sickles, knives and the like. My heart sank as once more the vision of mob violence rose up before me. What should we do? Whither could we flee? We looked, and behind, as before, an armed band was coming. The Han- tien riff-raff were in pursuit, and in a few minutes the two companies had met and were hemming us in on every side.

Once more we gave ourselves up to inevitable death, and quietly sat down by the roadside to await the end. But the tramp evidently had other thoughts — an object of his own in view which he was loth to lose sight of. Calling to us to get up and move on, he directed us to a wayside booth on the outskirts of the village, and, thankful to have the strain of such a situation relieved in any way, we obeyed the injunction, the motley crowd following at our heels.

The sun was now at meridian heat, and glad indeed we were to avail ourselves of the shelter afforded by the rush thatch of the booth. But no; the " Chang- knei-tih" who owned it would have none of us, and ordered us off the place. A grassy slope just outside, shaded lightly by a group of saplings, offered a more friendly resting place, where we had no sooner settled ourselves than we were surrounded as before.

During the three hours or so passed in that spot, we tasted again in full measure the bitterness of death, and the sweetness of the consolations of Christ. There was no question as to the intentions of our enemies. It seemed as though their mind was to play us first, as a cat plays a mouse before killing it; and as they stood around, they mingled coarse mockery with cruel suggestions of the way in which the deed of slaughter should be done, whetting their implementsthe while on stones before our eyes. The moving spirit of it all was the wicked tramp. "We'll strip them first, and then break their heads," we heard him say, and the word was readily taken up and passed round.

We had been seated thus in harrowing suspense for some little time, when a Boxer officer arrived on the scene — a young man of soldierly bearing, with clear-cut, handsome features, but an expression pitiless and cruel as the grave. Relieving himself of his forage bag, he unsheathed his sword, and entered into con- versation with those about him. His oft-repeated "Ai-ia!" as he looked across at us rings still in my ears, and the look itself even now my blood curdles as I recall it.

"What are you doing, letting these foreign devils sit here? Why don't you kill them?"

"We are going to beat and strip them first."

"Beat and strip them, indeed! No; kill them outright that's our first business."

Then stepping forward immediately in front of us, he closely scrutinized each one, asking us from what country we came, what it was that brought us to China, and what we now intended to do. Our answers provoked a sarcastic curl of the lip, as he sneered some contemptuous word, and turned for further conference with the rest. The result of which was that he sheathed his sword, shouldered his forage bag, and with the remark that he was on his way to the Boxer camp, (20 li off — 7 miles), but would shortly be back with his company to finish the work, hurried off.

Thus marvellously was another respite granted us, in the infinite mercy of our God. True, it was only for a little while, but the officer's unexpected withdrawal brought a faint, faint gleam of light into the prevailing darkness, and strengthened us to lean hard on Him with Whom all things are possible,

So we continued to sit on, while the crowd, which had swelled considerably by this time, continued to hem us in. They were now becoming bolder and more aggressive in their attitude. The wide ring was gradually narrowing towards us, until the foremost were but a few paces from us. We saw that they were evidently bent on taking matters into their own hands, without waiting for the arrival of the Boxers; and once more my beloved wife and I spoke words of farewell. I also gave her directions how to act, as well for little Hope as for herself, in the moment of attack, while I undertook to act for Hedley.

Meantime, Sheng-min's care for us revived, and elbowing his way through the crowd he brought the dear children a small three-cornered cake each of rice and dates. Dear little souls! they were hungry enough, having fasted for twenty-six hours, and their eyes glistened at the sight of the tempting morsel. As they put it to their mouths, one who had made himself increasingly obnoxious snatched it from their hand and ate it before them.

By this act the barrier of restraint was broken down, and the one cowardly deed was quickly followed by another. The man standing immediately in front of my wife suddenly darted forward, and seizing her left hand attempted to tear the wedding ring from her finger. In a moment the hot blood shot to my temples, and as my beloved one looked at me appealingly and closed her hand to guard the sacred symbol, all the feeling of resentment natural to the flesh rose up in me with strong temptation to strike. But the power of God kept me, as He brought to remembrance the word, "Avenge not yourselves, but rather give place unto wrath. Recompense to no man evil for evil," and I just whispered, "Let it go, darling. Don't grieve over it. The Lord will give you much more than this." So, meekly opening her hand, she yielded up the treasure. What it cost her thus to part with it, and what it cost me to see her subjected to such insult, no words can express. But the memory of that gentle act of resignation is a more precious possession to me now than ever the lost ring could have been, for it was the substance of that of which the ring was but the shadow the Christ-like expression of her true wifehood and womanhood.

This overt act of violence was the signal for a general attack. With a wild shout of "Rob!" they rushed upon us. There was not a moment to think how one should act. We were each one seized and hurled out into the road, into the midst of the raging mass. I never thought it possible that any one of us could or would come out alive. For myself, I was torn away from wife and children, and knew nothing, saw nothing, heard nothing but the mad tumult of what I was convinced must be a murderous onslaught. By a painful process not far removed from lynching, my clothes were torn from me, and when I was left alone alive, to my amazement it was to find that, save for socks and cholera belt, I was naked.

It was as well that my mind had other thoughts wherewith to occupy itself than with my own condition. Where were my loved ones? and where was Miss Gates? As I turned to look, the fighting crowd parted, and I caught sight of my precious wife standing alone, and anxiously looking for her little ones. She was flushed from the violence with which she had been handled; her gown was gone, and the "san-tsi" (or shirt) that was still left to her with her nether garments was torn. But she had sustained no serious injury, and was heroically calm. She greeted me with, "Oh, thank God you are alive!" every other thought was for the moment swallowed up in that for both of us. Then, "Have you seen the sweet lambs? Oh, where are they?"

It was a heartrending sight when, a moment or two later, we did see them. Not dead, thank God, not, apparently, injured, but in uttermost terror and bewilderment wringing their baby hands and crying piteously for us, as they ran distractedly hither and thither among the hurrying mob. To recover them was the work of but a moment. Poor little darlings! their joy at seeing us seemed to eclipse all the terror, and very soon the tears were forgotten in the comfort of having their hand fast in ours again. Nothing had been left to them save their light gauze combinations and socks.

And Miss Gates? She was lying in the roadway some thirty yards off, stripped of her gown, face down- wards and quite motionless. We thought at first she was dead, but Sheng-min was with her, and as I went forward he raised her, and she opened her eyes.

Presently, with his support, she was able to move, and together we all retraced our steps to the booth, where we were allowed a seat on a low plank beside the door of the food-shop behind.

I may here relate what actually occurred to my wife, Miss Gates, and the little ones, at the moment of attack, when we were torn one from another. It would seem that our sister was dragged along for some distance, the violence with which her head struck the ground producing unconsciousness. Hedley was roughly stripped at once, but little Hope, being a girl, was cruelly mauled as they tore at her clothing. She told me that "a man came towards her with a sword, and she prayed in her heart to God not to let him hurt her, and then he turned away from her." As for my dear wife, she was knocked down at the first rush and dragged hither and thither, by head or feet, in the process of stripping.

It seemed now as if we had been brought to the lowest point of distress and humiliation to a condition of things, in fact, in which it would be easy to choose death rather than life. I cannot utter the thoughts that overwhelmed my spirit as we sat there in our utter destitution. I can only say that the realization of all that our circumstances involved for the weak women and children under my care, together with the bitter shame of my condition, com- pletely overcame me, and for the first and only time in all those sad weeks, I gave way to my grief. When my beloved wife saw the silent tears, she gently said, "Darling husband, why do you cry? Remember, this is the fellowship of Christ's sufferings. He is counting us worthy to suffer shame for His Name." Thus, through the tender ministry of her love, He poured His balm into my heart.

The food shop at Sha-Ho-K'eo where we were stripped of our clothing.

Some degree of pity at the sight of our misery seemed to have been excited in the heart of a few, and a bowl of "mi-t'ang" (thin millet gruel) was passed to us to drink. For this we heartily thanked God, praying that He would bless the giver, and taking it as a fresh token of His near presence and watchful care for us. Not long afterwards, a short coat of filthy rags, such as professional beggars wear the like of which could only be seen in China was handed me over the heads of the bystanders from within the food-shop behind, by one who was none other than the tramp, arrayed now in a garb of re- spectability which I recognized as none other than my own. So now our friend had realized his object: he had my garment, and I could have his. He and I had changed places. It would have required much grace, under ordinary circumstances, even to have handled such a disgusting thing;

but as it was, I could only thank the grace of God which provided me a covering at all; and, bowing my acknowledgments to the man, I readily adopted it.

Yet a little later, one of my stolen shoes was returned, which proved of the greatest service to me afterwards; the dear children's shoes also were recovered. But the kindness of God was crowned by the arrival of our boy, P'ao-ri, on the scene, with a pair of pants which had formed the major part of his own kit for the intended journey to Chau-kia-k'eo. They were well patched, and came to about half way up my leg; but what of that? They met my sore need; and more than that, they were the embodiment of the love of Christ, offered me in His Name and for His sake; and as I thanked the dear lad in the Name of the Lord Jesus, I thought with joy of the King's recognition awaiting him: "I was naked, and ye clothed Me. Inasmuch as ye did it unto one of the least of these My brethren, ye did it unto Me. Come, ye blessed of My Father."

Questions to Consider

1. Stripped and feeling shame, how did Glover's wife help him?

2. Would you have difficulty giving up a wedding ring or other important family item?

CHAPTER ELEVEN

The Great Conflict of Sufferings

"Father, forgive them!"

"Father, forgive them!"

The day was wearing to late afternoon, and ere long we must expect the return of the Boxer officer with his braves. We had no reason to believe that the people were any the less disposed than heretofore to complete the programme they had set themselves, the first part of which they had already carried out. The stripping, doubtless, was but the prelude to the killing, as they had said. They still swarmed menacingly about us, giving us to believe that it was merely a question of time a brief respite only, not a final reprieve. A clear indication of this seemed to be given when the boothkeeper at length came out, and once more ordered us off the premises.

There was nothing for it but to resume the old seat beneath the saplings. We knew that we were doomed that, humanly speaking, all hope of escape was gone, and that any moment now the Boxers would be on the spot. Besides, to attempt to leave the place would only call forth suspicion and provoke the ever threatening attack. So we quietly sat down again on the slope, to be once more confronted by the instruments of death.

It was at this particular period that the climax of suspense was reached. For we could not but realize that, according to their declared intention, the next event was to be death. They had taken what they wanted; what else was there left to them to do but to kill us?

The inner experience of that hour was a singular one, in the way in which anxiety and rest existed side by side. How anxiously my eyes were for ever turning in the direction of the spot where the Boxer leader disappeared, expecting momently the dread sight of his reappearance; and then how fearfully would they wander back to the actual evidences of the destruction awaiting us! And yet, over against all the dread, how marvellously balanced was the deep peace of God!

As we sat, I need hardly say we prayed, not so much for ourselves as for our would-be murderers. It was no light compensation for the bitterness of the cross that we should be given by His grace, in the fellow- ship of His sufferings, the fellowship also of His con- straining love; and even the very prayer from His own Cross, "Father, forgive them; for they know not what they do." To find it possible to be possessed at such a time by the spirit of divine love and com- passion instead of by the natural spirit of resentment and hate, was to us a tangible evidence of the truth of the Gospel we had preached such as no philosophy in the world could reason us out of.(1)

What, I wonder, would the rationalism of the so- called "Higher Critic" have done for us, as we sat for hours facing our murderers and watching them make ready the instruments of a cruel death? I could almost wish that the wise who affect to speculate on the verities of the Eternal Truth by their comfortable fireside, and so lightheartedly from the ease of a pro- fessor's chair cut "the lively Oracles" with the pen- knife of an impious exegesis, were put for a few hours into the crucible of a Boxer persecution, with their "higher" reasonings for their only stay and solace. I do not envy the man who should find himself compelled to make the experiment. One thing, however, I must believe. If he were spared to come out of it sane, it would be minus his make-believes, with the wholesome conviction of his sinful folly stamped upon his heart, and upon his lips the honest confession that of all men he had been the most miserable.

I can never sufficiently thank God that, when I received His Word, I "received it not as the word of men, but as it is in truth, the Word of God, which effectually worketh also in them that believe." Had my faith not been founded upon that Rock before the flood arose and the stream beat vehemently upon it, in those awful weeks of the ever-shadowing presence of the king of terrors, I know that my reason must have given way. It was "by every word that proceedeth out of the mouth of God," as recorded in the Book of His inspiration, that I and those with me lived then. Our mental and physical, as well as our spiritual life, was supernaturally sustained by it.

Through the written Word laid up in our hearts, the Eternal Word manifested to us both Himself and the Father. Jesus Himself drew near and talked with us by the way; and the words that He spoke to us, they were spirit and they were life.

It was literally as though I heard His living voice beside me. Now He was breathing in my ear, "Fear not them which kill the body, and after that have no more that they can do; but fear Him, which after He hath killed hath power to cast both soul and body into hell. Yea, I say unto you. Fear Him."

"Fear thou not, for I am with thee; be not dismayed, for I am thy God; I will strengthen thee; yea, I will help thee; yea, I will uphold thee with the right hand of My righteousness."

"Fear none of those things which thou shalt suffer. Be thou faithful unto death, and I will give thee a crown of life."

Then He would speak in the word of the promise: "When thou passest through the waters, I will be with thee; and through the rivers, they shall not overflow thee: when thou walkest through the fire, thou shalt not be burned, neither shall the flame kindle upon thee."

And I knew it for my Lord's own voice when the words echoed within: "Said I not unto thee that, if thou wouldest believe, thou shouldest see the glory of God?" " erily, verily, I say unto you, If a man keep my saying, he shall never see death."

These passages in particular stand out with peculiar distinctness from amongst the many that were borne in upon my heart that day. I rested my whole soul upon the "Verily, verily I say unto thee" of Him whom I knew to be the Truth, and whose "saying" I had, in His strength, sincerely and earnestly sought to "keep"; and I relied upon Him to fulfil to me the promise, "Thou shalt never see death" "thou shalt see the glory of God." How graciously and abundantly He met my expectation! I proved the literal truth of His words; for I bear record that He gave me such a sight of the glory of God as to eclipse the sight of death and to deliver me from all my fears.

I remember well the comfort wherewith I was comforted of God over the story of Stephen's last hour. My thoughts dwelt much upon it; for, in a certain sense, our circumstances resembled his; and I prayed the Lord Jesus to be to each one of us then what He had proved Himself to His servant in the same great conflict of sufferings; and the testimony of each one of us afterwards was that we had seen "the glory of God and Jesus," as we sat on that slope beneath the saplings. In a letter written from Hankow by my be- loved wife to a dear friend of hers in Dover, I find her summarizing her own experience thus :

"The first message that meets me after our terrible journey seems just to express all He has done for us — 'If it had not been *the Lord* who was on our side, then they had swallowed us up alive"; and, oh, yes, our hearts do say, 'Blessed be the Lord who hath not given us a prey.' I can only write a little, but it may bring comfort to know all is well. All is deep praise to Him; for the experience has been so blessed — the experience of His power to cover and keep in perfect peace, *only seeing glory when face to face with death* — the experience of His tender carrying and enabling love when brought nigh unto death on the road all has been blessed experience of *Him*."

And Miss Gates has had the joy of giving publicly at home the same personal testimony to the grace of God.

One thought that was largely used of God to my comfort, especially in regard to the weak ones with me, was that the dismissal of Stephen's spirit from the body was not the effect of the stoning, but of a direct loosing act on the part of Christ, in response to His call, "Lord Jesus, receive my spirit." For, only the moment before, he had "cried with a loud voice": his life was yet strong in him. Again, he was in full possession of consciousness at the moment he breathed his last, for he prayed, "Lord, lay not this sin to their charge"; "*and when he had said this*" — immediately following upon it — "he fell asleep." The expression, too, "he fell asleep," seemed to me at variance with the thought of a dissolution involving conscious pain and distress. And so I gathered from these considerations that, however distressing the attendant circumstances of our end might be, yet the end itself would not be so. The flight of the spirit would be taken in obedience to the loosing touch of its Redeemer, and would be directly dependent on that touch alone. The moment of its separation from the body would be the moment of its reception at His hands; and the experience to the faithful servant of his spirit's entrance into the rest of God might only be set forth by the idea of a " falling asleep " so gentle, so quiet, so easy is his departure.

And so I rejoiced to think that, however terrifying to the natural man the mode of death awaiting us might be, our compassionate Lord would, in response to our call, Himself set the spirit free, and that we too should know only what Stephen knew not a struggling, agonizing dismissal under the blows of torturing weapons, but, under the painless loosing of Love's gentle hand, a placid "falling asleep."

One other passage I cannot but refer to, as having formed the foundation of God's consolations to my soul in the hour of death :

"But now in Christ Jesus, ye who once were far off are made nigh by the Blood of Christ."

How those unspeakably precious words, " made NIGH BY THE BLOOD OF Christ," stood out before my eyes in letters of light! The ground of my settled peace then was the knowledge that God had made peace through the blood of His Son's Cross, and the certain assurance that through faith in His blood I had redemption, the forgiveness of my sins. When all the humbling and distressing sense of sin as a believer, and of having fallen short of the glory of God, rose up before me (as at such a time it could not fail to do), to know that the precious blood of Christ had fully met for me the claims of God's holiness, and that He, the Propitiation for my sins, was Himself my Advocate with the Father — this was the sure foundation of rest for my soul. The Spirit of God witnessed with my spirit that I was, on the ground of the atoning sacrifice of my all-holy, all-sufficient Substitute, a child of God, in the nearness of actual sonship; and the knowledge of my acceptance in the Beloved of the Father gave the peace that passeth all understanding. I desire to bear this testimony that the blood of Christ, Who is our peace, was the alone ground of my perfect peace in the immediate prospect of my appearing before God, the Judge of all.

This, then, was the comfort wherewith we ourselves were comforted of God, in all the tribulation of those weeks of daily dying. My experience was not unique. It was shared by my companions in suffering to a degree which led me again and again to glorify God in them. And I know that many others, who were called to pass the same road at that period, will find in my testimony an echo of their own inner experience.

How long we continued to sit there I could not say. The time seemed interminable. The sun was dropping to the west, and still the mob held back, and still the Boxers had not come. At length, to my amazement, one of the men (probably a "shae-sheo," or village elder) called to us:

" What are you sitting there for We don't want you here. Be off with you! Tseo pa!"

The cry, "Tseo, tseo!" was taken up, and I saw our God-given opportunity.

"We have no wish to stay here," I said. "If my respected elder brother will allow us to go quietly on our way, we will go at once."

We got up and moved off. Once more the crowd fell back before us, as if held by an unseen power, and not a hand was lifted to touch us as we passed on to the Kao-p'ing road.

We had not gone far, however, before they caught us up again, and made it pretty clear that they intended to dog our steps. Upon this, we again seated ourselves on a grassy sward by the roadside to attempt to go on seemed idle; and once more we were surrounded. A supercilious young scholar, seeing us sitting thus as he drove by, dismounted in the hope of getting some sport out of us; and our answers to his questions upon our religion called out horrible execrations from the rest.

Up to the time of our being stripped, my wife had been able to retain her tiny pocket edition of the Oxford Bible, which she carried within the inner fold of her gown. The one, of course, had disappeared with the other; and the loss of the precious little volume was to her, and to us all, irreparable more keenly felt than any other. And now, as we sat, we caught sight of it in the hands of one of our captors, who was toying carelessly with it or showing the curiosity to the bystanders. Who should that one be but the tramp! My dear wife's joy at the sight of her lost treasure was very touching It was, however, only to be an aggravation of the trial of its loss; for the man's hard heart was proof against all her tearful entreaties, and the last we saw of it was its dis- appearance most sad irony! into my pocket. This may seem a trifling matter to record; but in reality it formed an integral part of the sufferings of that most suffering day, and as such I could not omit to notice it.

The incident of the scholar had the effect of breaking the people's reserve to us, and they showed greater readiness to talk to us than at any previous time. Though it followed the line marked out for them by their superior that of rude, contemptuous questioning yet it gave us an opportunity of preaching to them Jesus. The word was vehemently opposed by an old man, who had been very demonstrative when the scholar was talking with us, but whose rage now altogether broke bounds.

" Je-su, Je-su," he thundered; "what do we want with your Je-su? We mean to drive you foreign devils out of China, and Je-su too. Away with Him, and away with you! Tseo pa!"

It seemed now in very truth that the end could not be delayed. The crowd made a threatening move towards us, as they again took up the cry, "Tseo, tseo! "We answered as before, in polite, conciliatory tones, that we had no wish to trouble them with our presence, but that it was themselves who would not allow us to go. If they for their part would undertake not to follow us, but just leave us alone, we would go our way and trouble them no more.

Once again they fell back as we rose to go. A fear seemed to have fallen upon them that paralyzed their arm. They made no attempt to follow us; and when we looked behind at the bend of the road, the way was clear.

How to make the best use of our liberty, and of the time at our disposal, was the problem now. Was there any way open to us by which we could baffle pursuit ?

Happily, the rising ground on either side hid us well from sight. Lifting the children in our arms, we left the road they had seen us take, and passing through a quarry made for the fields beyond. Here we were overtaken by a sharp shower of rain, and having no shelter at hand were soon wet to the skin. In this, however, we saw the hand of God working for our good; for the friendly shower would both serve to deter the people, and also to convince them how false was the superstitious charge they had brought against us. On we pressed, seeking a temporary hiding place. But in vain. Nothing in the shape of cover could we see, look which way we would.

By the time the rain was over we had made some little distance, and my heart was beginning to take fresh courage when, as I turned to reconnoitre, I saw against the sky-line the figures of scouts on the look-out, and I knew that we had been sighted. We at once made for the lower ground, where we should be for awhile hidden from their view; and in doing so, we came upon a small hollow just off the beaten track, and sufficiently high up to elude the observation of passers by. It was partially screened by shrubs, and large boulder stones were tumbled in it. Here was the very refuge we needed; and one by one not without difficulty, owing to the treacherously balanced boulders we stepped down into it. In another hour or so the sun would have set; and if only we could escape detection so long, we might then hope to get well away under cover of darkness. How anxiously we listened, as we crouched together, almost fearing lest the loud beat of the heart might betray us!

We had not been long seated when our ears caught the sound of voices and hurrying feet. They passed without seeing us, and we breathed again. A few minutes later, others were heard approaching; and they too passed ignorantly on. At last a couple of men happened to turn when they were all but past the spot, spied us huddling together, and stopped. The game was up. There was nothing for it but to put a good face on our discomfiture and descend to the road- way. The men then hastened on to report their discovery.

Worn out with all that we had already gone through that day, rain-bedraggled, and oh! so hungry, our plight seemed more hopeless than ever. It was just now, when in sore dejection we were wandering on to we knew not what of fresh buffetings and cruelty, that the Lord gave us another token that He was with us and tenderly caring for us, according to the word that He kept in our hearts, "I will in no wise fail thee, neither will I in any wise forsake thee." Two men were seen coming over the field, and presently they called to us. Not knowing whether they were for or against us, Sheng-min answered the summons, and after a word with them bade us come. One of the two proved to be a gentleman from Lu-an city. With much compassion in his look and voice, he said, "I am so sorry for you. I would assist you, but am helpless to do so. Certain death awaits you: you cannot escape it. There are people there and there" — (pointing warningly) — "waiting to kill you. I would urge you, however, under any circumstances, to avoid the village before you. And yet I know," he added, "that you cannot go far without losing your lives. It is very, very hard for you." And with that he handed me twenty-five cash, saying, "Take this; it is all I have on me."

His companion then came forward, and without saying more than "K'o lien, k'o lien!" "I am so sorry for you" thrust into my hand a tin of condensed milk which he had recovered from the plundered supply of our Utters.

What these words and acts of mercy meant to us at that juncture I cannot express. We were much moved. Indeed, my dear wife, with her thoughts centred on the needs of her little ones, could not refrain from tears at the sight of the milk, and again and again we thanked our kind benefactors in the name of the Lord Jesus.

Following our friend's warning, we turned our steps in another direction, towards the village of Uang- fang, where an evangelist of our church (Chin sien-seng) was living; his wife only, however, being at home at this time. Our hope was that, if only we could reach her house unobserved in the darkness, she might be able to hide us in the loft until the storm had blown over. Fond hope, that was neither realized nor realizable! And yet God allowed it, for the sustaining of our courage and the guiding of our steps in the prepared path.

Our change of direction was quickly noted, and a large body of men gave chase. We were now pressed hard, and the threatening attitude of the men kept us in constant expectation of attack. At length they made a rush for our boys. Sheng-min, a big, powerfully built fellow, defended himself; but the odds of thirty to one were too heavy, and he was borne to the ground. For several minutes the scene resembled a wild football scrimmage. Every now and again the poor lad became visible for a moment, struggling desperately; and my wife and Miss Gates covered their eyes as they cried out, "Oh, they are klling him, they are killing him!" Then he was wholly lost to sight, and we could but conclude that all was over with him. It was a time of awful suspense as we sat and waited for we hardly dared to think what; for surely our turn would quickly succeed.

Then the gang scattered, some running in various directions, others eagerly scouring the ground. Some half-dozen ran for poor P'ao-ri, who had escaped their hands when the first rush was made, and was now standing near us. As he offered no resistance, they contented themselves with searching him from head to foot, and after robbing him of what little silver and cash he had on him, they made off.

Meantime, to our unspeakable wonder and joy, Sheng-min reappeared, bearing the evident traces of his conflict, but still sound of limb, through the miraculous keeping of God. Unknown to us, both he and P'ao-ri had secreted a portion of our silver in various parts of their clothing before leaving the inn at Han-tien, and had jealously guarded it until now against our future need. The discovery that he had ingots on him was enough. They wanted nothing else, and were content to let him go when they were satisfied that his all was in their hands. In the fierce scuffle, some of the silver and much of the cash in his wallet had scattered on the ground, and it was owing to this that many were kept from the further pursuit, so intent were they on the search for what they could pick up.

The path we had taken brought us out upon an open space, where we were met by an expectant crowd, who at once pointed us in a particular direction. Here again we experienced a remarkable interposition of God. A woman of their number, touched at the sight of our pitiable condition, compassionated us so far as to lend the ladies a needle and thread to mend the rents in the garments left to them. Hearing the talk that was going on around her, to the effect that they intended to kill us near the village towards which they were pointing us, she set up the customary wail for the dead, whereby we divined their intent, and, with Sheng-min and P'ao-ri to lead us, followed another path of their choosing.

Only to find, however, further crowds awaiting us and coming to meet us all along the road. As they met us, they turned and went on with us. It was a steep incline all the way, and how wearily now we dragged along it!

The presence of our native servants was an untold comfort God's own gift to us for such a time. But He was pleased now to remove one of them. I saw P'ao-ri forging on ahead, and then, at a point where the road curved to the right, disappear in the crowd. I imagined that he had gone on to reconnoitre, and that he would reappear farther on. But we never saw him again. This was a sore trial at the time; but the Lord was our confidence, and we rested in the assurance that it was the ordering of His perfect wisdom.

The reason of P'ao-ri's disappearance I learnt long afterwards. As the village of Uang-fang was our objective, he decided to go on before and prepare Mrs. Chin against a surprise. In this way there would be no disturbance created by our arrival, and no un- fortunate waiting at her door. As a matter of fact, he was doomed to the coldest of receptions. In her terror at the threats held out by the Boxers to all who professed "the foreign religion," she (poor soul!) had recanted, and was burning incense as he went in. Her fright at seeing him was such that she affected not to know who he was. As for any thought of receiving us, it was out of the question. Indeed, it was as much as her life was worth to have even him shadowing her doorway; and she entreated him to begone without delay.

Baffled in his endeavour, P'ao-ri retraced his steps and sought for us high and low, but to no purpose; until at last, utterly wearied out and unable to find any clue to our whereabouts, he gave up the search and returned sadly home.

Questions to Consider

1. Glover says he wishes the "higher critics" of the faith could experience just a few hours in the "crucible of a Boxer persecution" to see if their "higher" reasonings would give them comfort. Think of the people you know who reject or dismiss the teachings of Christ. What do they put their faith in?

2. Glover says they missed the Bible. Would you miss the Bible if it wasn't available? How often do you refer to it on a daily basis?

CHAPTER TWELVE

A Hairbreadth Escape

"I flee unto Thee to hide me."

*"The beloved of the Lord shall
dwell in safety by Him"*

The long and toilsome path brought us at length to an elevated ridge, which fell away on one side in a steep declivity to a dry torrent bed. A little farther on was a small temple standing by itself; and beyond this a certain village. By the time we reached the ridge, the crowd had not only swollen considerably in numbers, but had begun to make themselves ex- tremely objectionable. They were not merely the riff-raff class, either. Well-to-do men of superior position were amongst them: indeed, we were pain- fully conscious that the rough jostling and coarse jesting to which we were now exposed was experienced rather at the hands of the more respectable element than of the less.

The shades of the short twilight were fast merging into darkness, and it was evident that a move with a definite object was being made. We were being swept on towards the temple; and as we neared it, for the second time that dreadful day the ominous boom of the processional gong broke on our ear. At a word from Sheng-min we stopped and faced round.

"Don't go on," he whispered;" they mean to stone you to death there. Turn quickly."

As we did so, the mob hustled us severely, and with hoots and yells urged us to keep the direction they Indicated.

It was at this most critical juncture that we experienced a really marvellous instance of God's direct interference. Sheng-min had read the peril of the moment. Knowing that we could go neither backwards nor forwards, he again whispered:

"Down the steep quick! Follow the track!" Instantly we obeyed the direction. A thin "goat" trail was just visible among the rocks and shrubs of the declivity; and in single file we threaded our way down, down, until at a bend in the track we were hidden from sight. Quickening our pace, we hurried on with a strength divinely renewed. In that hour we proved what it was, in the extremity of physical weakness, to "run and not be weary, to walk and not faint."

The moment we disappeared over the side, the mob simultaneously stopped dead at the spot, as if arrested by a sudden and irresistible power. The loud yells and cries of a moment ago were stilled to silence absolute, awful silence. So startling was it that I dared to turn and take one look. I could scarcely believe my eyes. The mob lined the ridge in hundreds, motionless as if spell-bound, helplessly watching us poor, miserable us, whom they triumphantly believed they had so completely in their power slip away from under their very hand. Not a single soul of them attempted to follow. Sheng-min alone was behind, bringing up the rear; and before us, in the bright moonlight, there was nothing but the white zigzag of the trail and the gleaming breadth of the torrent bed.

Will any one venture to explain the above phenomenon on the hypothesis of mere natural causes, in the common acceptation of that term? Only he, I imagine, who would under any set of circumstances seek to shut out the supernatural from the plane of the natural, and deny to the Lord God omnipotent the sovereignty of His own right, will and power to rule in the kingdom of men, or to show Himself strong in the behalf of those whose heart is perfect towards Him, in the way He chooses and at the time He chooses. The most "natural" of all causes are the supernatural, if we would but be honest with our own hearts; and in the phenomenon I have recorded, I rejoiced to see again the simple operation of the natural law of cause and effect in accordance with the simple statement of the law by Him Who framed it, "*Call upon Me* in the day of trouble; *I will deliver thee*; and thou shalt glorify Me."

On we sped with wondering hearts, in the consciousness that God had, for the third time at least that day, wrought for us a great deliverance. Without halt or pause we crossed to the far side of the wide river bed, keeping cover as far as we possibly could, and hugging the deep shadows cast by the bright radiance of a full orbed moon. On, on we pressed, not heeding the stumblings and trippings of our weary feet over the boulder-strewn and stony path. Uang- fang was the near goal before us, and every step was bringing it nearer.

It seemed strange, after the all day noise and excitement of large crowds hemming us in, to be alone, with an unbroken stillness reigning all around. Could it be true that we really were alone at last? I looked this way and that; and there, as I cast my eye across the river bed, I saw emerging from the dark shadows four stealthy figures, parallel to us and keeping pace with us. Ere long they came out into the full light of the moon, and crossing directly over to our side were soon up with us. As they passed, they casually accosted us, asking (as is usual in China on the road) where we had come from and where we were going to. They were walking in single file, and we observed that they were armed with pole-axes carried over the shoulder at the slope.

In the early part of the evening Sheng-min had been called aside by a man in the crowd and warned that "the Boxers were going to kill us down at the bed of the river." A certain smartness and bearing about these men seemed to indicate that they knew something about drill, and to justify our fears that the warning was a well founded one.

There was nothing for it now but to keep on in the direction we were taking, with our eyes upon our God. If it was as we feared, escape was impossible; for they were narrowly watching us, though at some distance, and cautiously adjusting their pace to ours. At last we sat down, partly to ease our excessive weariness, but more in the hope that they would be disconcerted thereby; and they too sat down.

It was clear, therefore, that these men intended to shadow us that, in fact, we should have to reckon with them in some way or other.

The men were, as I said, some little distance from us, and we took this the first opportunity afforded us of opening the milk tin, and giving the dear little ones a tiny quantity of the precious food, the only sustenance they had had since noon of the preceding day. By common consent we agreed to keep it entirely for the children's use; for we were again absolutely moneyless (the gift of the 25 cash committed to Sheng-min's care having shared the fate of his other property), and this was the only means under our hand for their support. Then once more we lifted our hearts in fervent prayer to God our strength and our Redeemer, that He would be pleased to stand up for our defence against the four Boxers who were seeking our life. And thus strengthened with strength in our souls, we rose and went on. The Boxers also rose and went on.

At a point where the torrent bed was intersected by cross roads, there was a knoll, and on it we saw, under the moonlight gleam, the four white-coated figures seat themselves. There could be no mistaking their intention. They were awaiting us there, to "kill us at the bed of the river."

As we drew near they rose and again accosted us. What they said I don't know; but whatever it may have been, Sheng-min's reply was to the effect that "it was no business of theirs." Thereupon they confronted us with an insolent demand for money. Seeing now that there was no hope of our being able to pass them, we quietly sat down on the grassy slope.

They utterly refused to believe the statement that we had no silver. Our destitute condition was no argument with them. Resuming their seat on the knoll, they mounted guard over us, while in every possible way they tried to drag out of Sheng-min the truth about our money. They doubtless imagined that we had buried the bulk of it, and before despatching us they were determined to have from us the secret of its whereabouts.

Here, then, was a situation as desperate as any we had hitherto experienced. The measure of that bitter day's bitterness was not yet full. But He Who had given the cup would also give the grace to drink it, and would so glorify Himself that our sorrow would be afterwards turned into joy.

For upwards of an hour we sat thus over against each other. On their part, the time was spent in noisy altercation with Sheng-min; on ours, in silent prayer. Every now and then one or other of the men would spring to his feet with a curse, and stand over us with his pole-axe, threatening to strike. Finding, however, that they could get no further with us either by ques- tion or by threat of violence, they sat down to discuss what the next move should be. While thus engaged, Miss Gates, who could overhear their talk, said:

"Unless God works a miracle for us, we shall not leave this spot alive. The thing seems an impossibility; but it is laid on my heart to ask Him to take these men right away — one and all. It is our only hope; and is anything too hard for the Lord?"

So we made our prayer in the Name of the Lord Jesus, according to the terms of this petition.

Then from the opposite side of the river bed we saw the figures of more men coming one or two at first, then more at intervals, until some dozen or fifteen had gathered at the knoll. They were apparently just foot passengers on their homeward way; but the unusual sight at the knoll arrested them, and they turned to see what it might be. Their sympathies were quickly enlisted on the side of the Boxer ruffians, and we found that we had to deal now, not with four, but with four times four.

Emboldened by this accession to their numbers, the Boxer four became more impudently aggressive. We were told that if their demands were not complied with, we should be stripped of the last shred of clothing. Seizing their pole-axes, they then planted themselves in front of us, and with horrid oaths and menacing gestures attempted to strike terror into us. It seemed amazing that they did not rather strike the axe-heads themselves into us, as they continually threatened to do. But I could not fail to observe a singular hesitation in them every time they made an advance toward us.

At last two of them big, stalwart young fellows flung their weapons down in their fury, and setting themselves immediately before my wife and Miss Gates threatened to strip them if we did not give the information they wanted. Their answer to our silence was once again to seize their pole-axes and advance towards the weak, defenceless women. If ever I felt ashamed bitterly, contemptuously ashamed of my sex, it was then. They advanced a few steps and retreated, then advanced again. The strange hesitancy was upon them still; to be dispelled at last (as I suppose) by a moonbeam glinting from the surface of the milk tin in my wife's possession. The brave opposite her made a dash forward and snatched it from the hand that so jealously guarded it. This was enough: the next step was easy. The two rushed simultaneously upon the women, and seizing them at the throat tore each their upper garment from them. Miss Gates still retained a light gauze vest, but my beloved wife was left naked to the waist.

Their meek submissive spirit of unmurmuring patience was beautiful to witness. But who can measure the burning indignation of my heart's crying sorrow at the sight of them, under tho cold-gleaming moon, stripped to the chilling night air? Three times in one day assaulted by murderous hate with cruel violence; and now at the end of it left out in the mountains in cold and nakedness two delicately nurtured women, and one of them the partner of my own being! I thank Him Who enabled me to pray, with them, out of a true though breaking heart, "Lord, lay not this sin to their charge!"

As the men faced us again with the garments in their hand, I looked at them and said :

"Ni-men tsiu shi ren, ie muh iu ren ch'ing" "You are human beings, it is true; but you have not the feelings of your kind" about as stinging a reproach as one could well address to a Chinaman's ears; containing, too, a righteous, pertinent and legitimate rebuke. I am bound to say that I was not prepared for the effect it produced. To my amazement the word went home like an arrow to the mark. Sullenly they took the garments, first one and then the other, and flung them back to their respective owners. I have that very garment of my wife's in my keeping at this moment a token that speaks louder to me, every time I look at it, of the living power of the living God, than any treatise could. Platform "Evidences of Christianity" undoubtedly have a use and value of their own; but they are dreary things to me beside that soiled and tattered "evidence" of a God that "worketh for those who wait for Him." It also speaks to my heart as nothing else does of a Christ that "liveth in" His own, in the manifested beauty of His own life a life that could only be divine.

What the effect of this incident was upon the by- standers I cannot say. I only know that one by one they melted away, and ere long the four Boxers alone were left with us. Resuming their seat on the knoll, they again talked together, while we continued to cry to God for their removal.

Once more they confronted us this time with the order to get up and follow them back to Lu-an city. We replied that it was impossible we were too tired to attempt it. If they wished us to go, they must fetch a cart for us.

"A cart for foreign devils!" they cried; "we'll fetch ropes, and we'll fetch men; and if you can't walk, you shall be dragged." And with a mocking laugh and the information that they would be back directly, they shouldered their weapons and walked swiftly away the whole hatch of them; and in a few seconds we were alone!

Our God had done for us the impossible thing that we asked, and the mountain that was ready to fall on us had been removed in answer to the prayer that gave glory to God. The faith that offered it had been severely tested when the natural impossibility had been only increased instead of diminished by the sight of added numbers, who also were against us. But "if God be for us, who can be against us?" "Therefore we may boldly say. The Lord is my helper, and I will not fear what man shall do unto me."

With real awe in our hearts at what God had wrought, we watched the men disappear. It seemed strange that they should not have left a guard; for two (or even one) would have sufficed for the errand on which they were bent. But no; the thing was of God, according to the terms of our petition that He would "be pleased to take them right away, one and all"; and to Him we ascribed the honour due unto His Name.

The moment the last was out of sight, Sheng-min said, "They are gone, thanks be to the Lord's grace ! Now come quick: we have not a moment to lose." In an instant he had caught Hedley in his arms, and I Hope; and the next, we were in full flight. The moon was riding high in the heavens, and I judged it must have been about eleven o'clock when we took the river bed once more and pursued our trembling way towards Uang-fang. The excitement of the situation was intense; for discovery now meant absolutely certain death. We had no conception, of course, as to how far the four Boxers had to go for reinforcements; but the fact that they all ventured to leave us, and that they spoke of a speedy return, seemed to indicate that it was near enough, in their idea at any rate, to preclude any suspicion of the possibility of our escape; and therefore near enough to make the thought of our being re-taken uncomfortably possible. Two things were against us the superb brilliancy of the moon, and the whiteness of the ladies' san-tsi. Added to this was the almost total absence of adequate cover. To this hour I can never look up at the full moon in the glory of its radiance without a shudder going through me. Instinc- tively and invariably it recalls that night of nights, and only that night; and I live again the fear and trembling of our race for life. If only its traitorous brightness could be obscured for one brief hour, and the darkness cover us! But we were to learn what it meant to lean upon the promise," He shall cover thee with His feathers, and under His wings shalt thou trust."

The grave difficulty of the white san-tsi was partially met by Sheng-min's careful thought. He threw his own dark blue coat over Miss Gates' shoulder, and his black "ling-kua-tsi " (a kind of short sleeveless overall) over my wife's, the white sleeves of her "shirt" alone being exposed. For myself, my beggar's rag was an excellent foil, and I wrapped it round the lighter garment of the little darling in my arms.

Thus we pressed on, our weariness forgotten as much in the joy and wonder of our new-found liberty as in the fear of re-capture. Dead silence, utter stillness, reigned on every hand. The lateness of the hour and the loneliness of the path favoured us. Anxiously I kept looking back to see when the knoll would disappear, as being the point where our pursuers would be sighted, if at all; and oh, the intense relief when the curve of the river bed swept it at last from view, and there was no sign of their return!

The prospect of realizing our hopes was now well upon the horizon; and with strength renewed and lightened hearts we sped on. Higher up the river, the character of the country became more favourable to concealment. We were in the neighbourhood of the Uang-fang hills, and their wooded undulations and coppices of thick undergrowth would afford us a temporary refuge in our present extremity. The discovery of our flight could not long be delayed, and once made, would give rise to a pursuit the swiftness of which we could never hope to compete against. It was therefore high time we found a hiding place. So, leaving the torrent bed, we struck across the fields and made for the nearest cover.

As we did so the boy spied a graveyard, with its firs and monumental stones. In the strong contrasts thrown by the moon's light, the cemetery's sombre shades looked blackest darkness. Hither we turned our steps; and in the deepest shadows we could find, beneath the firs and behind the stones, we laid our weary bodies down at midnight, and in the peace of God, under the shadow of His wings, we slept.

The graveyard where we hid from the four Boxers.

Questions to Consider

1. Glover felt powerless to protect those he felt it was his responsibility to protect. Have you ever felt that way?

2. Glover says "The most 'natural' of all causes are the supernatural." Do you agree or disagree?

CHAPTER THIRTEEN

In the Mount with God

"Eye hath not seen, nor ear heard, neither have entered into the heart of man, the things which God hath prepared for them that love Him"

The event proved that we were not far out in our calculation. We could not have been sleeping more than half an hour when Miss Gates was awakened by the hue and cry of the Boxers in full pursuit. Quickly rousing us, she bade us be prepared for the emergency of discovery or further flight.

It was a sudden recall indeed to the realm of sad reality. Judging from the noise, the men had done what they said, and had returned with a strong reinforcement to find the bird flown. Baulked of their prey, they were now scouring the country; and unless our ears were deceived, we might hope for no mercy if they succeeded in the search. What if the deeper darkness of our hiding place, instead now of being our protection, should prove the occasion of our discovery! for it might well furnish to our pursuers the same reason for their search that it had furnished to us for our concealment. The sounds came near enough to lead us to fear that it was so in very deed. But they hurried on and passed by; and we were left with the deep consciousness that we had been covered by the Hand of God.

Again we lifted our hearts in praise to our Deliverer, and sought guidance in prayer. Miss Gates' conviction was that we could not long escape detection where we were, and that in any case it would be needful to find another hiding place against the morning light. But where? To attempt to reach Uang-fang now was out of the question, with pursuers on the track; and the woodland cover around, whatever it might be worth at night, would certainly fail to suffice us by day. Our only chance seemed to hang upon a suggestion of Sheng-min's. There was a lonesome cave in the locality known to him; to this he would try and pilot us, if we would take the risk.

Short as it was, the snatch of sleep so graciously given had much refreshed us; and realizing that the call to move was of God, we knew that, being in His will, we could count upon the sufficiency of His grace for all our need, whether of strength for weakness or whatsoever else. So committing ourselves and our perilous way into His Hand, we took the sleeping little ones in our arms once more, and "went out" from our hiding place, "not knowing whither we went."

And now the providential mercy of our God met us at the outset in a remarkable way. Our main anxiety hitherto had been the almost preternatural brilliancy of the moon. It was so still. The risks of breaking cover were such that it almost amounted to courting re-capture. And yet we were all of one mind in the conviction that it was God's way for us now. As we passed out from the deep shadows of the firs into the peril of that remorseless glare (I can call it nothing else), I feared; and my heart's cry went up to God to cover us. In almost less time than it takes to write it, the dread light was quenched beneath a rolling sea of cloud; nor did it appear again until we were in the place to which He would bring us. So dark indeed did it become, that at times we had the greatest difficulty in keeping together.

How can I describe that weird and awful midnight tramp? We kept to the fields, away from beaten tracks and haunts of men, seeking as far as possible the con- cealment of grove and coppice. Now we were climbing walls of ragged stone ; now dropping at a guess to lower levels. Anon we were plodding over ploughed fields or struggling with the stunted undergrowth. Once my dear wife sank almost to her knees in a bank of soft soil, and while seeking to extricate herself lost both her shoes; in recovering which I also was snared; while the rest had gone on into the darkness — (we were walking in single file)— and we dared not call aloud to them to stay. Often our feet had well-nigh slipped on treacherous ridges or into unsuspected holes. And how often we stumbled almost to a fall! But Thy mercy, Lord, held us up.

He Who was keeping our feet was also guiding our way. Sometimes it was so dark that I could scarcely see my wife's form, though she was but a couple of yards in front of me.

More than once I lost sight of the rest altogether, to my terror. But beyond all this, Sheng-min found that in the dim uncertainties of night, he had lost his bearings, and the hope of reaching the cave was gone.

What was to be done now? He knew of nothing else than to seek the covert of some disused temple, such as are constantly to be met with in isolated places. Slowly and cautiously we crept on in the hope of finding such a refuge, pausing continually to listen. At length the dark outline of a rural shrine stood out close before us. Warning us on no account to leave the cover of the grove and to await his return, the boy went warily forward to reconnoitre the building. The report he brought back was not only not reassuring, it was alarming. The temple was full of men, to judge from voices he heard issuing from within in all likelihood the very men who were hunting our lives. So, turning our steps back again, we made haste to flee whither, we knew not.

Yet He knew — He in Whose Hand our breath is, and Whose are all our ways. I remember so well the feeling of absolute helplessness that came over me. Knowledge we had none; and the little strength remaining to us was fast giving out. And I just said: "'The Lord is my Shepherd' Lord, shepherd us now, for we have no strength to go on. 'He leadeth me' Lord, lead us now; for we know not which way to turn. In our utter ignorance, be Thou our wisdom. In our utter weakness, be Thou our strength; for the glory of Thy Holy Name."

Then we remembered that there was one resource still open to us the hills. But, benighted wanderers that we were, how should we find our way thither?

We had succeeded in getting well away from the direction of the temple, and were now cautiously threading a coppice, when the shouts of our pursuers again startled the silence, and made our hearts stand still. Evidently they were making in our direction; for the dreadful sounds were growing nearer and more distinct. We stopped dead where we were, and stood rooted to the spot, not daring to move hand or foot. Then, just when it seemed that they were about to break upon us, the direction of the cries suddenly changed, and we knew that they had passed on to another track.

Our position had now become extremely critical, and we realized how easily the smallest indiscretion might betray us. Happily, the darling children were given over to heavy sleep, and past all thoughts of crying out a blessing compared with which the exaggerated deadness of their dead weight was to us who carried them a trifle. We waited until we were satisfied that the sounds were sufficiently distant, and all immediately around us quiet as before; and then, with our heart fixed on God, we crept forward again. At no great distance the cover was broken by a gully cutting the coppice. Just as we reached it, we heard a roar as of riot, and the baying of dogs. Then a lurid light shot up into the darkness. The sky glowed with the red glare of palpitating flame, waxing fiercer and fiercer, and outlining the bolder features of the landscape. Wonderfully did our God make this to work for our good. For there against the ruddy background of the sky, standing high before us, we saw the mountain we were seeking!

Patiently we waited till the glare had fallen. Then, swiftly crossing the gully, we entered the coppice on the far side, and ere long we found ourselves where we had prayed to be on the mountain slope, working towards the summit.

The glow had faded from the sky, and darkness covered us once more. Just at the needed time; for the hill side was innocent of anything that might serve to screen us. Had the moon unveiled or the flames revived, we could not have escaped detection as we moved upon the face of that open expanse. But our God was with us to give us an expected end; and the darkness that hid us was the covering of His Presence. Slowly and painfully we made the ascent. It seemed, in the particular circumstances, the counterpart of the words which came continually to mind

They climbed the steep ascent of heaven Through peril, toil and pain: and our stricken hearts took up the refrain, as they travelled on in thought to the spiritual reality

O God, to us Thy grace be given
To follow in their train!

With feelings of devout thankfulness the summit was reached at last. It was circular in form, with a diameter of about fourteen or fifteen feet, absolutely bare of trees, and very exposed. As a hiding place in the day time it would have been of no value but for a remarkable feature. The cone was

indented in such a way as to form a basin, of sufficient depth
to admit of our sitting (or even standing) in it without being
seen, provided we kept away from the margin. Into this basin
we now crept shall I ever forget how thankfully! with a deep
realization of the provision and safe-keeping of our Shepherd
Lord. A few minutes sufficed to make the needed preparations
for a short night's rest the unearthing of several large stones;
and with these for our pillows we lay down to sleep, in the
assurance that He Who had been so marvellously about our
path was also about our bed.

The mountain top. Sheng-min stands in
the basin where we hid.

The Lu-an district forms a plateau with an elevation of
some three thousand feet above the sea level; and on the
summit of that hill, in our condition of semi-nakedness, we
tasted the inner meaning of the dry geographical fact. I never
suffered from cold, before or since, as I did that night. We
huddled together as close as we could to keep in the vital heat,
with the little ones wedged in between, doing our best each

one to make our single garment serve the purpose of coverlet for them as well as coat for ourselves. But in vain. For myself, I know my teeth never stopped rattling all the night through, try as I might to prevent it.

Sleep there was none for any of us, save the children. The clouds drifted from before the moon, leaving us exposed to the full power of its beams exposed, therefore, to the proving of the promise, "The moon shall not smite thee by night." Far down, away in the distance, we heard the hoarse shouts of our pursuers as they pressed the chase, almost till break of day. And then a sweet spell of restful stillness, relieved of all unquiet alarms, and only the consciousness of the shadowing of Jehovah's wings.

******

I come now to one of the most solemn crises in the history, not of this solemn period only, but of my whole life. Among the many spots which I can look back upon as "holy ground," I might find it difficult to say which stands out before me as pre-eminently so.

And yet the dealings of the Lord with us, alone on the mountain top, were so peculiarly distinct, so definite and searching, that it would almost seem as if the title must rest there. Or should I say that, if other places were "holy ground," this was "most holy," standing out in my experience amidst all the other manifestations of Divine grace, as Mount Moriah must have stood out before Abraham and Isaac, or the Mount of Transfiguration before the three disciples. In very truth it was to each one of us three "the mount of the Lord" in which "He was seen" "the holy mount" where we "were with him"; and by a striking coincidence of His pleasure, the day was His own day Sunday, July 8.

The sunrise was one of glorious splendour. As the huge disc of fiery red showed above the horizon, its colour seemed prophetic of what the day should bring forth for us of "fiery trial." Not a cloud flecked the sky as, higher and higher, it rose into the azure.

After the bitter cold of the night, the genial warmth of its early rays was very comforting. But ere long, as its power increased, it became a source of grave anxiety and distress. I have already indicated that the summit was wholly destitute of tree life, or of covert of any kind. In the hollow where we lay, the coarse, burnt-up turf boasted of nothing beyond a plant or two of the stunted date shrub.

With no "blinds" between them and the bright morning light, the dear little ones were awakened all too early. We dared not stir from the two positions of lying or sitting (indeed, we had no inclination to, even had we dared) nor durst we speak in tones other than just above a whisper; and, from a child's point of view, such an outlook was not over cheerful. But the trial that was to test us was to test them, too, and to bring out in them qualities of character that we had no idea of previously. Sweet little darlings! how readily they fell in with our every wish! Not a murmur; not even a question, after we had given the reason why. Just the patient sitting there, or crawling a yard or two now and again, and not a sound above the regulation whisper.

After uniting together in prayer we began to think of breakfast; or, shall I say, to be forcibly reminded of it from within? For what we had to "think of" was not breakfast, but the lack of it. It was just forty- two hours since anything solid had passed our lips (Friday, at noon); and here we were, fugitives in hiding, with nothing to sustain us, and no hope of getting anything. It was wonderful how we were kept from the suffering of excessive pangs of hunger. I felt the gnawings, certainly, but not the pangs; and I believe that we could all testify to the same experience. Well, we made the best of our circumstances, and realizing that the eye of our God was upon us, according to the word, "Your heavenly Father knoweth what things ye have need of before ye ask Him," we were sure that He would feed us with food convenient for us. If He gave us nothing but the grass around us to eat. He could so order it that the grass should sustain us. So the dear children, happy in having something to do, began to see what delicacies they could find for "break- fast" among the weeds. To their delight they were able to bring of several kinds, which they doled out as "meat," with the leaves of the date shrub for "bread." Then lifting our hearts in thanksgiving to our Father, in the Name of the Lord Jesus, and asking His blessing upon what He had graciously given in our extremity, we made our herbal meal; for is it not written, "In everything give thanks. Whether ye eat, or drink, or whatsoever ye do, do all to the glory of God"? I learnt then, as never before, the true blessedness of "saying grace." The dry, uncooked weeds and leaves were truly "the bread of affliction"; but, being "sanctified by the Word of God and prayer," and "received with thanksgiving," they were found to be "the bread of blessing."

By seven o'clock the power of the sun was becoming distinctly perceptible; and, as it increased in intensity, we began to realize what it meant to be bareheaded. The gauze combinations, which formed the dear children's only covering, left their arms wholly exposed from the shoulder, and their legs from the middle of the thigh. It was not long before the skin, so sensitive in a child, was burning red as from a scald.

As the moisture of the skin dried, so also did that of the tongue, and ere long a great thirst was upon us. The trial of hunger was as nothing compared with this, for which there was no assuagement of any sort at hand. The little ones' plaint, "I am so thirsty; please give me something to drink," soon became a piteous cry, "father, dear father! do give me water. Mother darling, won't you give me water?" We sought to hush them tenderly, for they could not now refrain from crying aloud in their distress, and we knew that this would, in all probability, lead to our discovery.

"Don't cry, darlings. We will ask God to send us water, and we will be patient till He does."

The simple laying of our deep need before our Father comforted them; and it was touching to see how heroically they wiped their eyes, and set themselves to "try and be good." We strove to divert their thoughts from their distress in various ways; but presently the piteous cry broke out again.

"Darling little pets, you mustn't cry out loud, or else the naughty men who took our things will find us, and take us away. God knows how thirsty we all are, and He will help us to bear it, till He sends the water."

Again the earnest effort to contain, as they sought to amuse themselves with grass and soil; and again at length the pleading cry, "Oh, do, do give me water; just one drop!" as they clung about us with their loving ways and tender endearments. Seeing how much it affected my dear wife, I said to them,

"Don't you think we would give you water, darlings, if we could? But you see we can't; and you see how very, very sad it makes sweet mother to hear you crying so. You surely won't go on making her sad, will you?"

Once more the resolute brushing away of the tears, as they set themselves to please us in this. But as the time went on, our precious little Hope was unable to control herself. Her involuntary wail, "Father! Mother! water, water!" continued without intermittence as long as she was able to articulate tore our very heart-strings. As for Hedley, I never saw (nor ever expect to see) a finer example of Spartan endurance. When he realized how sad the sounds of his distress made his mother, the dear little chap (not five years old) set himself determinedly, for her sake, to absolute silence. There at her side he sat without so much as a murmur or a groan passing his lips. For hours, through all that burning heat, with his mouth parched and his limbs scorched, he sat quietly on, resolutely toying with the grass, a very miracle of suffering self-control. Some days afterwards, I was asking him a few questions about that particular time, and amongst others, this:

"Why did you keep so quiet, when all the time you wanted water as badly as Hope did?" His answer came so naturally and simply:

"I saw how sad it made darling mother to see me cry, and I asked God to help me not to cry once more till the water came." Truly out of the mouth of babes Thou hast perfected praise!

At length we could bear the sight of our little ones' sufferings no longer, and we sent Sheng-min to the edge of the ring to survey the country. But the news that he had sighted a goodly rivulet about three li from the foot of the hill seemed only to mock our grief. How was it possible for us to get the longed- for draught? To leave our hiding place was death.

To despatch the boy was to run a risk of losing him that we hardly dared contemplate. And yet our extremity was fast passing to a crisis, and could only have one issue at last. So we decided to send him, in reliance upon the guiding and keeping grace of God; and forth he went, with the promise to hasten his return.

With mixed feelings I may almost say misgiving we watched him disappear over the rim. From the human standpoint, all our hopes, even of life itself, centred in him. The temporary separation, at the time we were carried out to die, had made us realize what it was to lose him from our side; and the risks were such that we could not count upon his return as in any sense a foregone conclusion. As it was, we were happy in having him actually with us: could it be other than mad folly to be deliberately sending him from us? The fact that we were brought to do it furnishes perhaps the most striking comment I could make upon the straits to which we were reduced.

And now, with our devoted servant gone, a sense of loneliness came over us which searched the very depths of our being. It was too subtle to be accounted for merely by the outward loss; for we were trustfully expecting to see him again, and shortly. The dear lad's departure may have been the occasion of it, but it was not the cause. That was to be found in "the power of darkness." The hour had come which was to be peculiarly the hour of our temptation.

Under the pressure of hunger, thirst, and burning heat, my dear wife began to show signs of exhaustion, which made me apprehensive, to say the least. Pitilessly the sun poured down its rays of fire. We cried to God, but it seemed as though He heard not. No clouds gathered at His command, as yester-night ; no "gourd came up over " us, " to deliver us from our evil case." The heavens were brass over our heads, and brass they remained.

At this juncture Miss Gates and I conceived the idea of improvizing some slight shelter for her and the children by means of our two garments. Slipping them off and holding the inner edges together, we stood side by side, with the screen drawn up over the shoulders to the level of the head, varying our position with the position of the sun. With the alleviation thus afforded, slender though it was, my dear one was not a little comforted, and strengthened to hold on.

As the sun mounted towards the zenith, darkness gathered over my soul. I think we were each one conscious of the same experience, to a greater or less degree. It was not difficult to believe that Satan had been desiring to have us, that he might sift us as wheat. That hallowed consciousness of our Lord's near Presence, which had hitherto solaced us and given us power to endure, was now withdrawn; and the language of our hearts (if I may dare to speak for my companions in tribulation as for myself) was, "O that I knew where I might find Him!" I under- stood, as never before, why Moses so earnestly pleaded for the Presence "If Thy Presence go not with me, carry us not up hence." To be destitute of the Presence of Jehovah, my Strength and my Redeemer, in the hour of sore temptation; to be no longer conscious of the light of His countenance; to realize, instead, only the awful nearness of "spiritual hosts of wickedness"; and to see our adversary the devil coming in the terror of his power as a roaring lion to devour us — !

And all the while our Lord was near, "in His love and in His pity," though for the time being He willed, for His own great Name's sake, that our eyes should be holden that we should not know Him." In all our affliction He was afflicted; "and He was only waiting for the moment when the Wicked One should have finished all his temptation, and the Angel of His Pre- sence would come and minister to us as of old. There were many days of "hardness" yet before us; and the trying of our faith was necessary to work in us" the patience of Christ," by which alone we should be able to "endure" it, as "good soldiers of Jesus Christ."

But there was another aspect, too. We were to be disciplined, not merely as soldiers, but also as "sons and daughters of the Lord Almighty." Judgment is to begin at the house of God; and this was nothing else than God our Father bringing us under His mighty hand, even as He did His own beloved Son. As He called Him to learn obedience by the things which He suffered, so also was He calling us to the same lesson.

"The cup which My Father hath given Me, shall I not drink it?" "Ye shall indeed drink of My cup."

Higher and higher rose the sun into the heavens, and Sheng-min was not back. Narrower and narrower grew the shadow thrown by the slender screen; and soon there would be no shadow at all. The children were barely covered by it now; but they seemed past noticing anything. Hedley sat vacantly toying with the grass, while poor little Hope was rocking herself deliriously to the monotonous moan "Water, water! Oh, dear mother, give me water!" Even the oft repeated assurance that Sheng-min would soon be back, and then they should have as much water as they wanted, seemed lost upon them, A distressing phase of the situation was that with the increasing thirst, the saliva in the mouth turned to a viscous consistency, which we began to find the greatest difficulty in getting rid of. If water did not arrive soon, articulation would become impossible, for even now it was often difficult to disengage the tongue from the palate.

And now the sun was riding directly over our heads, and the last hope of shade was taken away. "A Man shall be as rivers of water in a dry place, as the shadow of a rock in a weary land." Had He not said it? Would He not fulfil the word to us in our extremity? Were we not "in a dry place," and "in a weary land "? "When the poor and needy seek water, and there is none, and their tongue faileth for thirst, I the Lord will hear them, I the God of Israel will not forsake them." Were not we "poor and needy, seeking water"? Was not our "tongue failing for thirst"? And again our hearts' cry rose up to Him: but He

answered us not a word.

In that hour all His waves and His billows seemed to go over me. As the sun poured its fiery heat upon us from above, the Wicked One hurled his fiery darts at us from beneath. How many times I threw back to him the challenge, "Who is he that condemneth? It is Christ that died, yea rather, that is risen again, Who is even at the right hand of God, Who also maketh intercession for us. He that spared not His own Son, but delivered Him up for us all, how shall He not with Him also freely give us all things? Who shall separate us from the love of Christ?" How often I fell back upon the word, "I have prayed for thee that thy faith fail not." Again and again did I give him my Lord's own declaration, "Himself hath said, I will in no wise fail thee, neither will I in any wise forsake thee." And over and over I said to the Accuser, "Though He slay me, yet will I trust in Him."

I would fain draw a veil over the solemn sequel. May He strengthen me to show forth just so much as He directs of His own marvellous works, to His own glory !

The Enemy's answer to all this was the collapse of my beloved Flora. She too had known the bitterness of those hours of darkness; but the language of her unwavering faith had been, "My flesh and my heart faileth; but God is the strength of my heart, and my portion for ever. I know Whom I have believed, and am persuaded that He is able. He faileth not." Indeed, the sight of her own steadfast endurance, and the sweet unmurmuring resignation of her spirit to the will of God, as " that good and acceptable and perfect will" which was all her delight, had been from the first a channel of Divine strength to me in seasons of special weakness. What it was to me on the mountain top, during those hours of fierce temptation from within and from without, none but God can ever know. And now she lay prostrate before me, overborne by physical weakness, and deeply troubled in soul. As I watched her panting and gasping for breath, with no power to alleviate her suffering beyond supporting her head, it seemed as though I heard the serpent's hiss, "Yea, hath God said? Where are His promised mercies and lovingkindnesses now? Has He not forgotten to be gracious?" The cruel taunt was winged to the heart of my beloved, too; and in an agony of soul she cried out from the deep darkness, "Oh, God has forsaken us! It can only be that we are not in His will, or He would surely never have suffered us to come to this." Her distress, physically, was such that I felt sure she was dying; but it was as nothing to the trouble of her soul.

Now indeed it seemed as if the Enemy's triumph was assured. The cup of sorrow was over-full; and con- scious that this was the "scourging" of the Lord, I was dumb under His rebuke. My heart was utterly broken before Him.

But "when the enemy shall come in like a flood, the Spirit of the Lord shall lift up a standard against him."The moment of our deliverance was at hand; and we were about to know what it was to "overcome him by the blood of the Lamb, and by the word of our testimony."

Scarcely had the words of anguish passed my precious one's lips than God put into Miss Gates' mouth the most wonderful song of praise I have ever heard. Kneeling by the side of her prostrate sister and holding her hand, she poured forth passage after passage, promise after promise, from the Word, exalting His Name, declaring His faithfulness, and proving His unchanging and unchangeable love, sworn to us in the everlasting Covenant and sealed to us in the Blood of His own beloved Son. Never shall I forget the music of that heavenly utterance. It was as if heaven were open above us, and the strains of the harps of God were being borne to us from glory. My beloved Flora drank it in, oh, how eagerly! with the avidity of a soul athirst for God, the living God. Together we drank "out of the wells of salvation" with what joy I cannot express deep draughts of the pure river of water of life, flowing freely to us now from the throne of God and of the Lamb. The time had come at last for Him to reveal Himself to us. Our eyes were opened, and we knew Him; and the word of His promise was fulfilled to the letter, "A Man shall be as rivers of water in a dry place, as the shadow of a rock in a weary-land."

Instantly the darkness was past and the true light was shining again. The heavenly expression in her countenance of joy unspeakable and full of glory, where but a moment before it had been one of un- speakable anguish and distress, was an evident token of what God had wrought. I see her now as she looked when, with the tears coursing down her cheeks, she said, "Oh, I will never, never doubt Him again." And I may add here that from that moment her glorious faith never wavered for an instant, but went from strength to strength through conflict after conflict, till she appeared before God in the heavenly Zion above.

Then together we repeated right through with parched lips and stammering tongues, but with hearts that had tasted of the wine of heaven the beautiful hymn, so true to our experience:

How sweet the name of Jesus sounds
In a believer's ear!
It soothes his sorrows, heals his wounds.
And drives away his fear.

It makes the wounded spirit whole.
And calms the troubled breast;
Tis manna to the hungry soul.
And to the weary, rest.

Dear Name! the Rock on which I build.
My Shield and Hiding-place,

My never-failing Treasury, filled
With boundless stores of grace

Jesus, my Shepherd, Brother, Friend,
My Prophet, Priest, and King;
My Lord, my Life, my Way, my End,
Accept the praise I bring.

Weak is the effort of my heart.
And cold my warmest thought;
But when I see Thee as Thou art,
I'll praise Thee as I ought.

Till then, I would Thy love proclaim
With every fleeting breath;
And may the music of Thy Name
Refresh my soul in death!

The effect of this divine cordial upon my dear wife physically was nothing short of miraculous. From an apparently dying condition she suddenly revived, and sat up with a restored vigour which amazed me. It was not merely a measure of revival from the extremity of collapse, but it was the incoming of a vital power quickening her for fresh activities. Indeed, it was to us all a literal manifestation of the truth of the word to which her faith had so resolutely clung, "My strength and my heart faileth; but God is the strength of my heart, and my portion forever."

By this visitation of God's grace, our hearts were encouraged to wait for His deliverance from a situation which was still gravely critical. It was past noon, and there was not a sign of Sheng-min. The sun's blaze was fiercer than ever; and the sensation of thirst was becoming well-nigh intolerable. Not only so: the power to articulate clearly was fast going from us.

Indeed, we had the greatest difficulty in making ourselves understood; and I saw that very soon it would be no longer possible to communicate with each other by speech. As I struggled to force out the syllables, I understood the meaning of the expression, "My tongue cleaveth to my jaws." Darling little Hope's moan was reduced to an indistinguishable sound, as she vainly strove to frame the word "water."

The situation, however, reached a climax when Miss Gates, who had been the chosen instrument in God's hand of my dear wife's restoration, suddenly fell to the ground and swooned away. It seemed as if it were a last revengeful thrust from our retreating foe, to cover the shame of his defeat (Luke ix. 42); and his malice must needs be directed against the one who had led the victorious attack.

It was a new and critical emergency, in the presence of which all the old helplessness came over me. As my dear wife and I were pleading with God for her recovery I heard a word behind me as distinctly as if it were spoken in my ear " Up, get thee down and tarry not." I said to my wife, "Come, darling, we must gather up what strength remains to us and go down to the water. It is not the will of God that we should remain here any longer." Then, taking Miss Gates by the arm,

I bent over her and said, "Dear sister, we must be going without delay. In the Name of the Lord Jesus, get up." In a moment consciousness was restored, and she rose up with strength renewed from on high.

With such a confirmation that the thing was of God, and in the assurance that the Lord our God, He it was Who was going before us, we left our hiding place, and once more adventured ourselves into the open. There below us, away in the not-far distance, was the thin streak of silver glancing in the sunlight the "still waters" to which our Shepherd-Lord was leading us at last What that sight was to our longing eyes I can never tell the joy of pointing it out to the darling children, and of seeing the faintest smile dawn over the sad, suffering little features!

Slowly and painfully we took our way down, making use of such cover as we could find on the lower slopes; down, to the ploughed fields below, and across them in as direct a line as the ground would admit of; down, to the lowest level; and then, by the shortest cut we could make, to the water's side. Regardless now of whether we were seen or not, we fairly ran, not to the river, but into it. Oh, the bliss of giving our precious little darlings the first draught, as we filled our hand and put it to their swollen lips! But the process was all too slow to satisfy the urgent need. Wading into mid-stream and putting our mouth to the surface, we drank and drank till the craving was satisfied. We scarcely noticed that the thin silver streak of the distant view was in reality nearer the colour of brass (or copper) than silver; for the water was heavily charged withh yellow silt, the consistency of which was forcibly impressed upon us by the fact that, after drinking, our tongue and palate were coated with a thick layer of mud! However, that was a minor consideration now. I can only say that, to me, those draughts could not have been more delicious if they had been the purest well water. Under the burning sun we dared to sit in the cool shallows for a few moments longer, laving hands and face. Then with hearts full of gratitude to our Father for so graciously supplying our need, we sought a place where we could lie down unobserved.

Not far from the margin of the stream there was a graveyard, similar to the one we had hidden in the night before. Dark yew trees were there, affording grateful shade; and high grass-grown mounds, amongst which we might hope to screen ourselves. It being a solitary place, and the time of day that known as "Shang-wu" the period of rest when few are about in the hot season we hoped and believed our sanctuary would not be noticed, or our privacy invaded, for an hour or two at least. But the events of an hour hence belonged, not to us, but to Him Who was guiding us with His eye upon us; and we could afford to leave them in His hands without carefulness.

Once more a heathen burial ground was to be the spot that should enshrine "the memory of Thy great goodness." What the shelter of that delicious shade meant to us, after being exposed for seven hours at least to the undimmed blaze and sweltering heat of a midsummer sun, no one can imagine. In the waters before us and the shade above us we found the counterpart on the physical side of the precious promise given us in the mount, and already so richly fulfilled on the spiritual side: "A Man shall be as rivers of water in a dry place, as the shadow of a rock in a weary land." According to His word, He had not failed us: but He had done to us as He said "When the poor and needy seek water, and there is none, and their tongue faileth for thirst, I the Lord will hear them, I the God of Israel will not forsake them."

Not least among the wonders of that memorable day was our miraculous preservation from sunstroke. Those who have spent a summer in China will be able to appreciate the nature of the fact that "the sun did not smite us by day," under conditions where, humanly speaking, a few minutes would suffice to do even fatal work. That we suffered terribly under its power only proves the marvel. The skin peeled from our faces, and the dear children's arms, from the shoulder to the elbow, were one huge blister. But the sun had no power to hurt us beyond that. The Lord had been our shade upon our right hand, to keep us from "the arrow " of its rays; and we are His witnesses that "He is good," and that "His mercy endureth for ever."

Nor can I leave this portion of my narrative without making mention of the supernatural power of endurance given to Miss Gates, and recording my deep sense of indebtedness to her, who, for over three hours, stood under that fierce blaze of heat covering my wife and children, in a ministry of self-sacrificing devotion which I can never forget, and the memory of which will ever remain with me as one of the noblest deeds of Christian heroism I have ever been privileged to witness. No words of mine can convey any adequate conception, I think, of what our actual experience was. I feel I can only say, as I look back upon it, "What hath God wrought!" It was indeed true of us in that hallowed mountain top — "We had the sentence of death in ourselves." But it was all to the end" that we should not trust in ourselves, but in God that raiseth the dead. Who delivered us from so great a death." Certain it is that "the excellency of the power" that brought us out alive, or that enabled us to endure what we did, was "not of ourselves, but of God," and God alone. And when we left the hill, it was with the consciousness that there we had "seen the Lord."

"I reckon that the sufferings of this present time are not worthy to be compared with the glory which shall be revealed to usward." As we laid us down, spent with long hours of watching and fasting, the hope of that glory was bright in our hearts. For, with a longing begotten of our experience, we looked on to the day when the redeemed " shall hunger no more, neither thirst any more, neither shall the sun light on them, nor any heat; for the Lamb which is in the midst of the Throne shall feed them, and shall guide them unto living fountains of waters; and God shall wipe away all tears from their eyes."

Questions to Consider

1. Do you believe God covered the moonlight with clouds to hide the Glover's from their pursuers?

2. Can God lead us when we don't know which way to go?

3. Do you have a "holy ground" in your life that you can look back on? A place where you knew you were in God's presence? Have you shared that with anyone?

4. Would you be able to thank God for weeds and plants?

5. Do you know what it feels like to go somewhere without the sense of God's presence?

CHAPTER FOURTEEN

Arrest and Treachery

"When my spirit waa overwhelmed within me,
then Thou knewest my path"

We had scarcely settled down to the enjoyment of our quiet retreat, when our ears were greeted by the sounds of music proceeding from a temple not far off. Worship was evidently going on; and I was troubled to think that ere long the worshippers would be out, and doubtless some of them coming our way. Turning in the direction whence the sounds came, I noticed that a narrow roadway skirted the tiny grave-yard, whence we could easily be sighted, lying as we were; so I advised a change of position. Too late!

As we were making the attempt, the first comers appeared from amongst the trees that hid the shrine from view, and passed along the footpath. They hurried on, apparently without having seen us; and I was beginning to hope that after all we were better screened than I supposed. Then the boom of a gong announcing a procession; and a few moments later, the usual motley crew of yamen tatterdemalions, with their clown's caps and sign boards, heralded the approach of an official.

It was idle to hope that we could escape detection now, though we lay close to the ground and absolutely still. Peeping from between closed eyelids, I saw one of the runners suddenly stop and look hard, then say something to those about him, who also stopped and stared. Then I caught the dreaded words, "lang kuei-tsi!" "The foreign devils!"; and I knew that we were again in the hands of our enemies.

As the mandarin's chair came into view, he craned his neck to see what it might be that his minions were so curiously occupied with, and forthwith sent a runner to the spot, while he ordered the bearers to stand. Needless to say, the runner was joined in his errand by a score or more, until the cemetery was alive with clowns' caps, sign boards and umbrellas. He needed to ask no questions one look sufficed; and he returned to his lord to report that it was the "iang kuei-tsi" who were lying there. Whereupon the Hsien (for it proved to be none other than the Lu-an sub-Prefect) issued some order in peremptory tones, and the procession went on its way.

Almost before we had time to take in the change of situation, a yamen "chiao-ch'ae" (or small covered cart) stood beside us. How it came there I have no conception. The thing was so sudden, it seemed as if it had shaped itself out of the invisible ether. A "small" official and two soldiers were in charge of it, the former of whom stepped forward and ordered us to get inside.

Meantime, poor Miss Gates had again relapsed into a prostrate condition. When I sought to rouse her, there was no response; and when at length, in the mercy of God, she rallied sufficiently to take in the position of affairs, it was only to say that she felt too ill to move. The official repeated the order to mount, adding that he had been sent by the sub-Prefect to take us on to the next magistracy at Kao-p'ing Hsien. The story seemed too good to be true; and believing it to be a Boxer ruse to have us quietly away and despatch us at leisure, we refused to get up. However, the officer produced a document as like a bona-fide "Uen-shu"(1) as official style and seal could make it, and as a guarantee of good faith pointed to a bundle in the cart, which he said contained clothing for us from the Lao-ie, and a certain sum of money. He added that they had been searching for us the night through; but that having now abandoned all hope of finding us, they had given up the search, and were just returning to the city with the Hsien's retinue.

How much of this we were to believe and how much to discredit we had no time to consider. Our incredulity must, I think, have been written in our faces as we looked at one another; for the official stamped his foot and ordered us again to "shang ch'ae." So I said to my wife and Miss Gates, "It may be that this is of the Lord for our salvation. Anyhow, one thing is certain: we cannot possibly live on as we are, tramping the road as beggars at the mercy of hostile crowds. If this is for life, then we shall live to praise our God; and if for death — well, we shall die any way. Let us trust in the Lord and take the cart."

The decision taken, we were not long in following it out. But a few moments sufficed to pack all five of us in, Miss Gates being lifted to her seat by one of the soldiers; and almost before we could realize the extraordinary turn of events, we were splashing through the water to the opposite side, and making for Uang- fang, en route to Kao-p'ing.

Now for one moment let me pause to point the significance of the events as they occurred. The cart, I need hardly say, proved to be the means of our ultimate deliverance; though I may here forestall my narrative so far as to say that our surmise was not wholly incorrect the intention was to carry us to execution. It was doubtless true that they had been searching for us all night: true also that they had now given us up, and were returning without us to the city. How marvellous, therefore, was the ordering of events whereby our arrival at the river synchronized with the mandarin's return from worship. *Twenty minutes later, and we should have been too late!* The procession would have gone on and the cart with it; and we should have been left to the rabble. Then it was that I understood the urgency of that Voice, "Up, get thee down and tarry not!" and how truly it had been the voice of God. Then too it was that I realized how the strength to rise up and get down was given where, humanly speaking, it was an impossibility. And, once more, I saw how the wisdom of God had overruled Sheng-min's non-appearance to our salvation; for, had he brought us water in the hill, we should not have felt it right to stir from our hiding place. As it was, however, we just had time enough given us to relieve the intense suffering of thirst and scorching heat before we were found.

So graciously did our compassionate God go before to supply our need, and then make for us the way of escape.

As for our faithful Sheng-min, we never saw him again. It appears that, after leaving us, he made his way towards the river to the nearest village, where he sought an opportunity, as best he could without arousing suspicion, of getting some vessel in which to convey the water to us. The difficulty, of course, was that he was moneyless: indeed, his condition was little better than our own. It was not long before he was recognized. He had been seen, they said, with the foreign devils, and must therefore be a Roman Catholic. Upon his affirming that he was not, they decided to settle the truth of the matter by ordeal. It was com- monly reported among them that by exposing the suspect to the full blaze of the sun, the sign of the cross would, if he were a Roman Catholic, come up in the forehead at noon; and his guilt would thereby be established beyond question. So they took him, bound him with ropes, and, planting his feet upon some mystic characters traced in the dust, compelled him to stand gazing up at the sun until noon a period of upwards of two hours. The test, of course, failed: but for some hours afterwards he was blind, nor was he released till the late afternoon. Then he returned to the hill, to find us gone; sought us in the hills and caves, and only gave up the search when he had exhausted every place in the neighbourhood. The next day he returned with a heavy heart to the city, and informed the sub-Prefect of the condition in which he had left us. He was told that a cart had been sent to take us on, with clothes, ten ounces of silver and six thousand cash. The first part of the Hsien's statement was true enough; the latter part may or may not have been so. I only know that

the bait was put before our nose by the cart official; but so far
as any personal benefit was concerned, clothes, silver and
cash were a myth.

Thus Sheng-min's ministry of self-sacrificing love to us
was finished. Both he and P'ao-ri had been given to us just so
long as they were needful to us; and now in the new
circumstances of our arrest, where they could no longer serve
us, they were withdrawn by the same gracious Hand that had
bestowed them on us.

As yet we knew nothing indeed, could know no- thing of
the purpose for which we had been picked up. It was only by
sad experience, as events developed, that we gathered its true
intent, namely that it was for death, not life. The fair-seeming
"uen-shu" was not the usual official passport, which would
secure us safe-conduct from one magistracy to another, until
'we were out of danger. It was, at the most, a semi- official
paper written by the sub-prefect to his friend, the Kao-p'ing
"Hsien" stating that "we had made a disturbance in our
district, and were to be taken out of Shan-si, never to return."
Thus, being rather of a private than of an official character, it
had no binding authority, and was practically valueless; and
also it was so worded that a magistrate was free to read into it
his own construction, whatever he might choose to make it.
What this meant to us the narrative will reveal.

The relief of finding ourselves under official surveillance,
after being for nearly three days exposed to mob law, was
greater than I can express, especially as the assurances given
to us bore distinctly in the direction of hope. At such a time,

when the heart was sinking in deep waters, it thankfully caught at the veriest fragment that came in the way wherewith to buoy itself up; and as we put one link with another in the chain of God's leadings, the hope of the promise given at the outset breathed its life into us afresh: "I shall not die, but live, and declare the works of the Lord." Thus the officer's assurances, flimsy as they might be in themselves, yet taken in connection with what we knew to be the orderings of God, were invested with a new value, and became a real ground of comfort. The mercy of a temporary shelter from the heat under the "p'eng" of the cart, and the knowledge that we were speeding in the right direction, contributed not a little to raise our spirits so great was the con- trast to what, but an hour before, had been the only prospect before us. As I sat in my beggar's rags on the shaft, with my dear ones just behind me, little did I care for the astonished looks of the passers-by. Few were about at this hot period of the day, and our arrest was not generally known; so that, until we reached Uang-fang (about 1.30 p.m.) we had nothing to trouble us in the way of crowds. The officer in charge rode immediately behind on horseback, while the soldiers urged the mule to a half trot an unusually quick pace for China. Seated as they were on the bare boards of the springless cart, with nothing to break the concussion of tracks that can only be called "roads" by courtesy, my dear wife and Miss Gates in their exhausted state suffered severely. However, in about half an hour's time we entered the little village of Uang-fang, and were halted at the food shop which did duty for an inn. Here we were ordered to dismount, and told to go inside, the option being given us of staying in the food shop on the street, or of going to the more private quarters at the back. There seemed to be no question that the latter would be the wiser choice from several points of view, and we elected accordingly, to the evident satisfaction of the escort. How wonderfully God was in the decision, though apparently a wrong one in the issue, will appear from what follows.

Passing to the rear of the shop, we were taken across a small courtyard to the opposite side and shown into a narrow, dingy room, thick with usual dust and more than usual dirt. But it was shelter from the heat, and its comparative privacy would, we hoped, afford us an asylum from the dreaded crowds. There was a mud k'ang, too, inviting rest despite its filth, whereto we thankfully betook our stiff and weary limbs. That room, so soon to be dark with the shadow of death! I can never think of it without shuddering.

By the officer's orders our wants were well supplied. Hot water was brought us to drink; and shall I ever forget the fragrance of the savoury "pien-shih," or pork dumplings, that were set hot before us! The sight of food and such food! was quite overcoming: and we thanked our God for inclining the officer's heart towards us in this unexpected way. We ate it with a ravenous relish begotten of a fifty hours' fast; for save the mouthful of grass plucked on the mountain top at sunrise that day, we had tasted nothing since Friday at noon.

The kindness thus shown tended to confirm our hopes that, after all, we had fallen into good hands. It was evidently designed, however, to be nothing more than a blind the apparent justification of the fair words by which we had been induced to enter the cart.

Meantime, the news of our arrival had spread, and the space before the food shop was soon thronged. Then they began to filter through into the courtyard, and once more we were under the stolid gaze of countless eyes, and the restlessness of a never-ceasing stream of comers and goers.

I was concerned to find, as time wore on, that our escort failed to show themselves, and that the usual limit of a midday halt was overpast. On the other hand, an activity painfully suggestive of the Han-tien experience was going on outside the room; and the significant looks and low-toned asides of the onlookers in the room increased the suspicion that all was not quite as it should be. This was the more confirmed, however, when the Boxer badge, now once more in evidence, revealed how large a proportion of the ever- shifting crowd belonged to the Ta Tao Huei. In due course, the door of our room was shut from outside, and a Boxer sentry set to guard it.

It now became certain that, unless our escort soon called for us, we should find ourselves in dire straits. The haunting dread, that had not been wholly laid to rest by the production of the "uen-shu" came back in force that this was none other than a Boxer ruse, and that we had again been betrayed. Was it possible that the escort had decamped, cart and all, leaving us to die where we were? I opened the door and looked out across the courtyard. Yes, there was our "Seng-k'eo," feeding quietly at the trough. Provi- dentially it had been brought inside, and tethered in a corner well within view; and as I caught sight of it, I thanked God for the hope inspired thereby that we were still safe. At the same time, I was wholly at a loss to understand the escort's long delay. The door was slammed to by the sentry upon my withdrawal, with a significance I refused to notice beyond reminding him that we were there as guests, with the Lao-ie's uen- shu, and that such discourtesy was unknown to Chinese etiquette. To save his face, he allowed us to open the door and take an occasional look out a privilege I was not slow to avail myself of.

As the afternoon wore on, the suspicion of foul play increased. I will not attempt to record the inward conflict of those hours of alternating hope and despair, of fear and strong crying to God. I reproached myself with having fallen so easily into the trap, first of taking the cart at all, and then of choosing the inner room, where we could be so easily cut off from escape. I began to doubt whether the mule was really our "seng-k'eo" after all; and even if it was, might they not have left it as a blind and gone off with another? And yet, all the while, these very things that I was deploring as mistakes were designed of God to be the ultimate means of our deliverance, as the sequel will show. How often in a time of perplexity do we take a step in entire dependence on God, after definite prayer for guidance according to His will; and then, when it seems to land us in situations that run counter to our expectations, mourn the "guidance" as "our mistake"! So strong in us is the Egyptian sin of unbelief, and its consequent the sin of murmuring against God in the desert, whither He Himself has led us in the wisdom which we profess to have trusted.

There was a passage at one side of the room, leading to a space at the back; and hither the crowds kept streaming to and fro, in a way ominously suggestive of preparations which to my mind boded death. I could only suppose that they were making ready to hang us at the rear of the building.

I have already mentioned that Uang-fang (the village where we now were) had from time to time been visited by us in past happy days, and that the people were by no means ignorant of the Gospel mes- sage. It was to the house of our evangelist Chin loh- han that our thoughts had turned when we sought a hiding place; and now our hearts longed to see his wife, who was alone at this time of need, and to streng- then her hands in God. As yet, of course, we knew nothing of her idolatrous compromise and denial of her Lord through fear of persecution.

Those who came into the courtyard seemed to be too intent on what was going on to remain staring at us, and so we were left more or less free of their company. A good many women had come in at one time and another; and now, towards the late afternoon, the door opened, and a little woman hobbled across to the k'ang and got up beside my wife and Miss Gates. They recognized in her one whom they had often seen in Chin ta-sao's house, and to whom they had spoken the Word of Life, being, in fact, none other than her next door neighbour. With scared expression and in scarcely audible tones, she told them that the Boxers had been all night searching for us, and had ransacked Chin ta-sao's house in the belief that we were hidden there. Disappointed in their hope of finding us, they had then seized everything she possessed. "And," she added, " I have come to tell you that, now they have caught you, they are going to kill you here. You are all to be burned to death in this room, and Chin ta-sao is to die with you. They are even now piling the wood to fire the building; and when all is ready, my neighbour will be brought across." And with a "k'o-Uen, k'o-Jien" ("I feel so sorry for you") she slipped off the k'ang and hobbled quickly away.

So then it was to be burning, not hanging. Once again we were face to face with the king of terrors; and once again we cried out of the depths to Him that is King even of that king, "mighty to save." The situation was as desperate and the outlook as hopeless as ever it had been at I-ch'eng, at Han-tien, at Sha ho-k'eo, or at the torrent bed. But it was not too desperate for Him Who had lifted us up from the gates of death not once nor twice. Nay, had He not, only just this very moment, brought us a fresh assurance of His protecting care in the knowledge that, when we sought asylum with Chin ta-sao. He had turned our steps into another path, so saving us from the Boxer search-party? The same God Who had wrought for us hitherto, was with us still "Emmanuel, God with us," "the Same yesterday and to-day and forever." And the same throne of grace was accessible to us still, where we might "obtain mercy and find grace to help in time of need." Yet surely if ever there was a time of need, it was now, when the preparations for burning us alive were being made before our eyes. If any loophole for doubting the truth of the good woman's words were left, it was blocked by the entrance of the innkeeper and his servant, who began hastily to clear the room of every vestige of furniture, even to the straw mats from under the ladies on the k'ang. Then, when they had gone out, the door was shut, the sentry mounted guard, and we were alone in the despoiled room; for all fled from us now, as from those "appointed to be slain."

The food shop where the Boxers attempted to burn us to death.

Through a paperless square in the window-frame I found I could still keep my eye on the mule without provoking either the wrath or suspicion of the sentry by continually opening the door. Idle as it seemed to suppose that the escort were still on the spot, I clung to the hope fostered by the animal's presence as a drowning man clings to a chip. With what intensity I peered through the tiny square! How I watched every movement, for fear of being outwitted by its sudden removal! I believed the hope was given me of God; and in the strength of that belief, I was enabled to impart a measure of reassurance to my dear wife and Miss Gates.

At length I heard the back gate, close to which he was tied up, open, and a man slipped in and quickly loosed the halter. "Now or never: come instantly," I said. Snatching up the children, we quietly opened the door, turned sharp to the right behind the sentry, and walked swiftly out through the courtyard gate before they had time to shut it. There they were our miserable escort, hurriedly preparing to put the mule into the shafts, all eagerness to bolt without us. Our unexpected appearance on the scene took them completely aback, and for a moment they seemed dumbfounded. It was impossible for them to say that they were not going on, for we had caught them in the very act; and as they knew they were bound by their orders to take us on to Kao-p'ing, they could not refuse to carry us without "losing face."

We were now hemmed in — escort, cart and all — by an immense crowd. At sight of us the people had given a shout, but not a soul attempted to touch us. It was evident that they were nonplussed by this sudden counter-stroke; for the back gate was the last place they expected to see us come out at. Indeed, they supposed we were nicely housed and a prey ready to their hand. From the conversation that passed between the escort and those about them. Miss Gates was enabled exactly to gauge the situation; for they talked freely among themselves, never dreaming that any one of us was able to follow the drift of what they were saying. There was no room for doubt that our professed friends were in collusion with the local Boxers, and had agreed to leave us in their hands, to be despatched as soon as they themselves were clear of the place. The programme having been abruptly interfered with in this inconvenient way, they were now discussing how it could be remedied. It was decided, on putting the animal in, to work him up to a restive state while we were attempting to mount, and then, on the plea that they were unable to hold him in, make off before our attempts had succeeded. Thus they would both secure their end and "save their face."

Little did they suppose their plot was known. As they whipped the seng-k'eo into the shafts. Miss Gates said to me, "They are planning to make off before we have time to mount. Our only chance is to get in now, before the mule is harnessed to the cart." No sooner said than done. To the dismay of the escort and the amazement of all, first Miss Gates and then my wife fairly leapt in; while I handed up the children, and in a trice had seated myself beside them on the shaft. The officer's bewilderment turned to fury as, with the soldiers, he cursed us and ordered us to dis mount. Quietly Miss Gates told him that we knew all their plans, and that, since there had been a "uen-shu" issued for our safe delivery at Kao-p'ing, we were not going to leave the cart until we arrived there.

Upon this refusal they once more debated what they should do, and it was proposed to fire the cart and roast us to death where we were. The escort, however, were unwilling to take the responsibility of a step so directly involving themselves and the property of the yamen; and the proposal was vetoed, under cover of the excuse that "there were Boxers farther on who would save them the trouble." To cover their discomfiture with us they said that the reason they wanted us to dismount was that they might be able to get at their money and coats, which were stowed away inside. To hand out the articles required was a very simple matter; and the chagrin of the men found vent in dark scowls and mutterings. When they saw that we were not to be moved by fair means or foul, the officer mounted his horse, the soldiers tore at the mule's mouth, and off we dashed, amid the curses, hoots and yells of the mob.

As I look back upon it all, I marvel at the deliverance God wrought for us. Not merely at the way in which He led us out of that sentry-guarded room, no man withstanding us; nor only at the way in which He confounded the devices of our enemies at every point; but (what amazes me almost beyond these) at the way in which He restrained them now from falling on us in their great wrath. As we drove through the street, the cart was pursued by hundreds of local Boxers, armed with bludgeons and gnashing on us with their teeth, as they cried after us and on every side of us, within easy striking distance, "Death to the foreign devils! They think they have escaped us. Wait till they get to Yin-ch'eng, and then see what will become of them!"

Questions to Consider

1. "Twenty minutes later and we should have been too late!" Glover says he heard God's voice. Do you believe God gives such specific directions?

2. Do you recognize His voice?

3. Do you follow His directions even in the little things?

CHAPTER FIFTEEN

With the Rain Processionists of Yin-Ch'eng

"I will deliver thee in that day, saith the Lord; and thou shalt not be given into the hand of the men of whom thou art afraid. For I will surely deliver thee ... because thou hast put thy trust in Me, saith the Lord."

Amid this outburst of diabolical fury God kept our hearts in perfect peace. The consciousness of the divine Presence and covering was never more real to us all, I think, than now. In the mere fact that we were on the cart at all we had a tangible evidence that He was with us; and we read in it the guarantee of the promise, "Behold I am with thee, and will keep thee in all places whither thou goest." Every fresh instance afforded us of His delivering grace and power became a fresh ground of trust, as it became also a fresh plea with Him in prayer, that He Who had delivered us from so great a death, would yet deliver us.

I have already had reason more than once to re- mark the experience of the quietness and confidence which such assurance is able to beget in the heart under the most disturbing circumstances; and with every recurring instance, I rejoice to put it upon record, as proving it to be a truth which holds good, not for this or that particular form of trial, but for all trials under all conceivable circumstances.

Thus we were cursed out of Uang-fang. The Boxer mob pressed us to the village bounds, and then, with the exception of a mere handful, who also soon disappeared, left us to pursue the journey unmolested to Yin-ch'eng. The sweet silence that now prevailed helped us to realize by contrast what the fury of the storm had been. When I recall the murderous looks and gestures of our pursuers as they ran alongside the cart, I marvel again at the power of the Hand that held them back and then dispersed them.

The temper of our escort made itself felt in the pace at which we were jolted along. But the sense of the protection of God, and the consciousness that every step was bringing us nearer the goal, kept us from giving the fact an undue place in our thoughts. In spite of their attempted treachery I clung to the hope inspired by their official character, and believed that, with the orders they had received, they would not dare to fall foul of their superiors. So reasonably unreasoning are we glad to become under pressure.

It must have been about 6 p.m. when we rattled into Yin-ch'eng. As a busy centre of the coal and iron industries of those parts, it was a town of some size and importance; a place, too, not unknown to us in our preaching itinerations. Not three months since I had visited it with Dr. Hewett on the way to Kao-p'ing, when we spent many hours preaching and distributing Christian literature on the streets. And now how different my circumstances and appearance! Worn with suffering, unshaven, unshorn, with matted queue and clothed in beggar's rags, a prisoner under arrest and on the way to execution.

Apparently the escort were anxious to keep the fact of our arrival dark. At any rate, we were not taken into the throughfares; but, entering by a quiet street, where scarcely a soul was about, we were almost immediately halted before some large closed gates. I noticed, too, that the officer did not adopt the usual noisy method of knocking up the chang-kuei-tih, but found some private way of communicating with him. We had not many moments to wait before the gates opened, and we were driven into the fair-sized court- yard of a comfortable inn.

I was relieved to find that we were the innkeeper's only customers, and it was a further relief to hear the gates close behind us, and to know that we were to have the premises to ourselves and the sorely-needed boon of a quiet night's rest. At the same time the sound of the Uang-fang Boxers' parting shout still rang in my cars: " Wait till they get to Yin-ch'eng, and then see what will become of them." There was nothing, however, to indicate trouble, or the approach of it; and as it seemed the officer's wish that we should be treated civilly, my confidence in his reliability was largely restored. A nice room was allotted us, and hot water brought us to drink. And thus in rest and quietness we lay down on the k'ang with hearts lifted in thankfulness to God.

We had not been reclining ten minutes before we heard shouting and battering at the gate. There was nothing for it but for the chang-kuei-tih to open, and some dozen or more pushed their way in to "have a look at the foreign devil." They were quickly succeeded by larger accessions, until we saw that there was no hope of our being left to a night of peace. The room was soon full to overflowing, and the crowd that had to stand without tore the paper panes from the window frames, clambering on back and shoulder to get their stare. The escort then forced their way through, and ordered us to sit outside on a form placed by the doorway, where all could see us.

On coming out into the open I was concerned to see that the large majority of men and lads who faced us were stripped to the waist, their heads wreathed with green fillets, and in every hand a stout cudgel like the Irish shillelagh. The significance of this was only too apparent. We knew at once that they were rain-processionists. Humanly speaking, nothing could have been more inopportune than our arrival at such a time, when the always excitable temper of the people is worked up to a highly inflammatory pitch. Even under ordinary circumstances it would have been dan- gerous to fall in with a rain-procession. How much more so now, when public feeling everywhere was running high against us?

Here, then, we sat for some little time, patiently giving them the opportunity they sought, and courteously answering the insolent questions they put to us. It was plain, however, that they had not come for the mere gratification of an idle curiosity. As they grew bolder, their insolence passed from words to deeds, and they began to thrust themselves upon us where we sat against the wall in a malicious horseplay, which would soon become open violence. Seeing the trend of things, the officer came and ordered us to a room on the other side of the courtyard, when he produced a padlock and proceeded to lock us in. This was too much. The Uang-fang experience was not to be repeated: once locked in we knew we should never get out aliye. The escort would decamp with the cart, and we should be left to the mercy of this fanatical mob. Remonstrance, however, was worse than useless. It only infuriated him; and seeing that there was nothing for it, we found it best to accept his statement that he was doing it for our protection, and gave him to understand that we implicitly trusted him to bring us in safety to Kao-p'ing. So the door was shut upon us and made fast with bolt and lock.

What a position was ours now! "Wait till they get to Yin-ch'eng!" It seemed certain that our doom was fixed. As we sat on the k'ang within, listening to the noise of the tumult and the cries for us to be brought out, we realized as much as ever before the helplessness and hopelessness of our position. And once more we stayed our hearts upon the word, "God is our refuge and strength, a very present help in trouble. Therefore will not we fear, though the earth be removed, and though the mountains be carried into the midst of the sea."

It is difficult to convey to the ordinary reader any adequate conception of the situation that confronted us. One glance at the windows was enough to terrify, as these half-naked fanatics glared in through the now paperless squares and heaped curses on us. The wreaths bound upon their heads served to intensify the wild savagery of the scene. Perhaps the riot of the Bacchanal might convey the nearest impression of it; only these were not the ravings of a festal crowd, but of a murderous mob.

The head and front of our offence now was not merely that we were responsible for the drought which was causing them such acute distress, but that, this being their day of special intercession for rain, we were there to frustrate the efficacy of their prayers. They had been crying to heaven all day; and now, as if to add insult to injury, the foreign devil to whom all their misery was due in the first instance must needs come along, and by his accursed presence spoil the whole day's work. As long as he was in the place, the gods would not hear them. For the honour of heaven, therefore, as for their own peace' sake, they must have us away. And with a riotous rush they forced the door and broke into the room.

What would have happened next I dare not think, had it not been for the concerted action of the officer and the landlord. Apprehensive for his property, the latter declared that he would keep us no longer on his premises, and that we must find a billet elsewhere. Together they forced their way in, and ordered us to get down from the k'ang and come out. Naturally I demurred. What? Deliberately adventure myself and those with me into the midst of a riotous mob of rain-processionists? As well might one think of walking with open eyes into a den of ramping lions. I freely confess that at that moment my heart sickened with fear, and as I turned to my wife and little ones beside me it was with a deep inward groan to God. The next instant I was torn from them, dragged from the k'ang and hurled through the door out into the midst of the seething mass. As I fell forward amongst them every trace of fear vanished. I knew well the end had come, but my only concern now was that I was apart from my dear ones. Not a soul touched me, and as I recovered my footing, I turned to see what had become of them. With admirable courage my wife and Miss Gates had leapt from the k'ang the moment after my seizure, and dragging the children after them were fighting their way through behind me. To my joy they were within reach, and in another moment we had joined hands.

Keeping tight hold of one another, we were borne along as by a resistless current through the courtyard gates. It might truly be said that bulls closed us in on every side. At times, too, the pressure was such that we were lifted off our feet, and my dear wife came near to fainting with the severe buffetings. I know it was nothing but the sustaining power of God that carried her and Miss Gates and the tiny children under it all; for as we swept into the road we were met by a cross current the main body of processionists who had been unable to find room in the courtyard. As when a rushing stream joins the swollen waters of a torrent, so was it now. Helplessly and tumultuously, as straws upon the swirl, we were borne on down the narrow street, whither we knew not.

It seemed strange that not a hand had been raised as yet to hurt us. Doubtless some feeling of respect for the landlord had held them back from falling on us in the courtyard. But here we were now in the open, on the street; what was to hinder them from doing all their pleasure? Close beside us, in the providence of God, was the officer in charge of us; and we had come to see so much at least as this, that, anxious as the man was to get rid of us, it must be in such a way as not to implicate himself. I observed that, as we came into the open country beyond the town and the pressure of the great crowd relaxed, he was evidently bent on getting away from our immediate neighbourhood, that he was indeed again scheming to give us the slip. I said as much to the ladies; and at my wife's suggestion we adopted a move which I believe, under God, was our salvation. Taking possession of his right hand and Miss Gates of his left, they two simply hung on. Thus in the eyes of all he was our declared guardian, and he dared not, or at any rate did not (as we judged he would not), repudiate the obligation. However, the unhappy man's heart was meditating evil. Miss Gates overheard him discussing our death with those about him, and saying,"I will get them to sit down and rest themselves at yonder stony spot, and once down they need not get up again. It will be easy enough there for you to trample them to death." She told us what she had heard, and urged us, should he or anyone else invite us to sit down, on no account to do so.

We were now able to form a better idea of the proportions of the huge crowd that swarmed about us. Between eight and ten thousand would be a modest computation. On a special occasion such as this, where so much hung upon the due observance of the appointed rites, the whole country side would pour in to the centre. Not only so, but with the continuance of the drought agricultural work was at a standstill, and many who would have otherwise been busy in the fields were simply hanging about with nothing to think of but mischief, and glad of anything that might offer in the way of a little excitement.

We were forced on till we came in due course to the whispered "stony spot." It was a wide, open space, where we were able to move more freely, and where the mob would have room enough to do anything they wanted with us. Here the officer stopped, and, as if by common consent the great procession stopped too. He then addressed himself to us, and under cover of the excuse that we should probably have to wait some considerable time for the cart, casually suggested that we would do well to sit down by the wayside. We thanked him, but replied that we would prefer to keep with him and remain standing. Poor, miserable man! His look of utter bewilderment was almost pathetic. It was evident that he was being torn two ways be- tween his desire to please the mob and get rid of us on the one hand, and his fear of official censure, if he failed in his appointed duty towards us, on the other. I remember well how the sweat broke out in great drops on his forehead, as after a respectable interval he urged us once more to rest ourselves. I need not say we again refused the delicate attention; but I added sadly to his confusion by asking him, as he was so considerate, to carry my little girl for me; and he actually allowed me to put her into his arms. This, of course, committed him more than ever, as I intended it should; for I was anxious to show him that we were prepared to trust him absolutely in his official capacity, as the one responsible for our safety; and not only that, but to make the fact patent to the wild rabble as well, that we were under the protection of the yamen. I hoped, too, and believed that the sight of a little child lifted up before them might prove a mute appeal that would find its way to the heart where nothing else could. In taking the little one as he did, it seemed to me that the man's conscience feared lest a refusal might betray its guilt; or else that he hoped a show of kindness might throw us off our guard, as proving the sincerity of his good intentions towards us. However that may have been, I record the simple, the amazing fact. There he stood before the whole vast throng of would-be murderers, himself one with them at heart, with little Hope sitting high above them all on his arm, our confessed ally and protector. There was no possibility of his eluding us, for the ladies had tight hold of his gown, one on this side and the other on that. It really seemed as though, like Balaam of old, he had no power to exercise the bent of his will God had determined to bless us, and he could not reverse it.

Remarkably, too, was his own impotence reflected in the mob. They hung about us like howling wolves, longing yet fearing to attack. They did all they could to induce us to sit down, and when we refused they threatened to fall on us as we were. Doubtless they would have done so, had the yamen official not been there to cover us. The only thing they could now do was to carry us beyond the radius within which our malign influence was supposed to work against their prayers. Thither we were borne, and once more they came to a standstill, hovering clamorously about us as they discussed what they should do to us.

The cautious irresolution of the officer led him to make another attempt at bolting. He had already given little Hope back to me, and now he was nervously looking this way and that, as though for some loophole of escape from us. It was so obvious that I thought it time to remind him once more of his responsibility, and said, "Your duty is to take us to Kao-'p'ing. If we can't stay the night at Yin-ch'eng, you must take us elsewhere." "How do you suppose we are to get elsewhere?" he replied. "Our cart is away yonder at the inn." "Very well," I said, "you have to get us somehow to Kao-p'ing, and your business is to send to the inn and have the cart brought to us here." This little colloquy was almost immediately followed by the appearance of two soldiers in uniform whether for life or death we did not know, but evidently for decisive action one way or the other. Driving the crowd to right and left with their cudgels, they made their way to the officer and entered into conversation with him. What the gist of their communication was I cannot say. I only know that under cover of talking apart with them he contrived to edge away from us and mingle with the crowd. We were able to frustrate the attempt just in time, much to his chagrin. It was well for us that we did; for the sun had set, and the short twilight would soon be merging into darkness, and who could tell what the rabble might not do then? We had learned enough of hostile Chinese crowds by this time to know that there comes a point at last when their temper will stick at nothing. It was so now with these Boxer processionists. Instinctively one felt that it would not be long ere that point was reached. Marvellous indeed it was that it had been held in check even till now. The event of the soldiers' appearance had been most timely in the mercy of God; for whatever the duty that brought them, their presence had a restraining effect upon the mob. In the light of after events, I think it not improbable that after conference with the officer they persuaded the people, as they went in and out amongst them, that we were being taken as Imperial prisoners to Kao-p'ing, where we were to be officially executed by order of the Emperor. All this anxious while we had been lifting our hearts in an unceasing cry to the Rock of our salvation. How deliverance could come to us we knew not. Death was as imminent still as ever it had been, for the officer's heart was full of treachery, and as yet we had no idea for what purpose the soldiers had come. Any moment a signal might be given for our destruction; and as for our request that the cart might be brought to us where we were, the words which framed it seemed to fall from the lips with a sound that mocked us. For myself, I fear my faith was hardly prepared for the answer God vouchsafed to our prayers. The impossible to us was again proved to be possible with Him, as with inexpressible wonder and thanksgiving we saw the cart speeding towards us at a fast trot, and then pull up parallel with us. No need for the officer now to order us to "shang ch'ae." It was no longer to us the probable vehicle of our destruction, but the evident channel of our salvation, and that of God.

The sullen silence amid which we took our seats broke into a confused roar as we drove off, the dominant note of which "Death to the foreign devils!" was so often to resound in our ear. But beyond this no attempt was made to stay us. Not a hand was put forth to touch us, nor a foot to pursue us. In a few minutes the wild hubbub had passed to a distant murmur;

and as darkness fell we were alone once more in the heavenly quiet of silent, lonely roads.

Questions to Consider

1. Would you have put your daughter in the soldier's arms?

2. Do you trust your family is in God's care?

3. How do you show that?

CHAPTER SIXTEEN

A Night to be Remembered

*"Weeping may endure for a night, but
joy cometh in the morning "*

Our escort were in no mood either to talk themselves or to hear us talk; so that the way was pursued in silence. And, indeed, we were not sorry to have it so, for we were unspeakably weary. The acute suffering, mental and physical, of the mountain solitude had been succeeded by a long, nervous strain of many hours in the very hands of those who were seeking our life, and we could not but be conscious of after effects. The marvel is that it was not followed by a serious reaction, in the case at least of the ladies. What God did for us in those days can never be fully told. From first to last it was one perpetual miracle. Where His power was not manifested in the more direct and obvious way of actual interference and deliverance from seen destruction, it was none the less evident to ourselves in the more hidden processes of strengthening and sustaining grace for spirit, soul and body.

As our thought travelled back over the events of the day, we were shut up more than ever to the conviction that the Lord had sent His angel and delivered as from all the expectation of the people. The escape from Yin-ch'eng was certainly not less miraculous than that from Uang-fang. One fact alone, apart from other considerations, will suffice to show the nature of it. In our parts, to cross the line of a rain procession was a crime to be visited there and then, in the case of a man, with a heavy cudgelling, in the case of a woman or animal, with death. The year before, our evangelist and I had narrowly escaped a severe handling when returning late one night from the street chapel in Lu-an city. Seeing the procession coming up the street, we drew aside into the darkness of a doorway, where we expected to be secure from observation. The vanguard, however, whose duty it was to clear the way, found us and ordered us to strip off our coats. Our refusal was the signal for a demonstration which showed us that no time was to be lost if we were to get away with a whole skin, and we beat a retreat just as the main body was upon us. Already the advance party had begun to strike at our legs; but happily we were not far from a crossing where four roads met, and the turning we took proved, in the mercy of God, to be off the appointed path for the procession. Had it been otherwise, we should have been hunted down, and the usual penalty would have been meted out to us without mercy. My concern, therefore, on taking in the position of affairs at Yin-ch'eng may be imagined; and when the officer gave out as the reason for our quitting the inn that the processionists regarded our presence in the place as a hindrance to the efficacy of their prayers, we all understood the real significance of the warning. It meant nothing else than that they looked upon us as having crossed their path, and intended to treat us accordingly. Under ordinary circumstances even a native could not hope to escape with anything less than a severe beating; and as for a native woman, the penalty for her was death. What, then, had we to look forward to, the hated "iang kuei-tsi" under circumstances, too, where the Empress Dowager's edict for our extermination was already known, and when Boxer placards proclaimed everywhere that our destruction would be regarded as a work of merit? Escape even under ordinary conditions would have been marvellous enough; but as things were it had been nothing short of miraculous, the result of a definite act of Divine interference. God had proved Himself again unto us a God of deliverances, and our united testimony was and is, that unto Jehovah the Lord, and to Him alone, belong the issues from death.

How long we had been traveliing I do not know, but it must have been over an hour when we entered a moderately-sized village. The long narrow street was deserted, and all was quiet as we pulled up before the crazy door of the only inn. To judge from the length of time it took the "chang kuei ti" to answer the summons, one would gather that custom seldom came his way, and that he was in a position to be independent of it when it did. Be that as it may, the arrival was an event of sufficient moment to be more particularly inquired into; and the discovery that he had a cartload of foreign devils to cater for, brought out all his native independence and something more, as he slammed the gate with a curse and bade us begone.

Driven off from the only shelter open to us, where should we find a resting place now? Every bone in our bodies ached with excessive weariness, until it be- came almost unbearable under the harsh jolt-jolt of a springless cart. There was nothing for it, however, but to go on. At any rate, our guards were so minded, and there was an end of it; so we passed out to the endurance of another hour or more of the unendurable. And yet even this had a compensation of its own. The quiet of the solitary roads, the freedom from mental strain, the cover of the darkness that hid us from recognition, and even the very fact that we were moving, brought each its element of comfort. Then, too, we were together and to ourselves in the cart; so that, other things notwithstanding, we could be "still praising Thee." Above ail else, it was a valued time for waiting on God without distraction, and in the opportunity of undisturbed communion we were able to renew our strength for what was immediately before us.

We arrived at the village which was our objective, to receive again at the only inn a similar rebuff to that we had just experienced. In very truth we were tasting what it meant to be despised and rejected with our Master. It seemed now as if this was to be the rule wherever we came. As we looked out into the street and felt the touch of the chilly night air, our heart and our flesh failed us; but we remembered that it is enough for the disciple that he be as his Master, and the servant as his Lord. If it was true of Him that no man cared for His soul, and that even He had not where to lay His head, why should we expect it to be otherwise with us? for even hereunto were we called — to the fellowship of His sufferings, a privilege that carried with it its own reward, and in the knowledge of it "the joy of the Lord was our strength." Clearly there was nothing for it now but just to take what we could get, and betake ourselves to the refuge of the destitute, the local temple. Such at least was the decision of the officer, and a few minutes later found us in the large theatre area in front of the sacred buildings. Here we were ordered to dismount. The escort then tethered the mule without taking him out of the shafts, and telling us they were going to negotiate a night's rest for us with the village elders inside, disap- peared behind the temple wall.

We believed, of course, that their reappearance was but a matter of a few minutes more or less, and looked to see where we could seat ourselves meantime. There was no other accommodation than a pile of stones, angularly tilted in such a way as to ensure discomfort all ways. But we were thankful for anything in our weariness, and with the weight of the sleeping children to support, were ready to make shift with whatever offered.

The little company of forlorn strangers could not fail to attract the notice of several groups of loungers on the place, who had no difficulty under the light of the clear moon in making out our identity. Of course, the news that there were "iang kuei-tsi" in the village was carried on to the street, and it was with no little anxiety that we saw the original handful increase to the dimensions of a crowd. Added to this was the consciousness that the escort were not to be relied upon, and that for aught we knew this was only another ruse of theirs for shirking the highly objectionable bit of work allotted to them. However, as long as the cart was before our eyes we had some tangible guarantee that they did not intend to abandon us, and with this hope in our hearts we kept watch.

How long I cannot say. Long enough to believe at last that they were never coming. Long enough to become acutely sensible of the cravings of hunger and to shiver with the cold. Long enough for the crowd to lose the silent reserve of curiosity, and give vent to the true expression of the thought of their heart.

By evil looks, threatening gestures, sinister innuendoes, and open avowals, they left no room for doubt as to what they meant to do with us if we stayed in the place much longer. They sang the praises of the Ta Tao Huei, and fell to discussing in what way they should put us to death. Close to the temple buildings and immediately in front of them a huge fire was burning, only too suggestively, in a large square grating, and the idea of roasting us alive (possibly, as at Han-tien, with the thought of sacrifice behind it) was proposed and adopted. Our hearts went out to the poor degraded people, darkened as they were in their understanding, alienated from the life of God because of the ignorance that was in them; and as opportunity offered we spoke to them of the life and immortality that Christ has brought to them through the Gospel, of redemption through His Blood and the forgiveness of sins. But there came a point at which they refused to listen further. We were in their eyes nothing more than the emissaries of the Evil One, and like him only devils, to be feared, hated, and got rid of out of hand. So that there was nothing left for us to do but silently lift our hearts in prayer for them.

Taken up with the attitude of the crowd, I was not on the alert, as I ought to have been, in the matter of the cart, when suddenly a cry from my wife startled me to my senses: "Quick, Archie, quick! they are bolting!" Sure enough they were. Surrounded as we were by the crowd, the escort had seen their opportunity and untethered the mule without our observing it. My wife just caught sight of them as they dashed through the enclosure, and they were away. Quick as thought I was on my feet, and after them. All sense of weariness was gone. I flew as on wings. The mule was a spirited animal, and making the pace under the driver's lash, but I got him before he was half way down the street. Gripping the reins at the bit, I held him until my wife and Miss Gates, who I knew would not be far behind, came up with me. The escort, I need hardly say, were furious; but either they were too taken aback or else too anxious to save their face to do anything. The excuse, always ready with a Chinaman, was that they were taking the animal to its night's stabling. "Very well; then you take us with him," we said; and in we bundled, to their infinite disgust. The crowd that had threatened us, not prepared for such a sudden turn in events, watched us drive off in amazement thankful enough to be well rid of us, as their parting volley of "Shah iang kuei-tsi!" testified.

The hostility of the village being what it was, we could not but thank God that we had been denied shelter there. A quiet night in the solitude of the open was preferable to the doubtful comfort of a room filled with plotting watchers. In the light of experience, however, it was not reassuring to find that we were retracing our steps and hastening back towards Yin-ch'eng, and we were bold to tell the escort that, take us where they might, we refused to think of passing the night at either of the two places, Yin-ch'eng or Uang-fang, where we knew well a reappearance would mean certain death. The answer was a storm of abuse. I remember how my heart quailed under it, for it seemed now as if they had reached the point where they could no longer tolerate our presence, and would even turn on us themselves. I need not say that, while we received it with outward silence, we made it the occasion of loud inward crying to God.

The quiet of the lonely roads, that had been so restful to us before, in the knowledge that we were leaving the scene of riot behind us, had lost its power to refresh us now. The old nameless anxiety came back (upon me, at any rate) as we drew nearer the town; but when at last we were near enough to hear the distant roar of riotous revel, and to know therefore that the processionists had not yet dispersed, I could no longer refrain, and said to the officer in courteous tones:

"We are not willing to enter the town. You know they wanted to put us to death there, and you are not wise in risking death for us again. We trust you to find us a suitable lodging elsewhere."

He turned on me fiercely. "We are going nowhere else to-night. Where should I find stabling at this hour if not at Yin-ch'eng? If you don't wish to come, get out and sleep under yonder hedge. You slept out in the open last night, and you can do it again to-night."

I thought that surely now the climax was reached, and that they were minded to turn us out forcibly by the wayside the more certainly that they pulled up short, and began to talk together apart. Not so, however. The conference ended, the officer gave a charge to one of the soldiers, and taking the other with him to lead his horse, hurried off on foot towards Yin-ch'eng.

The hour or so that we were kept standing in the roadway awaiting their return was of a piece with the rest of that troublous day. Ordinarily we should not have had to reckon with wayfarers at that time of night; but we had fallen upon a great exception, and we knew that before long the processionists would be taking the homeward tack. Thankful we were that we had not been driven back into the thick of it all, as at one time seemed inevitable. But we were still in the presence of a very real danger, and one that called for the staying of the mind afresh upon God.

A cart standing stock still in the middle of the road, under a bright moon, was an object conspicuous enough, and one calculated to excite curiosity; and the curiosity of processionists who had sought our lives once that day already was not a cheering prospect. So again from under the p'eng of the cart went up the cry of the helpless to God mighty to save.

In due course they came, one here and another there, singly and in groups. One and all, arrested by the unusual sight, stopped at the answer to the customary inquiry, "Who have you got there?" "The cursed iang kuei-tsi." The bitterness with which the soldier gave it out went through me; for it amounted to an invitation to the bystanders (about twenty of them) to fall on us. But though they joined him in heaping scurrilous abuse on us, no one lifted a hand against us. That endless hour of suspense under the cold moon was one that left its mark upon my own soul. Though the situation was not so acute, perhaps, as on some occasions, yet I recall it as one of peculiar suffering, as well as of signal mercy. For the hostility of the guard, openly avowed as it had not been before, removed even the semblance of protection from us. There was nothing on man's side to hold them back from doing all the desire of their heart; and yet they feared a fear, and we knew well that it was a fear from God Who stood as a wall of fire between us and them.

The suspense was ended by the return of the other two. We had dreaded, indeed, lest it might only prove an aggravation of the trouble, but in the mercy of God it was otherwise. The officer's manner seemed to indicate that he had business on hand that required haste. After addressing a few words which we could not catch to the several groups around us, he gave an order to turn the carts (which owing to the restiveness of the mule had been facing in the opposite direction) for Yin-ch'eng; and away we sped with lightened hearts, leaving the dreaded wayfarers to go their way and think their thoughts.

With lightened hearts; for no one can imagine the intense relief of finding another peril left behind. And yet with hearts not wholly without care; for were we not heading for Yin-ch'eng? Sad experience was teaching us that we were to escape one phase of danger only to confront another; and the inward attitude to be constantly maintained, was by necessity one in which praise for "mercy obtained" in deliverance merged into prayer for "grace to help" in view of a "time of need" that lay on immediately before. Thus only were we enabled to go on from hour to hour; and as the care of the hour brought us into touch with Him Who careth for us, we learnt in a very practical way what it meant to be "lifted above above all," and with our hand in His to be "without carefulness."

The moon's light was at intervals obscured under masses of drifting cloud as we hurried along the now wholly silent and deserted road. It was after mid- night when the gate of the town was reached. There was no question about it they meant us to spend the night there; and once more we entered the place of sorrows. Instead of taking us, however, into the town to a respectable inn, we had no sooner drawn within the gate than the cart pulled up. Here we were ordered to get out, and the place indicated where we were to pass the night. It was the stage of the small stone theatre, open, of course, in front and facing the long main street. Such places are the customary sleeping ground of tramps, outcasts and professional beggars; and doubtless it was chosen now to mark the contempt in which we were held, and suitably to impress the sense of our degradation upon us. So far, indeed, as our outward appearance was concerned, there was everything to suggest, to the ordinary observer, a natural correspondence with our environment; for we looked by this time as nearly professional, *qua* Chinese beggar, as the genuine article specially I, in the orthodox dress of the order. It was evident to us all that we had no choice but to obey the direction, though not before we had required and received the solemn assurance that they would call for us at dawn the next morning, 'ere the town was astir.' Not that their word went for anything, but an appeal to their honour was the only resort left to us from man's side; and then from God's side, might He not use that very appeal as the lever for the accomplish- ment of His saving purpose? At any rate, faith took hold of it thus, and the prayer that it might be so in His good pleasure turned into the hope that it would be so to His glory.

The small stone theater where we slept with the beggars.

The officer planted our feet in the small, narrow steps of the steep stairway, and one by one, with heavy hearts, we mounted to the stage. Happily for us the darkness hid from sight the horrible filth amid which we were to lie. Nothing was discernible save the dark forms of some five others, beggars and outcasts like ourselves, stretched in the attitude of sleep. One of these a woman the officer roused up, and telling her who we were, bade her watch us carefully till the morning, and on no account allow us to escape, as we were to be put to death next day. Then, throwing us three or four small breads of steamed dough, he jumped on the cart and was gone.

Yes, really gone this time our one hope of escape; and we were alone once more, publicly exposed in the very midst of our enemies. I shall never forget what I felt like as the rattle of the cart died away in the street. With the knowledge that they had twice attempted to abandon us, how could we reasonably expect to see the escort again?

The old woman in whose charge we had been left affected no small solicitude for us. She mourned our plight, deplored the fate that awaited us, and then urged us to lay ourselves down to sleep beside the rest of her gang. Finding, however, that we withdrew to the farthest corner and the deepest shadows, she came and settled herself beside us, watching us intently, and giving vent to her inner feelings in a series of sighs, mutterings and ejaculations. It was dreary work listening to a voice in the dark, with its hoarse, low monotone, "Ai-ia! ai-ia! they are all to be killed in the morning"; and the consciousness of being thus narrowly overlooked by a hag who, for aught we knew, had a stake in our destruction, as well as of the near neighbourhood of her lawless clique, was disturbing enough (to say the least) to make sleep out of the ques- tion. She was too suspiciously anxious to see us sleeping for us not to fear that there was a sinister motive in it all. How much the poor old soul took in of the Gospel message, lovingly given her by Miss Gates, it is impossible to say; but when all was still enough for her to suppose that we were asleep, it was not encouraging to see her steal away to her four male companions where they lay, softly rouse them to a sitting posture, talk low with them for a while, and then resume her moanings beside us. It was now time to let her know that we were not so oblivious to her move- ments as she had hoped; and the sound of Miss Gates' voice bidding her go and rest in her own place instead of sitting where she was, evidently took both her and her companions by surprise. To our unspeakable relief she left us to lie down and feign sleep with the rest.

How we managed to keep awake that night I really do not know; but the situation demanded it, and I can only say that Divine grace was given for it. In spite of the known and felt (if unseen) filth, in spite of vermin and distressful pose of body, in spite of cold that pierced to the bone, my eyes were so heavy that I knew not how to force them open. We had agreed to take each a short watch, waking one another by turns; but the snatch of sleep thus afforded, for all its imperativeness, was yet so troubled that after all it amounted to little more than a series of apprehen- sive starts. It was a night of terrors. I cannot describe what it was. "Lord, I am oppressed, undertake for me!" was the burden of all my waking moments. There was the continual suspicion that the beggars were only feigning sleep, and watching for an expected opportunity of falling on us; and every movement of theirs kept fear alive. Peering out into the street, there was the constant dread of seeing the forms of our enemies emerge from the darkness to hurry us away to death. And then with all the longing for the darkness to be passed, there was the terror of the morning light the gathering of the hostile crowds as we had known it yesterday in that place, and no man now to cover us from violence. The condition of nervous apprehension to which we were reduced appears in the fact that when some six or eight men came past the theatre in the small hours, Miss Gates insisted that they were crouching beneath at the foot of the stage, ready for the work of death in the morning an illusion which was only dispelled by my creeping forward to the edge to verify the assertion. We were sitting in darkness in more senses than one that night; but we thought upon Him that quickeneth the dead, and remembered that our Advocate at His right hand was One that had been tempted in all points like as we are; and the words of Micah vii. 8 became a literal experience: "When I sit in darkness, the Lord shall be a light unto me."

The break of day brought home to us the full in- dignity of our position. As my eye turned from my beggar associates in all their filth and squalor, to the forms of my wife and children beside me, and saw them where they lay, my heart bled at the sight. To any passer by we must have looked, in our rags and dirt, as one company with the rest. And yet with it all we had the sweetest solace, to which even the darling little ones were not insensible, in the knowledge that unto us it was being given in the behalf of Christ to suffer for His sake. Many times in the course of our sad journeyings some moment of peculiar darkness would be suddenly shot through with heavenly light, by a word from the Ups of our babes, uttered in all the simplicity of childlike innocence and trust. There was one such moment now. The sorrow of seeing the extent of their outward wretchedness was broken in upon by Hedley's voice.

"Father dear?"

"What is it, darling boy?"

"I think Jesus must have slept in a place like this,when He had nowhere to go to?"

"Yes, darling, I think it very likely."

"Then we ought to be glad that we are like Jesus,oughtn't we?"

Little did the dear child know what that baby message meant to me. "We ought to be glad that we are like Jesus." I could see that it was a reality to him — a power that really kept him amid all the very real suffering from complaining, and little Hope too. Yet there they were — hungry, blistered, all but naked; their bed the hard cold stone of the stage floor, their bedding filth unimaginable. Tiny as they were, there was given to those little ones that believed in Christ, not only to believe, but also to suffer in His behalf in a way that often put my own faith and patience to the blush, while it also imparted fresh courage, joy and strength in the Lord.

The beggars were astir with the dawn. For a while they sat over a fire of sticks talking together and eyeing us askance; but they did not attempt to meddle with us in any way. An early opened food shop close by supplied them with a meal and with broad daylight they decamped, as if fearful of us, and glad to get away from our neighbourhood. The old woman probably considered that, having been charged to watch us till the morning, she had fulfilled her trust, and that indeed there was no further need to watch, as escape by day was out of the question.

In accordance with the promise given by the escort we hoped against hope, and kept an anxious watch for the cart's appearing. With the experience of yesterday before our eyes, we had nothing to look forward to in Yin-ch'eng but hostility, all the more certainly that we had dared to come back and were now unprotected. I need not say that our time of quietness, when we found ourselves once more alone after the beggars' departure, was one of diligent waiting upon God for guidance and protection, and of definite committal of ourselves, our burden and our way, into His hand.

The promised time of dawn had gone by, and no cart appeared. Dawn had melted into clear daylight, and daylight itself into the brilliance of cloudless sunshine; and still no cart came. In another hour or so the town would be astir, our presence in the place would be noised abroad, and all hope of escape cut off. It now became a question of the first moment. What would be the right thing to do to stay on where we were and take the risk of waiting for the cart, or to make off across the fields while yet we had the chance of escape on foot? If ever I felt the need of a wisdom other than my own, it was in that hour of awful responsibility. Life and death were in the balance the life or death, not of myself, but of those committed to my trust; and the final decision one way or the other rested with me. The hopelessness of the escort ever turning up again, rendered almost certain by the length of time that had already elapsed since the promised hour of dawn, combined with the certainty of our being taken for death by the hostile crowd of yesterday, led me to favour the desperate idea of getting away into hiding while the opportunity was in our hand; and but for my wife's conviction that the cart had been given us too definitely to be thus presumptuously set aside, I should have taken the latter course. And yet as I looked the alternative of sitting still square in the face, it seemed sheer suicide. Look which way I would, I was borne down at every point by the overwhelming odds against us. Flight was madness, and sitting still was madness; and we, whither should we go, where every way was death? I never remember coming so near despair. But "it is good that a man should both hope and quietly wait for the Lord"; and I was being brought to an end of myself, that I might cease from myself and be shut up to God. Eventually we were all brought to one mind in the matter; and as we resolved to remain where the will of God had set us, and committed the keeping of our souls to Him, in the well-doing of patient, trustful waiting, as to a faithful Creator, a sure consciousness possessed us that, whether He made a way of escape or no, we were in His hand; and "the peace of God that passeth all understanding " garrisoned our hearts.

In due time the usual signs of awakening life ap- peared, and the ones and twos that came down the street stopped curiously at the sight of the stranger group against the back wall of the stage. For a while they were content to survey us from below; but as the numbers increased and mere curiosity lessened they pressed up on the stage and stood or squatted before us, eyeing us in an evil way, and talking together of the doom that awaited us. At last it became so offensive that we were forced to leave the stage for the street, where we found a seat on some stones a few yards from the theatre. Here we sat, with the sun beating down upon us, until we became faint under its power and the closing in again of the crowd; and we returned to the stage for breathing room rather than for shelter. We were careful to treat the people with all respect, and to give courteous replies to all inquiries, but we found it advisable to speak as little as possible. Any attempt to speak on Gospel themes was received with derision; and experience taught us that silence helped to maintain the feeling of reserve common to these crowds, and eminently helpful as a barrier of restraint.

I believe there were always some amongst them who sincerely pitied and sympathized with us. There was one notable instance now. We sat well forward on the stage to keep them from crowding up; and from amongst the sea of faces staring up at us, we noticed one old woman who really looked the pity that she felt. Miss Gates was moved to make an appeal to her as she stood near by, and pointing to the torn condition of my wife's garments entreated the loan of a needle and thread. The dear old soul readily complied, and had the satisfaction of seeing the rents sewn up and of receiving our fervent gratitude for her kindness.

This little incident, I doubt not, was very helpful in restraining any immediate expression of hostility, and of course every such delay was of consequence in view of the cherished expectation that any moment might bring the sight of the cart.

But the long minutes lengthened into hours — hours of long-drawn suffering — and still there was no sign of it. Anything seemed preferable to the suspense of hope deferred with the momently expectation of attack before us. The power of the sun drove us to the back wall of the stage, where a slender strip of shade now showed itself; and again the crowd from below pressed up in front of us with menace of rude jest and gesture. We bore it until it became insufferable as before, and then sought refuge again below on the street.

The state of exhaustion to which we were being reduced by hunger and thirst, combined with the oppressive heat of sun and stifling crowds, forced me to crave a little water from the food shop hard by the theatre. In the compassionate mercy of our God the request was not denied, and I had the joy of reappearing with a bowl of "k'ai-shui" in each hand. Not only so, but the chang-kuei-tih repeated this kindness until our thirst was satisfied. The Lord remember those cups of water given us at a time when to befriend the foreigner was to court the foreigner's doom.

Another of those gracious tokens for good which had never failed us just at the time of special need, this little incident, as may be supposed, cheered our hearts more than it refreshed our bodies. It afforded us, too, an opportunity of witness before the people that we sought their good alone; for as we lifted our hearts in thanksgiving to God before drinking, we prayed Him in their hearing to send them the rain for their fields and the living water for their souls. They were noticeably quieter after this, having nothing against us that they could lay hold of.

The situation, however, was too precarious to last long. Superstition works by fear as well as by hate, and there was enough to show us that if we were not quickly relieved by the escort we should be driven out from very fear of our presence in the place. To have to sit on and on and see the restless spirit of uneasiness gradually rising and working to a head, was to me a form of ordeal more dreaded than any other. But it was allowed of God only that we might learn what it meant to be "strengthened with all might according to His glorious power unto all patience and long suffering with joyfulness"; and that we might know that "salvation is of the Lord."

It was going on for noon now, and still there was no cart, or any sign of it the cart that had been promised at dawn! But the comfort was ours that we were in the appointed place of God's will, and, in spite of all, our hearts were in peace because we "trusted in Him." Shall I ever forget the bounding joy of the sight which at length rewarded our faith the officer with his long pipe hurrying past on foot! He paused for a moment to tell us in an off-hand way that they were soon coming to take us on; then, tossing us a morsel of steamed bread, hastened away. Here, at least, was a double mercy the known presence of the escort in the place, and the supply of our present need of food; and out of a full heart we gave thanks to Him Whose mercy endureth forever.

Questions to Consider

1. As they looked back on the events described in this chapter they were convinced "the Lord had sent His angel and delivered" them. Do you think that is really possible?

2. Glover asks the Lord to "remember those cups of water given us at a time when to befriend the foreigner was to court the foreigner's doom." Do you ask the Lord to remember those who show kindness to you?

3. "Our hearts went out to the poor degraded people, darkened as they were in their understanding, alienated from the life of God because of the ignorance that was in them ..." This view led the Glover's and Miss Gates to pray for and share the gospel with their Chinese captors. Was this a feeling of cultural superiority or the view of people who recognized the nature of spiritual warfare?

CHAPTER SEVENTEEN

Travelling to Execution

"We are accounted as sheep for the slaughter:
NAY :
We are more than conquerors,
through Him that loved us. "

Some considerable time elapsed before the officer's promise was finally redeemed. Indeed, so long did it seem that my fears began once more to work against my faith, and to suggest that after all his words were only "hsii-kia" "empty and false" a current expression in relation to the world of morals in China which unhappily is only too well understood. And yet what reason had he, if he wished to decamp, for showing himself to us again? Surely the hand of God was in it; surely the man was yet to be the instrument of His will in our deliverance.

The restraining effect of his appearance upon the people was evidently due to the fact that they took it as the guarantee of our destruction by the officials themselves. This alone, I believe, hindered them from taking matters into their own hands. If the escort had really abandoned us, there is no question that we should not have left the place alive. As it was, their talk was of nothing but our approaching death. About noon two horse soldiers with drawn swords passed out of the town by the gate close by, and we were informed that they were our executioners, with orders to await our coming and despatch us on the road. Thus our minds were directed perpetually to the thought of death rather than of deliverance, until it was borne in upon us irresistibly that, even if the escort had decided to discharge their duty and take us on to Kao-p'ing, it was (as they themselves had given out) only for eventual execution. The cherished hope that the cart had been given for life died within us, though it died hard; and its place was taken by the earnest expectation and the hope that in nothing we should be ashamed, but that with all boldness Christ might now be magnified in our body by death, since the will of God was so.

The sequel to the passing out of the horse soldiers was all in keeping with the one thought. About half an hour later the officer reappeared, and, ordering us to follow him, led us outside the gate. Two carts were awaiting us instead of one, and I was dismayed to see the kind of vehicle provided. The covered "chiao-ch'ae," which was originally sent for us, had been exchanged for the low coal trolly of those parts, with spokeless wheel and axle all of one, locally known as the "mountain tiger" from the facility with which it traverses the steep and narrow passes. The body of the cart was simply a strong wooden frame — nothing else; no side supports, no p'eng over our heads, and nothing beneath us to break the concussion. The ladies and children were ordered to seat themselves on the one, while I was to follow by myself alone on the other. What else could this mean than that we were common felons, riding to a felon's death? Amid a silence that contrasted strangely with the experience of yesterday, we passed away for the second time from Yin-ch'eng, the officer on horseback leading the way. There was no hostile demonstration. Rather a fear seemed to be upon them, or at least an awe, cast, it may be, by the shadow of our impending doom. Silently the great crowd watched us out of sight, and once more we were alone.

Separated now from the fellowship of my companions in suffering, I was left to my own reflections. The bitterness of that lonely ride who can tell? The iron of an unutterable desolation entered into my soul. Some perhaps may wonder why, after such signal manifestations of delivering and sustaining grace, it should have been so why faith did not rise superior to it. God knows. I only record the fact that it was so. Seasons of darkness do not necessarily argue the failure of faith. Often the very reverse. For faith needs to be educated, and its schooling has to be done in the valley of Baca as well as on the hill of Zion. In leading His people from faith to faith, God asks them to follow Him at times where His path is in the great waters and His footsteps are not known. And after all, was it so much to be wondered at? There was a good deal to account for it from the physical side alone, for it was a month that day since we first took the road, and what had we not endured within that time! Then, too, the hope that had buoyed us up, of deliverance by the cart, for which we had waited in the will of God, was gone; and what that meant no words can express. Moreover, with this barbarous trolly work there was the ever present consciousness of what my precious wife was enduring; its every jolt and bang, as it climbed the rugged passes, went through me in that consciousness, and the sight of her thus under the scorching blaze of the noonday sun, with no alleviations of any sort or kind, was like the tearing of a wound. I had represented to the officer before starting that, situated as she was, such a mode of conveyance was the refinement of cruelty; but the only answer vouchsafed was a callous "Muh fah-tsi" "There's no help for it"; or in other words, "She will get nothing better."

I may also add a remark which is not out of place in this connection. It so happened that the period of this distress of soul synchronized to the hour with the awful tragedy which was being enacted within the governor's yamen at T'ai-yiien Fu. Who shall say that there was no relation between the two events? For is it not a law that if one member suffer all the members suffer with it, in a far reaching sense beyond the grasp of comprehension? And is it too much to believe that we were being touched by the fringe of the same dark cloud into which so many of our beloved brethren and sisters were at that moment entering? At the boundary where the Kao-p'ing jurisdiction commenced we were halted before a small yamen, whence the officer presently emerged carrying two small pennons of Imperial yellow, each inscribed with four characters, "Ch'ang Chi Hsien ch'ai" "Offici- ally forwarded by the Ch'ang Chi district-magistrate" (the official style of the Lu-an sub-prefect). These he carefully affixed with his own hands to the mules' harness of either cart, and then gave the signal to move on. Thus certainty was made doubly sure. As I pondered the meaning of it, I could find not the faintest gleam of hope that those yellow symbols represented anything else than our death-warrant, displayed for all to read as we passed along. The sub-prefect's reference to a secret edict of the Empress Dowager's came forcibly to mind, and I could see in them only the declaration that we were Imperial prisoners, being conveyed under guard to execution. The whole demeanour of the escort, as well as the mode of conveyance, were against any other conclusion. But perhaps the strongest confirmation of it was found in a most singular incident. Just as we were about to resume the journey, a man came out of the yamen habited in a rough garb of coarse white calico, tied at the waist with a girdle of string, a cap of the same white material on his head, white shoes on his feet, and a white braid in his queue in other words, in the customary dress of a mourner attending a funeral. This man significantly attached himself to us, and joining the officer headed the cavalcade. I give the incident for what it is worth; but the kind of impression it made upon us all, under the circumstances, can be readily understood. It seemed to be designed to impress upon us that this was none other than a funeral procession, and to indicate China's mock grief at the extermination of the "iang kuei-tsi."

With such positive evidence to go upon I felt it right to prepare my dear wife and Miss Gates. To sit thus alone with the thoughts that sprang out of it was unendurable; and leaving my cart I dared to run on and speak with them. How sweet was the solace of those few moments of intercourse to me! I found them with the same conviction, but calm and in perfect peace; and together we lifted our hearts to God for grace to glorify Him in the death we were shortly to die. I was then ordered back to the lonely cart.

Some little time after, as I sat praying and reminding God of the mighty deliverances He had already vouch- safed us, and of that Name, "Wonderful, the Mighty God," which He has given to His beloved Son for us, the thought flashed upon me as a revelation that after all, might not the yellow flags be the symbol of Imperial protection, set there to proclaim the fact to all for our greater safety in a district known to be peculiarly anti-foreign? It reads like an absurd anti-climax, unreasonable to say the least, in view of the evidence against it. Nevertheless, God used the absurd and the unreasonable to bring back to my heart the hope I had lost, and to strengthen my hold of Him as the "Mighty to save." Guards notwithstanding, I leapt from the cart and ran to impart the comfort of its inspiration to my companions. The words of the promise given to my wife on the morning of the flight, "I shall not die, but live and declare the works of the Lord," revived in our hearts to the quickening of our faith; and once more He turned the shadow of death into the morning, and gave us the garment of praise for the spirit of heaviness. I learned then that God had taken away the hope of deliverance by the cart, upon which I had come to lean unduly, that my faith and hope might be in Himself alone. I needed the reminder that the walk of faith can never be by sight, that my expectation must be from Him always, only, immediately from Him. It was to be enough for me that God was with us, apart from seen possibilities of escape, and that I might safely rest the issue, whether it were life or death, with Him. Again and again He had to bring this to remembrance, in His patient forbearance with my slowness of apprehension.

As we reached the summit of the pass and began to descend on the Kao-p'ing side, the travelling became too awful for words. Our guards seemed to have lost sight of the fact that the trollies this time carried a load of animate, not inanimate, matter. Absolutely no account was taken of our humanity. Probably they would have looked more carefully by a good deal to their going, had the freight been coal or iron instead of foreign flesh and blood. If what we had endured hitherto was suffering, this was torture. The declivity became a succession of ledges, down which "the moun- tain tiger" plunged, leaping from one to the other with a recklessness all too cruelly facile. The jolt and bang of the previous record now gave way to a series of crashes, the concussion of which was alarming. So impossible was the endurance of it that even the escort relaxed so far as to allow us to make the descent on foot. In this way we were brought once more together, and under the burning sun we toiled down to the foot of the pass.

The words "in weariness and painfulness" were as applicable to our condition now as ever before. The scorching heat not only fell on us from above, but was refracted like a furnace from the rocks around. No refreshment either of food or drink was given us, and our bones ached again with the severity of the ride. What all this meant to the weaker vessels the women and the tiny children needs no effort of the imagination to conceive. Yet dear little Hope sang to us by the way, a fact which speaks for itself as to the unmurmuring spirit inculcated by her mother and Miss Gates; and one of the liveliest memories that I have of that memorable journey is the sweet voice in song of my sunny little darling borne to me in my loneliness from the trolly on before.

There came a time at length when the intent of the yellow flags was settled beyond a doubt, in the open declaration of the escort that we were under sentence of death by Imperial decree, and were being taken to Kao-p'ing for execution. Yet though the comfortable meaning of the symbol as that of protection was gone, the comfortable hope in God which it had been used to revive remained. We were allowed still to see nothing else than death: but our eyes had been taken away to the Living One at the right hand of God, and rested on Him to Whom all power in heaven and in earth has been given.

All things have an end, even a never-ending 60 li of jolt and crash and sweltering heat; and at seven o'clock we entered the city. The two horse soldiers who had preceded us from Yin-ch'eng, and who had been pointed out to us as our executioners, had not been en- countered on the road. In all probability they had been sent on to prepare the Hsien for our coming. At any rate, our arrival was not unexpected, to judge from the enormous crowd that met us and thronged us to the yamen. I feared when I saw it; for I remem- bered how, when Dr. Hewett and I entered the city two months previously, they had hooted us out, and we had to confine our preaching to the suburbs. The shame, too, of our rags and dirt and the degradation of the trolly carts would not tend to induce a kindlier feeling; while the Imperial yellow, with its official authorization of hostility would remove all restraint.

As we entered the yamen enclosure the huge crowd pressed in with us. The trolly carts were driven away, the escort went to report themselves and deliver their papers, and we were left standing alone in the thick of it. The experience was not a pleasant one. All attempts made by the runners to quiet the people and keep them back were unavailing. With hoots and yells they thronged in upon us, and forced us up the steps by the inner gate. I shall never forget darling little Hope's shrieks of terror as she clung about my neck, entreating me to take her away. What with the great heat and pressure, we were nearly suffocated. The excitement grew in intensity, and but for our timely admittance to the inner courtyard it must have gone hard with us. In the mercy of God the gate opened just at the moment of extremity, and we were pulled inside and locked into a small room containing two small k'ang. Prison though it was, it seemed the calm and rest of Paradise after the howling storm outside. The yelling and battering at the gates continued for hours afterwards till nearly midnight; and we blessed God for our hidden retreat, at the same time beseeching His mercy for the people and sufficient grace for ourselves, whatever the issue before us might be.

Once more He proved Himself better than our fears, and magnified His Name as the Lord merciful and gracious. An excellent supper was sent in to us by the Mandarin, of rice, bread and eggs; and though he did not come to interview us himself, yet he sent his son, the "Shao-ie," to reassure us with the promise that we should be sent on to the next magistracy the prefectural city of Tseh-cheo in the morning, and to give us a sum of a thousand cash for the road. We were also visited by several small officials and many of the gentry, who plied us with a running fire of questions of the usual curious sort, without betraying either sympathy or antipathy There was one remarkable exception, however. A gentleman of the yamen, looking hard at me, said :

"Surely you are one of the two pastors who were over here about two months ago preachmg in the south suburb?"

"Yes," I replied, "I am."

"The Jesus doctrine is a good doctrine, and your words were very good. It is pitiable to see the honourable pastor in a beggar's rag. Will you please exchange it for this of mine?" And he presented me with a gown of blue calico one certainly that had been well worn, but still most presentable, and to my eyes at that time a princely garment.

I need not describe the impression this unexpected act of kindness made upon us all. It was at least an indication that there might be others among them who at heart were well disposed towards us, little as they might care to show it. At any rate, the treatment we were receiving, negative and positive, did not look like execution; and the assurance given us that we should be sent on next day strengthened the belief that our life would not be taken here. Happily for us we knew nothing of the events that were transpiring elsewhere in the province, else we should have been a good deal slower in taking account of yamen professions. For as I have already indicated, this proved to be none other than the day of the massacres at T'ai-yiien Fu, the provincial capital, where at the governor's yamen, whither they had been decoyed by fair seeming promises, a devoted company of men, women and children — 44 souls in all were ruthlessly put to the sword. I may here add that, but for the delivering Hand of God, we ourselves would have been of that company. Yii-hsien had issued an order that every foreigner in Shan-si was to be sent up to T'ai- yuen for execution. Why, therefore, we were not sent north instead of south is among the secret things that belong to the Lord our God. Our escape from the province is all the more remarkable in that we were sent on under arrest, with nothing but a criminals passport, as the sequel will show. The meaning of this was, that the magistrate was under no obligation to send us on. Had we travelled under the safeguard of the full official "uen-shu," they would have been bound to pass us through without question. As it was, each magistrate was free to exercise his own discretion in one of four directions. He might either pass us on to the next magistracy, or send us back to our own city, or forward us direct to the governor's yamen at T'ai-yiien, or put us to death himself. He might also, if he chose, wipe his hands of us altogether and turn us adrift at the border where his jurisdiction ended, as in fact was done with the Lu-ch'eng party three days later, and by this very magistrate of Kao-p'ing. Thus we never knew when we left one city what awaited us at the next — and this in Ho-nan as well as Shan-si. More than once we were on the point of being sent back to Lu-an; and once certainly it was all but decided to forward us direct to Yu-hsien himself. The fact, therefore, that with such odds against us we ever crossed the Shan-si border into Ho- nan, or the Ho-nan border into Hu-peh, is itself a standing witness to the reality of God's direct interference. Of the nineteen yamen we passed through, fourteen were, to our knowledge, so far anti-foreign that it was a moot point with each one whether or no we should be passed on, while even with the remaining five the severe tension as to whether they were for or against us was never once relieved previous to arrival.

These things, however, were graciously hidden from our eyes, and only revealed as we were able to bear them. When at length, at a late hour, our inquisitive visitors withdrew, we stretched ourselves on the stone k'ang and slept a sweet, restful sleep with one pillow between us my beggar garment, which we rolled up and put under the children's heads. I need hardly say that before we lay down we gave definite thanks to the God of all grace Who had brought us through another day of extraordinary peril and hardship.

Chief among the wonders which He wrought for us I count the return of the escort. So false were the men at heart, and so evidently anxious to be rid of us, that, humanly speaking, there was nothing to account for it. Whatever the influence at work in their own minds which led them finally to take us on, the efficient cause behind it was the determinate counsel of God. That is patent on the face of it.

July 10, at break of day, we were knocked up and ordered hurriedly out. An escort of six, four of whom were soldiers in uniform armed with bludgeons, was awaiting us, and two carts to my distress the coal trollies of yesterday. I remonstrated and entreated them at least to give the ladies a litter; but the request was set aside with a hard impatience which made our hearts sink. There was no time, they said, to think about a "shan-tsi" now. If we did not wish to be attacked by the city mob we must begone. And off they hustled us without further ceremony.

Thankful as we were to be away before the city was awake, yet the behaviour of our guards was such as to create the apprehension that the very mischief from which they professed to be taking us was purposed in their own hearts. Whether they intended to bring us to Tseh-cheo at all became more and more question- able as time went on. While preserving an outward show of civility, we found that they were inwardly as false as their comrades of Lu-an.

That long, long way of 90 li (30 miles) is a terrible memory, whether I look at it from the inward or the outward point of view. The whole journey was of the same suffering nature as its predecessor crash, crash over mountain roads and boulder-strewn passes. Throughout the entire day, with the exception of one bare hour at an inn, we were exposed to the full power of a burning sun, in the same unprotected condition as heretofore. In my own case there was one mitigation over the experience of yesterday. I was allowed to have my little son with me on the trolly a comfort the more appreciable from the taste of its privation.

To break as far as possible the force of the concussion I took him on my knee, for I feared for his little spine. The violence of our modes of travel were such as to call again and again for special prayer and for definite committal of our bodies specially the delicate frames of the mother and the children into the safe keeping of our heavenly Father; and it stands amongst the miracles of those days, and the answers we received to believing prayer, that we sustained no serious injury under it.

About 9 a.m., when we had made some 30 li (10 miles), we drew near to a large market town. Before entering it the escort were at pains to warn us that the folk were notoriously anti-foreign, and that we should never get through; the effect of which was to bring us once more to the Throne of grace with the cry of the poor and needy. We had no sooner entered the gate than we were driven into an inn and taken to a back room. We were now able to join unitedly in prayer; and again we put up the definite petition, that God would be pleased, for His great Name's sake, to put His fear upon the people of this town in such a way that it might not be possible for them to lift a finger against us. Our little store of road money gave us a measure of independence, and we had the satisfaction of buying our own food for the first time, and also of investing in the luxury of a wooden comb.

Meantime a crowd was gathering at the courtyard gates, which had been closed behind us, and the yelling and battering that now ensued told its own tale. The terrible cry "Shah kuei-tsi!" ("Kill the de- vils!") was its own confirmation of the escort's warning.

We noticed, however, that the soldiers of the guard were not with us; and with their prolonged absence the painful suspicion gained ground that they themselves were at the bottom of the uproar. When at length they called us to "shang ch'ae," it was significantly to repeat the warning that there was

no chance of our getting out of the town alive; and in the prospect of immediate death we passed out on to the street.

"The floods have lifted up, Lord, the floods have lifted up
their voice; the floods lift up their waves. The Lord on High is
mightier than the noise of many waters." What was it that
paralyzed the arm and tied the tongue of the vast crowd that
lined the way ? We saw it with our eyes the people, who but
now were at the doors yelling for us to be brought out to them,
as though turned to stone at the sight of us. Hundreds of them
(I might almost say thousands), massed on either side,
watched us pass slowly along the narrow lane they left for us,
without speaking a word or lifting a finger against us. A few
lads echoed the shout that had so lately rent the air, "Shah
kuei- tsi!" but there was no response of any sort or kind a fact
which only served to point the phenomenon. Once more we
were allowed to witness the mighty power of God, and in the
fearsome awe of a murderous mob to read the literal answer to
the prayer we had offered in the inn. And our hearts were
bowed in worship before Him as we freely acknowledged, "
This is the Lord's doing, and it is marvellous in our eyes."

As the escort talked amongst themselves we learned that
the wonder of it had not escaped their notice. It had been as
we suspected, a plot of their own de- vising, upon the success
of which they had confidently counted, and its inexplicable
failure was only the more remarked upon in consequence.
From the scraps of conversation that caught our ears, we
gleaned that, whatever their orders may have been, their intention was to get rid of us en route in an indirect way that
would not involve the yamen.

With such a prospect before us the journey was pursued in the certain expectation of death, whether through treachery by the way or by direct official action at Tseh-cheo. Three hours more of it under the midday blaze and we entered a large village, where we were driven to the farther end and halted before a small shrine. The animals were taken out and led to the refreshment of the inn; the guard betook them- selves to food and rest, and we were left on the trollies in the scorching heat and to the uncertain temper of an ever growing crowd.

One might have thought that, with all we had already passed through, surely the bitterness of death was passed. And yet in this place we were to taste it once again, with no abatement of its sharpness once again to enter the swellings of Jordan and know no decrease of its surging flood. The food shop attached to the inn where the escort were lodged soon became the centre of a busy throng; and from the way in which we were being held up to scorn and contempt it was not difficult to infer that our would-be protectors were again playing us false. The inference was justi- fied by the reports that floated down to us from time to time, showing that beyond question they were busying themselves with schemes against our life. Foreign blood must be spilt by reason of the drought; but the question now seemed to be, How much? Should all be put to death, or only one? And should the victim be taken from the children or the adults?

As the topic was discussed amongst the bystanders, the covert expressions of sorrow and sympathy that fell from many of them were as touching as they were unexpected. The uncertainty was, however, laid to rest when a message was brought from the inn to the effect that it had been decided to put the ladies to death on the spot, and to take on only the children and myself to Tseh-cheo. The reason of this seems to have been that foreign women were credited with possessing an evil influence of peculiar malignity, and that to them the drought and other ills were mainly attributable. More than once in the course of our journeyings expression was given to this sentiment; and the generally cruel treatment of the two ladies, and the often brutal indifference to their sufferings, certainly seemed to bear it out.

What the agony of that message was to each one of us can be known only to God. As my beloved wife received it, the momentary spasm that shot across her face revealed the depth of the inward suffering, to be replaced immediately by the heavenly light I had seen more than once before when in the immediate presence of death. Turning to me she said, with unfaltering voice, "I do thank God that you and the children are to be spared. It is a comfort to me now to think that they will have you to care for them." But the thought of having first to witness and then to survive the murder of my wife was insupportable; and for the dear children as for myself I could not but desire of God the mercy of deliverance through death from such unspeakable anguish.

I may not dwell upon the unspoken agony of the long hour of suspense that followed the announcement. It was the very concentration of the sorrows of death. At Han-tien and elsewhere there was given at least the consolation that we were to die together; but the prospect before me now was one that, in the natural view of it, might well unsettle the reason. The talk around us was of nothing but the death of the two ladies, even the spot being indicated where the deed was to be done yonder field to the right of the shrine.

One sometimes hears it said in this so-called Christian land that "religion drives men mad." Let those say it who wish to tell it out to their shame that they have not the knowledge of God (I Cor. xv. 34). I bear witness that in the accumulated sufferings of those days of "daily dying," and above all in that most awful hour, it was religion and only religion (in the true sense of the term) that saved me from going mad. Thank God, I knew Whom I had believed; and I was not disappointed of my hope in the persuasion that He was able to keep that which I had committed unto Him. We knew, each one of us, that these sufferings were "for Jesus' sake"; and we each one proved in a definite experience that, "as the sufferings of Christ abounded unto us, so our comfort also abounded through Christ." Even as my beloved wife and I exchanged in secret once again the last farewell, the sting of death was gone in the consciousness of the love of Christ that passeth knowledge, though the anguish remained.

Notwithstanding the fact that the word had gone forth, and that everything pointed to its accomplishment, we still did not cease to make our prayer to God our Refuge and Strength, that He would even now show Himself strong in our behalf and save us from the very jaws of death for His own glory. As the escort emerged at last from the inn, followed by the mules, we knew that the critical moment had come.

The animals were put in and the order to "go on" was given. Amid a silence strangely like the hush that had prevailed when we left our morning inn, the trollies moved forward. An awe that rooted them to the spot where they stood settled upon the crowd; and instead of being driven to yonder field at the right of the shrine, we passed on through the gate to the Tseh-cheo road. At the last moment the decision had been reversed whether through the irresolution of the village elders, or from whatever cause, matters not. The simple fact remains, "to the memorial of Thy great goodness," that "I sought the Lord and He heard me, and delivered me from all my fears." I needed to fall back upon no second causes for what was so evidently supernatural. Indeed, Elisha's experience in Dothan was not more real than ours in that nameless Chinese village. For just as then, "the mountain was full of horses and chariots of fire round about Elisha," so also were we given to know now that "the Angel of the Lord had encamped round about us who feared Him and had delivered us."

That it was in no sense due to any change in the escort's disposition towards us was evident, not only from their conversation, but also from the fact that they made one more determined effort to get rid of us before the journey's end. They sent on two of their number to warn the people, at the last place of any size that we should pass, of our approach, and to incite them to fall on us at a given signal, which signal was to be the raising of the bludgeon at the "present." My heart quailed at the scene before us as we approached. A mob of several thousands had assembled to meet us, and it seemed incredible that we could run the gauntlet of the long street unscathed. Never shall I forget the feeling of momentary terror when, as we entered the gate, I saw the soldiers suddenly bring their bludgeons to the "present." What happened? The sense of terror gave place to that of perfect peace as the word came almost audibly to me, "Fear not; for no man shall set on thee to hurt thee"; and then of awe and wonder as I saw the tumultuous crowd fall back on either side, and like the waters of old "stand upon an heap." The same mysterious hush we had known before was upon them as we slowly traversed the narrow path between; and to the unconcealed amazement of the disgusted soldiery, not a soul broke bounds, or gave heed to the summons to fall on us.

This was the last attempt the escort made to hurt us; and marvelling in themselves at the things their eyes had seen, they brought us in due course to Tseh-cheo. Faint and weary indeed we were at the end of that terrible and wonderful journey; but hunger, thirst, and aching limbs were forgotten in the realization of its threefold deliverance. Jordan had been driven back before our eyes; and driven back, we knew well, "at the Presence of the Lord."

Questions to Consider

1. When they realized they were going to die, they asked God to glorify Himself in their death. Do you ask God to glorify Himself in your life?

2. One of the "liveliest memories" Glover had was the sound of his young daughter singing as they were being taken to their execution. Have you seen people praise the Lord during difficult times? When? Have you done it? When?

CHAPTER EIGHTEEN

Left to the Mob

"The very hairs of your head are all numbered.
Fear ye not therefore."

The traditions of the city of Tseh-cheo Fu were, as regards its attitude towards foreigners, the reverse of reassuring. The Roman Catholics had, it is true, succeeded in settling within its walls, but only by dint of a characteristic policy of pressure and threat. They were not wanted; and on occasion they were made to know it. Protestant missionaries, acting on the inspired principle that the weapons of a spiritual warfare may never be carnal, had visited the city with the Gospel message, but as yet had received no encouragement to stay. Indeed, more than once they had been denied the right even of sojourn, and had been driven from their inn and expelled the city. The atmosphere was charged with hatred of the foreigner; and the prospect, therefore, of entering it, even under the most favourable circumstances, would call for a special act of faith and prayer. How much more in circumstances where the Imperial Government had declared against us, and where our condemnation was written in the manner of our advent! Whatever else the trollies carried, they carried at least a load of prayer.

As we neared the city, a mounted courier dashed past at a tearing gallop and disappeared within the gate. What his errand was I know not, but it looked as if it had to do with us. Anyhow, it was one of those incidents which, trivial perhaps in themselves, yet go to make up the sum total of experience, whether of joy or sorrow, and instinctively it connected itself in my mind with a presentiment of coming ill. Its special use was that it led me to watch and pray the more carefully against surprise in the temptation before us.

The sun was nearing the western horizon when we arrived at the great gate. The ponderous arch that gloomed over us seemed like another portal of the Valley of the Shadow of Death, and its shade struck chill to the soul. No one can realize what it meant to face the thought of entering a hostile Chinese city. Villages and towns were trial enough, but the mere sight of the brown battlemented walls towering high before one, in the knowledge of what lay behind them, had for me a dread of its own which never grew less. And never was the Lord's "Fear not" more comfortable than at such times, as it certainly was never more needed.

We had made but a few paces within the gate when our progress was arrested by a party of yamen officials at the head of a waiting crowd, amongst whom we recognized the evil face of the foremost of our Han-tien accusers. In the most violent and offensive way they seized the animals' heads, and forcing them round ordered us to leave the city. For several moments our fate hung in the balance, as they abusively refused to hear of our admittance; and we had before us the alternative of being either taken back to Kao-p'ing or turned adrift to tramp the roads. Meantime, the officer in charge had produced the papers which he was deputed to carry to the sub-prefect; and the presentment of these changed the situation. The officials quickly ran them over, conferred for a while together, and then gave the order to take us to the yamen.

If ever we needed to realize the encompassing of the invisible host of Grod, it was in the streets of Tseh-cheo Fu. The trollies were followed by an ever increasing and tumultuous mob of men only, the dimensions of which, by the time we reached the yamen gates, were alarming enough. As we drove into the enclosure they thronged in after us; and when a moment later we were dismounted and the carts driven off, we found ourselves, as at Kao-p'ing, alone and unprotected in their midst. Even the semblance of help, in the shape of runners to keep back the crowd, was dispensed with here, and we were practically left a prey in their hands. There was nothing for it but to stand where we were, amid the scorn and buffetings of the wild mob about us, and quietly wait to see what would be done with us.

We had not to wait long. In evident fear of a riot within the precincts of the yamen the Hsien hastily ordered the underlings to clear us off the place. With the Kao-p'ing experience before me I believed that they had come to take us to quarters in the inner courtyard; but when they began to hustle us towards the outer gate the terrible truth revealed itself that it was intended to abandon us to the mercy of the people on the street. The crying injustice of it, let alone the cruel prospect before us, was more than I could stand; and, refusing to go, I demanded the right of a personal interview with the Mandarin. My request was answered with derisive laughter, and my refusal to move by forcible ejection. Amid hoots and yells we were driven to the street and told to await there his Excellency's pleasure. It was virtually an attempt over again to get rid of us in the irresponsible way of mob violence.

The long interval that followed was, I need scarcely say, a distressing one. In the fear of being swept out on to the open street, and hopelessly away, we kept hard by the yamen gate, where we were pressed up into a comer face to face with the thronging, struggling, yelling crowds. We had aU our work cut out to soothe the children and to shield them from the crush; for it was a "tight comer" in a very literal sense. As I think of it now, I marvel at the way God kept the mob back; for many times as the great human wave surged up, it threatened to crush the breath out of us. At length the deputies appeared with the Mandarin's instructions. We were to be lodged for the night in an inn on the street to which they would conduct us, and be sent off the next morning to Huai-k'ing Fu. Spend the night at an outside inn? What was this but simply giving us straight into the hands of the mob for death? And again I remonstrated, pleading with the officials to take us into the yamen and allow me to see the Kuan. Their answer was that if we had anything to say we must put it in writing; for it was the only way in which we might hope to approach him. This was tantamount to saying that his Excellency would have nothing to do with us; for they knew perfectly well that we had no means of getting a letter written, and that, even if we had, it would never be delivered. Whereupon we were driven on to the street, and ordered to follow them, with the great crowd at our heels.

The inn to which we were taken was in the principal thoroughfare, where we should naturally be exposed to peculiar danger. Behind the open food shop, through a narrow passage, was a tiny courtyard where a small room was allotted us, into which, having settled us, the officials withdrew, leaving a single rabscaliion to represent the yamen.

For some hours yet we were to be "made a spectacle unto men." Until long after dark the narrow passage discharged its confused stream in never ceasing flow into the tiny square, whose only other outlet was our room. In order to spare my dear wife and the children as far as possible. Miss Gates and I sought to stay them at the threshold by giving them their full opportunity of seeing and questioning us outside. For a while it answered; then the pressure forced us in; every inch of the ground was occupied, the k'ang itself was besieged, and there we sat immured between walls more cruel than of stone. I have a lively recollection of the suffering of those hours; for apart from the vicious attitude of those who were watching us, the heat and stench were overpowering. The cravings of hunger and thirst were intense; and head and limbs and every bone ached again with the hardships we had already endured.

Once more in our extremity we hid in God. As the men stood about us and over us on the k'ang, threatening every moment to drive us out on to the street, our hearts were kept in peace, so that we feared not. The restraint that held them in check was from Him alone; for no human power was for us in that hour. Nay, "the powers that be" were avowedly against us, and the people knew it. Every opportunity for the gratification of their anti-foreign hatred was now theirs. And yet they touched not a hair of our heads.

Not until the hour for closing the inn did the crowds withdraw. Many hundreds, running probably into thousands, had swarmed about us since our arrival; and a reaction after hours of bullying cross-examination and imminent attack was hardly to be wondered at. The quiet in which we were left at last seemed almost unintelligible after the continuous uproar of the hustling mob. Could it be possible that all that was left of them was the half-naked underling, where he lay across the courtyard yonder, placidly fusing the opium pill over the lamp flame?

When all was quiet and the shop door barred, I made my way to the chang-kuei-tih and ordered food. The several attempts I had made before had been in vain; and even now the request was treated with casual contempt. He refused to cook for us, and we had to make shift with the dregs of the copper in which the evening millet had been boiled. Thankful at least for so much, we praised our God and committed ourselves into His Hand for the hours of darkness.

My determination was to keep the night watch. But alas for resolutions, even under circumstances of such grave peril! I remember an evil-looking band of men being let into the room, and the close examination they made of us as we lay. After that I remembered nothing. I confess with shame, for the sad selfishness of it, that I slept solidly until daybreak. When I awoke my wife said to me, "Oh, what an awful night it has been!" "How do you mean, darling?" I said. "Haven't you slept? What is it that has troubled you?" " Thank God you slept through it! Miss Gates and I would not wake you unless we saw absolute need for doing so; but it seemed as if hell were being let loose against us. For hours they have been yelling in the streets and battering at the doors to have us brought out and put to death. Is it possible you have heard nothing of the pandemonium?" With amazement and confusion of face I had to confess that it had been possible; for my sleep had been the sleep of absolute oblivion. I was grieved beyond measure to think that I could have taken my rest while they were watching and praying and suffering alone. But the act was involuntary; and it may be God saw that it was a necessity, for indeed I knew not how to go on. The only consolation I have in the memory of it now is that it served to bring out into beautiful evidence the characteristic unselfishness and devotion of those with me. Here, at any rate, was one occasion and I fear it was not a wholly isolated one when the weaker vessel shamed the stronger, and proved its own superiority in the power of endurance and the strength of self-denying love.

It was not until afterwards that we learned how gravely critical the situation had been, and how marvellous, past understanding, the deliverance God wrought for us. At midnight the whole city was in riot. With horrible cries and yells they rushed to the Roman Catholic quarters first and fired the premises, the priests barely escaping with their lives.

Then they came on to our inn, and for what seemed an interminable time, amid the clash of gongs howled for us to be brought out to them. How they came to disperse without having their wish gratified we could never learn. I only know that when I awoke it was as quiet as when I lay down. And together we gave God the glory for another signal interposition for our salvation. The fact is all the more remarkable when it is considered that not two days later our sister, Miss Rice, of the Lu-ch'eng party, was brutally done to death not far from the walls of this very city.

It was full early, perhaps about seven o'clock, when a petty official from the yamen entered with the underling and some half-dozen soldiers and ordered us out. We were to be sent on to Huai-k'ing Fu, and to start immediately, to prevent further rioting. I inquired what sort of conveyance had been provided for us. "The Lao-ie has been pleased to give you three donkeys"; and the tone of loud contempt in which the reply was flung back implied that we were to credit his Excellency with extraordinary magnanimity in making provision at all for such carrion as we. My dismay may be imagined when I saw that the saddles provided for a 30 mile ride were the bare "kia-tsi," or wooden frames with which pack animals are saddled for the carriage of goods! It was preposter- ous; and I said with considerable warmth, "You ought to be ashamed of yourselves for imagining that two delicate women and infants like these could endure such a mode of travel. We don't budge from this inn till you have brought us two mule litters." I need not describe the lively demonstration that followed. The calm resolve and the strength to hold to it was doubtless Divinely given; but I am bound to say that I was as amazed, as I was thankful, to find that, instead of falling on us there and then, as they threatened to do, they took two of the donkeys back and returned in half an hour with a single mule litter (or an apology for one) for the women and children. It consisted of nothing but the bare poles, with wide meshed rope work lashed to them, and for a seat a fragment of an old straw mat, dirty and frayed, to cover the meshes. P'eng (for privacy and protection from the sun) there was none. Its occupants were to be carried as so much cargo.

I saw that it was not expedient to make any further demur; and accepting the inevitable with as good a grace as we might, even to the extent of a "thank you!" for the exchange, we prepared to go. It was pitiful to see the crushed, constrained position of the four who were for the litter. My wife and Miss Gates faced each other, with their backs against the transverse poles, and between them, in a space which could ill accommodate their legs, the two children were somehow jammed in. Then they were hoisted to the mules' backs. I got astride the saddle-rack provided for my torture, the escort surrounded us, and we were hurried off. An immense concourse had gathered at our heels as we passed along the main thoroughfare to the south gate. The momently expectation of an outbreak drew the eyes away to God, and we were strengthened to endure as "seeing Him Who is invisible." After the night's riot it was a marvel that we got out at all; still more so, that it should be accomplished without molestation. A general impression, however, seems to have pre- vailed that we were being taken to the "ing-p'an," or military camp, for execution; and that sufficed them.

Another burning day was before us. Even now, as we passed out through the suburb we were only too sensible of the heat; and the prospect of a repetition of the past three days' experience was full of dread. In the mercy of God we had now a sufficiency from which to meet the urgent need. The one difficulty was that, as foreigners and doomed prisoners withal, we were not allowed to buy for ourselves. So there was nothing for it but to part with the bulk of our small horde to the underling for the purchase of the requisite hats and fans. The rascal returned in course of time with five tiny rush fans of the commonest make, and the ready lie that "no hats were to be found — all sold out!" He chuckled as he slung the cash bag over his shoulder, the heavier by several hundreds of our cash; for what was the weight to the windfall? The lie that weighs the pocket down lies light in any clime. And now we were nearing the dreaded "ing-p'an." The news travelled on that we were coming, and the military element was soon in evidence. Uniforms mingled largely with the crowd; and as we skirted the mud-wall enclosure scores of soldiers were seen hurrying to the gate. Meantime the escorts' in-flammatory talk and gestures as they parleyed with them seemed to indicate that we were in very deed arrived at the execution ground. Again and again we caught the sound of a rhythm which was to be dinned into our ears all that day, like the burden of a refrain, to this effect:

See the rain does not come —

The sky is as brass;
Foreign blood must he spilt.
Or the season will pass.

They were terrible moments; for an appeal to the soldiery at such a time would be considered certain death. But we passed on covered by the Hand of God, and were hurt by nothing more than shouted curse and scorn. It was evident, then, that no formal orders had been issued to the Commandant for our execution; and at length the crowds dwindled away, the roar of the city streets grew faint, and we were pursuing our way amid the comparative quiet of country roads.

Comparative. For when travelling by day we could never count upon being wholly free from the anxiety of a Chinese crowd, even in secluded spots. Often and often I have wondered where in the world the men sprang from. They seemed to rise from the dust as if by magic, where but a moment or two before one was alone. Now, however, we were taking the high road; so that, with the busy border traffic of two provinces, it was scarcely to be wondered at. And so it came to pass that all the long morning through our ears were regaled with the same refrain, as the escort answered the queries of the many passers by: "Where are you from?" "The Fu" (that is, Tseh- cheo). "Who have you got there?" " Foreign devils." "Where are you taking them?" "To death;" and then the terrible refrain again.

The wrath of the gods
For vengeance doth call;

Foreign blood must be spilt
Ere the rain can fall.

Soon after passing the "ing-p'an" the escort was joined by a mounted trooper armed with sword and pistols, who took over the command. His stern silence and brutal manner boded ill. At any rate, it was all in keeping with the dominant note of the dirge-like refrain.

As the day advanced and the power of the sun increased, we suffered greatly. The endeavour to screen our heads as far as might be with the tiny rush fans was in vain. They were, of course, wholly in- adequate; and then, too, they were needed in the fainting heat to put a little air in circulation, and to keep off the flies that swarmed about us. I have a lively recollection of that pitiful journey. Of the sad, sad picture of the ladies in the litter with the children in between, jammed into the cordage with no power to alleviate the constraint of their position. Of my precious wife's face marked deep with the sorrows of the way we had already come, and now drawn with the pains of dysentery, which had just taken hold of her. Of the dear little ones sobbing uncontrollably with the smart of raw blisters, their arms an open sore from shoulder to elbow under the burning blaze. Even the underling was so far moved that he loaned his own broad-brimmed straw hat to my wife, and allowed me without remonstrance to pluck leafy twigs from trees by the way with which to cover the children's blistering legs.

As the morning wore on towards noon, and the cravings of hunger and thirst asserted themselves, we longed for the midday halt, and in all innocence asked when we were to "ta-chien." The answer made one's blood run cold. "Ai-ia! 'Ta-chien' indeed! There will be no need for such as you to *ta-chien'" a significant way of reminding us that we should be dead ere the day was out.

Thus in sorrowful silence we journeyed on over the rugged mountain road. At length we were halted in the narrow side street of a small village, before a crazy looking hovel, and the mules taken out. A poor miserable looking woman, the occupant of the hovel, was told to look after us; and, thankful for any shelter from the awful blaze, we followed her inside. Her pitiable poverty revealed itself, not only in the condition of the house, but more than all in the pinched and sorrowful face. The circumstance of suffering common to us all seemed to draw her to us, and later on, when an opportunity presented itself of talking quietly with the ladies out of earshot of the guards, she expressed a very touching sympathy with us in the knowledge of our impending execution, and then poured out the heartrending tale of her distress and that of her neighbours under the rigours of the long drought. It was a God-given opportunity for the Gospel message; and the dear woman's heart seemed ripe to receive it. All the hunger and thirst were forgotten in the deep joy of ministering the bread of life and the water of life to that needy soul, and the sorrows of death itself were swallowed up in the sweet consolation of pointing a weary and heavy laden one to the Saviour of Whom she had never yet heard. I remember still the radiance of the sisters' faces, as they returned to me at the hovel and made me partaker of their joy.

Meantime many were coming and going; and to every inquiry one and the same answer was given by the guards, "We are taking the devils to execution." On resuming the journey they maintained as before a morose silence, and if anything a sterner and more forbidding manner. The muleteer in charge of the litter was hard and cruel to a degree in his treatment of the women and children; and any appeal to him to mitigate their sufferings was met with a storm of cursing and abuse that brought us well within the zone of death. For myself I had been walking almost continuously since we left the Fu; for the pack-saddle so galled me that I found it impossible to ride it for more than a few minutes at a time, and at last was compelled to abandon it altogether. At length there came a time when the trooper dismounted to ease his limbs, and, worn with the long toil over the burning, rocky road, the heat of which sorely drew my shoeless feet, faint under the scorching sun, and spent with hunger and thirst, I looked longingly at the well-padded, comfortable saddle beside me, and was con- strained to beg him to let me occupy it until he was ready to remount. The request was treated with contemptuous silence; but the look he gave me was its own warning that if I dared to repeat it he would not give me a second chance. I have often wondered since that we came out from under the hands of such an escort alive; especially in view of the fact that not a few of our martyred brethren and sisters of Shan-si fell under precisely similar circumstances by the sword of their official guard.

Questions to Consider

1. Did God let the Glover's suffer just so the woman who sheltered them could hear the gospel?

2. Do you think God would let you suffer if it led someone else to come to Christ?

CHAPTER NINETEEN

The Death-Plot
of Lan-Chen Cheo

*"Why should it be thought a thin^ incredible
with you that God should raise the dead?"*

"God is able to raise up even from the dead."

And now we were drawing near the confines. But a little more, and we should be over the border and out of Shan-si, a thought that made the heart beat faster with a glad impatience; for, so far as we knew, the Boxer movement had not spread to Ho-nan, and every step southward increased the hope of final deliverance. I well remember the unutterable longing that possessed me to be clear of the province whose very name was now a synonym for terror.

We had not taken the road more than a couple of hours, and the sun was still hot, when we arrived at a large town on the frontier called Lan-chen Cheo, high in the hills. What was my surprise and concern to find that, instead of pressing on towards our destination (Huai-k'ing Fu), we were halted, the litter set down in the street, and its occupants turned out. From the house immediately opposite, which proved to be the "li-kin yamen" (or customs barrier), two men came out and officiously examined the papers which were handed over by the Tseh-cheo underling.

"Ai-ia! What's this? They are irregular," we heard them say, as they took them inside for more careful scrutiny; "*there is no 'uen-sMi.'*"

The purport of the discussion that ensued upon this discovery could to some extent be gauged by the voices, looks and gestures of the men within the open door. It meant detention, to say the least; and to me, with the prospect of being over the border and out of Shan-si so near realization, the thought of delay was intolerable. I was hardly prepared, however, for the actual issue. We were ordered into the room and on to the k'ang, whence, to our dismay, we saw the escort, whose duty it was to safeguard us to Huai-k'ing Fu, calmly lead out our animals, and take the road back to Tseh-cheo!

Never shall I forget the despair of that dark hour. Abandoned! — and still in Shan-si! Should we even now get out alive? Nay, how could we, with our only source of escape cut off, our papers worthless, our escort gone? Not only so, but the manner of the men who held us quickly confirmed our suspicions that we were their prisoners. Five men mounted guard over us, and all our movements were narrowly watched.

Meantime, our arrival had created the usual stir, and the inevitable crowds were soon coming about the door. To allay the excitement — with perhaps a more sinister motive behind it — our guards ordered us outside; and for some considerable time we sat on the doorstep, not knowing what the next moment might bring forth. Under pretext of putting the children to bed, my dear wife was at length enabled to withdraw, while Miss Gates and I remained to keep the mob at bay. When darkness fell, we were called inside and locked in, with a roomful of men about us.

From the noise without it was evident that the excitement was growing in intensity. The sound of blows soon mingled with the indescribable hubbub, followed by the shrieks and cries of women. These were quickly succeeded by a simultaneous yell, "Shah iang kuei-tsi! Shah, shah!" and battering at the door. The situation was now so critical that a council was held in the room as to what should be done with us. Strengthened by the irregularity of our papers, the verdict went against us by a large majority; and on the popular plea that "no rain could fall till foreign blood had been spilt," they separated with the decision that we were to die there.

Nothing could exceed the desperateness of the situation. All semblance of official protection removed; all means of escape taken away ; the people howling for our blood on the street, and the sentence of death already gone forth from those with whom the shadowy burden of official responsibility was now supposed to rest! I can only describe our affliction which befell us in Lan-chen Cheo, on the Ho-nan border of Shan-si, in the words of St. Paul: "We were weighed down exceedingly beyond our power, insomuch that we despaired even of life: yea, we ourselves had the answer of death within ourselves." Look which way we would, nothing, nothing but death confronted us. All room for trust in ourselves, or in any human soul, was cut clean away from under us: nothing, absolutely nothing, was left us but the cry, "Save me, God, for the waters are come in unto my soul; I am come into deep waters where the floods overflow me." Already delivered unto death, we were as good as dead. Our deliverance, if it came at all, could only come from one source — "God, *which raiseth the dead.*"

It was an intensely hot midsummer night. The room, in size about twenty feet by twelve, was very low and very filthy. Ventilation there was none (unless an occasional puncture, finger-made, in the papered squares of the tiny window-frame could be dignified by the name); for the door, the only real avenue by which air could reach us, was now fast barred and locked. The fire, which had been in use all day for cooking, was kept in all night; and ten persons withal in the room! Moreover, the atmosphere reeked with the sickly fumes of opium and tobacco, blown from the pipes of the five gaolers, whose forms were revealed by the opium lamp, lying stark naked around us. To add to these miseries, the k'ang was infested with vermin, whose depredations were reinforced by the attacks of mosquitoes.

Our lying down was not to sleep, but to watch and pray. At any moment the death summons might come; and we must be prepared. Now and again during the night the guards would exchange a few words; but beyond this, and an occasional looking over at us to make sure that all was right, nothing took place. The long weary hours were spent in the light of God's countenance; and in the multitude of our thoughts within us. Thy comforts refreshed our souls.

At daybreak the crowds began to reassemble. The decision of the council that we were to die had doubtless exercised a quieting effect upon them the previous night, and induced them to withdraw until the morning. Now, however, they would demand the carrying out of the sentence to the letter; and ere the sun was up, the terrible cry rang out upon the air once more, "Shah! Shah! Shah!" We knew well that the crisis had come, and that nothing but the direct and immediate intervention of God Himself could deliver us out of their hands.

At this moment the promise was borne in powerfully upon my heart, "Call upon Me in the day of trouble; I will deliver thee, and thou shalt glorify Me." My faith was strengthened to take hold of it, and to plead it with God as a promise, to which He had pledged His Name, for *the present hour* of our trouble. Our part was to "call upon Him"; and realizing as we did that the assigned cause of their rage against us was the long continued drought, we were moved, under the impulse of the promise, to make a united cry to God to interfere for His great Name's sake on our behalf, by sending rain enough to satisfy the need of these poor sufferers, and because of our extremity to send it now. Accordingly, kneeling up upon the k'ang, we poured out our hearts before Him in Chinese, that the gaolers might know exactly what we were doing, and what we were asking.

Fools! to suppose that out of a cloudless sky, as brazen as ever before, with every prospect of another day of devouring heat, rain could fall, and fall at once! Had not the guards already caught up the cry without and warned us that our hour was come that there was not the faintest indication of rain, nor would there be until our blood had been shed? The contemptuous incredulity with which they listened showed what was in their heart.

How long we continued in prayer, I cannot tell. I only know that scarcely had we risen from our knees, when the windows of heaven were opened, and down upon the howling mob swept the sudden fury of a torrential flood of waters. In a few seconds the street was empty, and not a sound was to be heard but the swish of the rushing rain.

Oh, I can tell you, dear reader, the words "God is a *very present* help in trouble" became a living, great reality to us in that moment of doom. In so marvellous a manifestation of His love, we found a true manifestation of Himself. His "very presence" could not have been more real to us in the prison-room if we had seen Him with our eyes. The throb of the heavy plash, plash of the waters without was the echo in our ears of His own Voice a music of God's own setting to the new song which He now put in our mouth. From that vile den went up the song of Moses and the song of the Lamb, "Great and marvellous are Thy works, Lord God Almighty: just and true are thy ways. Thou King of saints." The prayer of the poor destitute was once more turned into praise, and the prison of our sighs into the temple of His song, who alone giveth songs in the night, even thanksgiving to our God.

The effect upon our gaolers appeared in more ways than one. Something akin to awe took the place of their hard incredulity; and though they still affected a rough indifference towards us, they relaxed a good deal from the cruel severity of the previous day. Then we had had the greatest possible difficulty in getting them to give us food at all, even at their own price; now we were supplied with a fair liberality, though never to the point of satisfaction. The door, too, was thrown open, and we were allowed to stand at the threshold and drink in the sweetness of the outer air.

One little incident will suffice to show how really impressed they had been, and how literally they had connected the double circumstance of the prayer and the rain as cause and effect. I was standing in the door- way with the two little ones, watching the swift rush of water as it hurried by at our feet down the long incline of the narrow street a veritable river where, but a few hours before, it had been the hard dry road beneath some inches of powdery dust. As we watched, we sang, giving glory to God in the words of some of their own childish hymns. One chorus especially they delighted to sing in Chinese :

Tsan-mei, tsan-mei Chu Je-su,
T'i shi ren shae ming tih,
Ts'ong si li fuh huo tih,
Tsan-mei Je-su ngen Chu.(1)

As we sang, the talk within subsided. Our keepers were listening intently over their pipe?, and presently one was heard saying to the rest:

"They are praying to their God 'Je-su' to send the rain faster; and just look! it actually is coming down faster."

Faster? Yes. It fell in solid sheets, as though some mighty reservoir had suddenly burst overhead and dropped its contents in bulk. Never in my life have I seen such rain. All that day, and far into the following night it poured, poured, poured with a greater or less degree of intensity, and never ceased. Blessed be God!

Two gracious results followed closely upon this miraculous visitation. The first was that every mouth was stopped against us. The pretext that had been given for putting us to death was thereby taken away; and the superstitious notion that our presence and prayers were enough in any locality to keep off the rain was unanswerably refuted. Notwithstanding, the gaolers took care to drill it into us that there was no hope for our lives unless the fall was in sufficient quantity to soak the thirsty soil through and through; and when, at certain intervals, we inquired: "Surely it is 'hsia t'eo loh' now?" the suggestion was first derided, then evaded where derision was no longer possible, until the fact was too obvious even for evasion; and the resolve to put us to death was revealed as a thing determined in any case, quite apart from the professed reason.

The second effect was to secure to us a day of quietness and comparative privacy. No words can express what this meant. True, the shadow of death was not removed; but the substance of the shadow (as I may well call it) the fiendish, yelling mob, athirst for our blood we were delivered from the consciousness of that, thank God! compared with which the other was as nothing.

The grateful monotony of an undisturbed morning was broken in upon at last by the arrival of a courier from the Tseh-cheo yamen. Greeting him in the usual native way, we asked him what the business might be that brought him there. I need hardly say that our impertinent politeness was treated with the disdain it deserved. From the way, however, in which he made his short communication to the gaolers, it was not difficult to infer the gist of it. The colloquy ended, he left as hurriedly as he came.

It was drawing towards dusk when two men arrived, whose bearing, in spite of their bedraggled garments and generally woebegone appearance, bespoke them gentlemen of the yamen, and officials. They were evidently expected, and were soon deeply engaged in conversation with the officer in charge. Meantime, two soldiers of their retinue, each bearing a stack of three guns, took up a station under cover on the opposite side of the street.

If any hope of ultimate escape from Shan-si had been fanned back into life by the timely interposition of the rain, it was absolutely quenched now. The three officers freely and openly discussed our death, and the mode of it.

"We can no longer make the plea of 'no rain' the incriminating charge against them. But what of that? Enough for us that they are ignorant foreign devils, who know nothing of Chinese and are the curse of China. Why should they be allowed to live? Nay, look at their papers. The instructions passed on to us from Kao-p'ing are that 'they be taken out of Shan-si, never to return!' What is the meaning of this 'never to return' but that they are to be put to death? Ai-ia! we will take good care that they are both 'taken out of Shan-si' and that they 'never return.' See, we have guns with us; and to-morrow morning we will have them away yonder and shot outside the gate."

When matters had come to such a pass as this, it was clear that nothing would be gained by silence. So I said to Miss Gates, who had interpreted to me the substance of their talk:

"If they suppose that they can put us to death with impunity simply on hearsay charges, it is time we disabused them of the idea. They think we are ignorant foreigners who know nothing of Chinese: let them know we understand more than they bargain for."

With admirable courage she left the k'ang, and, facing the chief official with calm dignity, said quietly and courteously:

"Your Excellency is talking of putting us to death, and upon no certain charge. You ought to know that this is contrary to the law and custom of your honourable country. You ought also to know that, as foreigners coming from Great

England, you are bound to protect us. If we have done anything wrong against the law of the land, your duty is to bring us before the proper authorities for trial; and if it can there be shown that we have committed crimes worthy of death, we refuse not to die. But our guilt must first be lawfully established before a regular tribunal, or a terrible retribution will befall both yourself and your country."

The effect of these fearless words was extraordinary. Coming as they did from the "ignorant foreigners" in terms that turned the tables on themselves, they reduced the two officials from an attitude of contemptuous indifference to one of obsequious politeness. The "li" (or right of the matter) was so obviously on our side that, to save their face, they were driven to deny that they were intending any harm towards us at all. Bowing low to Miss Gates, to cover their con- fusion, they added:

"We assure you, you have nothing whatever to fear from us;" and went out into darkness and driving rain.

Thankful as we were to be rid of their presence, we yet knew that their assurances were pure "hsii-kia" "hollow and false" as their own hearts. It was not for a moment to be expected that they would go back upon their intention after such an open avowal of it, especially as they had gone the length of bringing the very weapons of death with them into the place. So we could only look upon their words as a blind, and set ourselves to face the certain issue death; death by bullet, on the morrow at latest.

We retired to the seclusion of the k*ang to face it, as so often before, in the presence of God. With the same calmness and composure as though in her own home, and with the same careful thoroughness, my precious wife prepared the dear children for bed. Then laying them down, we sang with them, as always after prayer, their evening hymn

"Sun of my soul. Thou Saviour dear!
It is not night, if Thou be near.
Oh, may no earthborn cloud arise
To hide Thee from Thy servant's eyes.
*****

"Be near to bless us when we wake,
Ere through the world our way we take;
Till, in the ocean of Thy love,
We lose ourselves in heaven above."

It was specially moving to hear their little voices in the words:

Be near to bless us when we wake,

and to know, as they did not, what the waking would be to. One thing, however, they knew as well as we, that whether it were to life or death. He would, as we had prayed, "be near to bless us." And in that sweet confidence, notwithstanding the pain of their open sores, they fell asleep.

When darkness set in, the door was barred and locked as before. The night air, charged with moisture, was heavy with a steamy heat; and shut in as we were under precisely the same foul conditions as had prevailed the night before, the atmosphere of the room quickly became insufferable. Somehow one seemed to feel it more on this second occasion than on the first. What with the nauseating fumes of opium, the stench of tobaoco, the "ch'i" (or gaseous exhalations) emitted from the "mei" with which the fire in the brick stove had been made up for the night, and ten pairs of lungs at work upon the few cubic feet of oxygen originally available the reader can imagine the condition to which we were reduced. All this, however, was as nothing compared with the outrage upon the feelings inflicted by the shameless indecency of the men around us.

In the midst of all these discomforts we set ourselves to watch and pray as aforetime. "Offer to Me the sacrifice of thanksgiving. . . and call upon Me." As we reviewed the marvellous lovingkindness of that wonderful day, our hearts were drawn out in extolling the God of our salvation and giving glory to the Lamb, the Overcomer, in the midst of the Throne. Sweet indeed were the moments, rich in blessing, which before the Cross we spent that night, on the eve of execution. Their fragrance has not departed yet: it is as fresh to me now in the memory of them, as it was then. A wonderful peace was borne in upon our hearts; and more than that a sense of triumph in our God, "Who is able to do exceeding abundantly above all we ask or think," so full and assuring, that again our trembling faith was quickened to lay hold of Him as "able to raise up, even from the dead," and to " deliver out of the mouth of the lion." Accordingly we agreed again to pray before our gaolers, in their own tongue, for the direct intervention of God for our deliverance from the death immediately before us; and kneeling up once more on the k'ang, we called upon Him in Chinese as "the Mighty to save." The definite terms of our petition were that for the glory of His great Name He would not permit the officials from Tseh-cheo, or our captors in the room, to touch a hair of our head, and that no power might be given them against us. To this we added earnest petitions for these our enemies, persecutors and slanderers, that God would be pleased, for His beloved Son's sake, to forgive them and to turn their hearts.

There was dead silence as the prayer went up. By the dull light of an opium lamp, we could discern the forms of the five men lying or sitting in different postures about the room; but it was not sufficient to reveal the expression of their faces. Presently, however, the silence was broken, and out of the semi-darkness came the words:

"They have been praying to their God to deliver them. Ai-ia! deliver them indeed! Too late for that now. *What is the use of praying when everything is fixed?"*

The atmosphere of the room had now become so intensely oppressive that we scarcely knew how to breathe. My dear wife's strength was ebbing perceptibly; for, besides the fact that this was the seventh day of extraordinary privations and buffetings (Thurs- day, July 12), the dysentery had increased upon her. Could it be otherwise, with no means of protection from the rain when forced to go out, no way of drying her clothes when wet to the skin, and no food obtain- able but that of the coarsest? And now, under the oppression of the heated and poisonous atmosphere, her exhaustion was extreme. It was only by my keeping the fan incessantly going that any relief at all was afforded. Her condition was such as to call for special prayer, in a definite committal of her body to the healing and strengthening hand of God.

It must have been shortly after midnight, as nearly as we could judge, when a stealthy knock was heard at the door, and a voice demanding admittance. The bolt was thrust from the lock, the bar drawn, and the form of the Tseh-cheo-Lao-ie showed big in the doorway.

"Up, up!" he said, "up and be doing! Now's your time. These foreign devils are under your hand and in your power; and you must put them to death. Do it in any way you choose; but do it you must, and do it now. Kill them at once, and don't be afraid. Poison them with opium, if you will; and to prevent trouble, stupefy them first by burning such and such a narcotic. Do as I counsel you, and never fear."

And with that he passed out into the darkness. The burden of this terrible communication was interpreted to me by Miss Gates in the whispered words:

"The end has come. The Lao-ie has instructed them to kill us now."

Without giving the gaolers the slightest intimation that we had understood what had passed, we made our prayer to our God, and set a watch against them. Meantime, the door was once more secured, and a short consultation held; after which the men lay down as before. In a little while they were, to all appearance, asleep.

Time went on, and we saw no indication that foul play was intended. Miss Gates was reclining in a half-sitting posture towards the back of the k'ang veiled in shadow, which the yellow glimmer of the opium lamp failed to penetrate; while my wife and children were covered by my kneeling form as I swept the fan above them.

At length one of the men got up and busied himself with preparing some stuff in a vessel. When ready, he put a light to it, and returned to his place.

Why did my arm move so heavily? and whence this overpowering sense of weariness? I changed my position, and stood up on the k'ang, to rouse myself; for at all costs the fan must be kept going in such a stifling atmosphere. Again I knelt, and then again stood up. It was a hard fight, but the battle, I felt, was against me. An unconquerable drowsiness held my eyes; I swayed to and fro; and a stupor, from which I strove in vain to shake myself free, clouded my faculties. The movement of the arm as I fanned became indolently mechanical; then spasmodic; and then the fan (topped to the k'ang, and I helplessly after it. It was no use. Sleep I must, whether they killed us or not. And dazed to "don't care" pitch, I passed into unconsciousness.

The noxious fumes of the burning drug were doing their work entirely to the satisfaction of the watching gaoler. The utter stillness that pervaded the k'ang proved it to demonstration; and leaving his resting board, he brought the lamp across to scrutinise his victims before giving the coup de grace. What was his amazement to find, as he held the light to Miss Gates' face, that she was wide awake, and that upon one of the "kuei-tsi" at least the narcotic had had no power! A quick movement, designed to let him know that she was fully alive to all that was going on, so took him aback that he could only blurt out a disconcerted, "Ai-ia! not asleep yet? The bugs are too lively for you to-night, eh?" and withdraw to his plank and his pipe. In the strength of God and the patience of Christ, our dear sister continued the lonely vigil of self-denying love and unceasing prayer, to which undoubtedly we owed the preservation of our lives.

It was still dark when I was startled out of my heavy torpor by cries and groans close beside me. I sprang up to find my beloved Flora lying up in Miss Gates' arms, in the throes of asphyxiation. She was gasping, panting, struggling for breath, and moaning for "air, air!" I turned to the gaolers and besought them.

"My wife is dying — can't you see it? Open the door, I entreat you, and give her air. Have pity upon her, oh, have pity, and open the door, if only for one minute."

Alas for the heathen heart of man, so far past feeling as to turn from such an appeal with callous indifference and contempt! It was refused with a curse. Yet, indeed, what else could I expect,when her death was the very thing they were aiming at ?

Praying God to forgive them, I seized two of our tiny rush fans — all that I had at my disposal — and plied them, one in either hand, with all I knew of vigour. The remarkable thing was that, during sleep, not only had I thrown off the effects of the narcotic, but had even in some measure renewed my strength. So far, therefore, I was, by the sustaining mercy of God, equal to the emergency. But oh, the distress of my precious wife's suffering, and no alleviation possible! And then came the word of the promise to my remembrance, given her at the outset of the flight, "I shall not die, but live, and declare the works of the Lord." So I worked the fans and pleaded the promise. Miss Gates uniting with me; and as the morning broke we had the unspeakable joy of seeing her breathing naturally and quietly again — prostrate in body, but rejoicing in spirit, giving glory to God.

The night was past, and the dark deed of death was not done. There was yet time for the men to do it before the world was astir, if they were so minded; and we dared not relax the watch of prayer. In any case, the breaking dawn reminded us that the hour of our execution was at hand, when we were to be shot outside the gate; and the call was still to readiness, that Christ might be magnified in our body by either mode of death, whether this or that.

Two anxious hours, and the men make no move. The sun is up, and the early clatter of hoofs tells that the busy day of traffic has begun; and we are still alive. The keepers shake themselves from their uneasy slumber, and as they don their clothing, we hear them discussing the events of the night, and the answer they shall make to the remonstrance of the Lao-ie; and it is this:

"These people have been praying to Shang-ti le-ho- hua (Jehovah God); and we could do nothing against their prayers."

Such was the testimony of the heathen around us of the same men who but a few hours before had mocked at the futility of prayer, and scoffed at the idea of a God that could deliver out of their hands.

* *

In due course the door was unlocked and thrown wide open; and into the noisome prison room streamed the blessed light and air of heaven. Its entrance seemed like another visitation of the personal presence of our God, to revive our spirit and to change our strength. As it poured in irresistibly, scattering the darkness and its terrors so long upon us, and driving before it the foul atmosphere that had poisoned the very springs of life, it spoke to our heart of a Power that was for us, against Whom no weapon that was formed could prosper; and the word came to me triumphantly, "He shall deliver thee in six troubles; yea, in seven there shall no evil touch thee." At the quickening Voice, hope sprang again into being — not the sickly uncertainty begotten of sentiment, but the strong consolation born of a living faith in the Word of the living God, which works effectually in those who believe; a settled conviction that what He had promised in the word whereon He had caused me to hope, He was both able and faithful to perform. Twice already since our imprisonment here God had wrought miraculously for our deliverance: might we not take it as a guarantee that His determination was to bring us over the border to Huai-k'ing Fu after all? But how ? The people were expecting our execution; and even apart from that, we had no "uen-shu" to pass us through, no animals to carry us, no officials to escort us.

"Look not around; for I am thy God." (2) If the situation was, to all outward appearance, as hopeless as ever, it was so only that He might prove us; for He Himself knew what He would do.

Wonderful to say, no exception was taken to our standing or even sitting in the doorway a mercy for which we could not sufficiently thank God, as the sweet freshness of the early morning was life to my wife in her exhausted state. The rain had ceased before daybreak; and now there was a crisp, delicious coolness in the air which revived her like a strong tonic. The sun was brilliant, and the sky cloudless again, giving promise of heat. But the rain had done its beneficent work. The parched ground had become a pool, and the thirsty land springs of water; rivers were running in the dry places, and streams in the deserts. The blessed effect of this, so far as it immediately concerned ourselves, was that, in their joy and satisfaction, the people had for the time being forgotten their enmity against us, and in their anxiety to improve the opportunity had scattered to the fields.

But what of the two officials from Tseh-cheo Fu? What indeed! I have not the faintest idea. Whether they went off in the night, after leaving instructions with the li-kin officer to have us privately destroyed, we never knew. Certain it is, they did not put in an appearance at the li-kin office, nor did we set eyes on them again. I cannot but think that God used Miss Gates' warning, as to their responsibility in having us informally executed, to work upon their fears; and that for this reason they first crept round in the dead of the night to incite others to do the deed they dared not do, and then slunk home, to be out of the way while it was in doing. Thus God removed these two officials from us. As we had prayed, so it proved. They were not permitted to touch a hair of our head, nor was any power given them against us.

Meantime, of course, we had no idea but that they were still on the spot, and that the possibility of our being carried out to be shot might be realized any moment. It was not our wisdom, however, to betray our thoughts by word or look, but rather to assume that our captors fully intended to discharge their obligations and send us on at once. When, the previous day, we had urged it upon them, the heavy downpour was made the reasonable excuse for detention. We were therefore bold to press the matter, and to demand that, as the only obstacle to our going forward was now removed, we should be taken on without further delay, according to the intention of the Tseh-cheo prefect.

For some considerable time we were kept in suspense. A long and excited discussion ensued, in the course of which it was evident that the council was divided. In all probability the lack of unanimity was due to their calculations having been upset by the perplexing disappearance of the two yamen officials. Some were for detaining us and putting us to death in the place; others for sending us forward and shifting the responsibility of the crime on to the shoulders of the next prefect. At length the question was settled out of hand in a most unexpected way. Who should appear on the scene but the muleteer that accompanied us two days before, and who we supposed had returned with the traitorous escort! Brutal as he had been towards us then, marvel of marvels! he now espoused our cause, if not in the sense of friendly advocacy, at least in the way of furthering the desired end. Standing out amongst them all, with that reckless air and defiant look of his, he said :

"I care not a straw for all your talk. My orders are to carry the foreign devils to Huai-k'ing Fu, and to Huai-k'ing Fu I carry them. Put them to death here? You would only be fools for your pains. Don't you know that, even if they get as far as the Yellow River, they will get no farther; for all the fords are held by the Ta Tao Huei. But, for that matter, there's a band of them not far off. They'll make short work of the 'kuei-tsi,' and save you a deal of trouble."

Upon this he walked over to the other side of the road, and dragged from a shed the framework of the litter. Oh, the sight of it, as he laid it in the street before us and set to work upon the lashings! It is impossible for the reader to imagine what one felt. The Lord was turning our captivity; and I can only express it in the words, "we were Hke them that dream." From that moment everything was done that could be done, in the leisurely haste of the Celestial, to hasten our departure. Three of the men from the li-kin yamen were deputed to accompany us; there was our escort. Our papers, such as they were, were endorsed and given into the hands of the officer in charge, whose presence with us would of itself be suffi- cient to carry us over the boundary; there was the adjustment of the "uen-shu" difficulty. And as to means of conveyance, two pack mules and a donkey, selected from a long string of coal-laden "seng-k'eo" passing through, were seized and calmly commandeered "for yamen use"; there were our animals! As I watched the men hoist the litter with its precious freight to the mules' backs, I almost wondered whether I was in the body or out of the body. No crowds followed us they were busy in the fields; no insults were shouted after us by those we left behind. Instead of being carried out tumultuously to die outside the gate, we were journeying quietly to our destination, set forward on our way by the very men who sought our lives.

Lan-chen Cheo behind us! What had God wrought! Three times miraculously delivered from death at the hands of the people, at the hands of the gaolers, at the hands of the Tseh-cheo officials. Signal answers to prayer, how many! together with the miraculous removal of the mountain of difficulties that stood in the way of our escape from the place.

The memory of Lan-chen Cheo will never be anything else to me than an agony. "Abba Father! if it be possible," seemed the only language in which the heart could utter itself. And yet over all was the coverimg Presence; and the memory of that can never be anything else than joy unspeakable and full of glory.

"Therefore with Angels and Archangels and with all the Company of heaven we laud and magnify Thy glorious Name, evermore praising Thee and saying:

Holy, holy, holy. Lord God of hosts!
Heaven and earth are full of Thy glory.
Glory be to Thee, O Lord most high!

Questions to Consider

1. They prayed for rain and rain came. Was this of God or just chance?

2. They prayed in Chinese so the jailers would know what they were asking. Do you pray so non-believers can understand what you are asking of God?

3. When the "reasons" for killing the foreigners was removed, the guards came up with new "reasons." Why didn't the jailers kill them?

CHAPTER TWENTY

New Perils in Ho-Nan

"He brought them out of darkness and the shadow of death. O that men would praise the Lord for His goodness and for His wonderful works."

Friday, July 13: the seventeenth day of the sixth Chinese moon; the eighth day of our second flight. A week to-day since we left Lu-an — a week that will probably stand alone in the history of my life for concentration of inward suffering and for manifestation of Divine power.

The road we were now taking lay through magnificent scenery, over the great stone stairway of the lofty Tai-hang range that divides the provinces of Shan-si and Ho-nan. The immemorial traffic of the great trade route has worn the rocky steep into a series of steps, so regularly gradated that one wonders whether skilled labour has not been employed upon them. The pass is a nearly continuous ascent of ragged and precipitous rocks, until it reaches an altitude of at least 2,000 feet, when it drops to the plains of Ho-nan. Its wild grandeur is most impressive; and the distant views that burst upon the eye at some turn of the road, or reveal themselves where the crags part, are striking and beautiful to a degree. At least, so they appeared to my unaccustomed eyes, in the light of a new found liberty.

Not that we were free. Though rejoicing truly in a gracious deliverance, we were captives still and made to feel it. Neither escort nor driver had abated one jot of their rooted enmity towards us. Rather they seemed to vie with one another in the expression of the hard-hearted contempt that sprang naturally out of it.

Nor were the conditions of travel less rigorous than on former occasions. The sun beat down upon our unprotected heads as fiercely as at any previous time. In the dear children's case, it is true, there was the slight alleviation of a "sheo-kin" apiece (or small square handkerchief of coarse native cloth) which my wife had contrived somehow to get for them; these twice folded just sufficed to cover the crown of the head. To render them as sun-proof as possible I kept them well wetted, dipping them in the wayside pools that abounded, since the great rain, in the holes of the rocky road. As the morning advanced and the sun's power increased, the water in these rock holes became hot well-nigh to steaming, so that at last the wet "sheo-kin" had no longer any cooling virtue to carry to the poor little burning head.

The furnace heat of that morning I shall never for- get. If fire was above us, it is no exaggeration to say that fire seemed also to be beneath and on every side of us. The arid rocks and the shimmering air were charged with it. As the donkey provided for my use was again saddled with nothing easier than the torturing "kia-tsi," I was driven to walk. And here how mercifully had God in His foreseeing love supplied my need! When my clothing had been taken at Sha-ho-k'eo, my Chinese socks had been left to me; and the stout calico sole, strongly sewn after the native fashion, was now my salvation. I could not ride for the sores produced thereby; and the heat of the rock was such (let alone the painfulness of its jagged formation) that, but for my socks, walking would have become an impossibility. Even as it was, I could only ease the foot by plunging it, sock and all, into the hot water-holes by the way, and by occasionally shifting the single shoe (recovered to me after we had been stripped) from one foot to the other.

The sufferings of the ladies and children under these climatic conditions were increased, not merely by the cramping squeeze of their close quarters, but by the nature of the ground traversed, and the careless con- struction of the litter frame. The ups and downs of the steep ascents and descents produced a motion very different to that of the level road; and the discomfort in their particular circumstances, huddled as they were like so much baggage in the rope work, can in some degree be imagined even by those who have never used a northern "chiao-woa-ri." As a result of the short, awkward jerks,, the sisters were severely galled by the jar and fret of the loosely lashed woodwork at their back; but even worse was the distress of finding that, in my dear wife's case, the mat under her was slowly giving way, and she sinking through the ropework! The parting of the meshes soon lowered her to the point where she had no choice but to hang on to the poles for dear life, in which desperate position she was thrown in the descents against the rump of the mule, who, kicking at the obstruction, involved not only her but all in the litter in the most serious peril. Yet when I urged the muleteer to halt for a few minutes to put the cordage right, the request only called forth a dangerous sneer, in spite of the appeal to his pity on the ground of my wife's condition. Her sweet unmurmuring patience, as she bore it all in the gentleness of Christ, was never perhaps more graciously brought home to me than then. Not one word of reproach or even of complaint; only the enduring meekness of her Lord. When the usual halting stage was reached the ropes were tightened not before.

The sun was at meridian heat when (joy of joys!) we crossed the long-looked-for boundary line, and could say at last, "Shan-si and terror are behind us; we are beyond the roach of Yu-hsien's power." Yes, we were actually in Ho-nan, and had begun the descent to yonder plains of living green! Never did my eyes feast with greater satisfaction on a landscape than in that hour on the soft brilliancy of the Paradise spread out before us. It would have been beautiful at any time; but just now it was rendered eminently so by contrast with the brown barrenness of poor drought- dried Shan-si; and especially by the promise of liberty it inspired as the realization at last of hope so long deferred.

We had yet to learn by sad experience that to be quit of Shan-si was by no mean synonymous with being quit of danger, or even of Boxer danger. The spirit of that terrible movement had already infected Ho-nan and inflamed the provincial governor, Yu-chang, with a hatred against the foreigner scarcely less pronounced than that of the Butcher of Shan-si. Then, too, if it was a fact that our papers were irregular, we were liable to be sent back to the dreaded province at any point of the journey, at the discretion of any one of the Mandarins through whose hands we had to pass. Again, events had been transpiring in this very province of which as yet we knew nothing. Of the reign of terror inaugurated here as elsewhere by the bloody edicts of the Empress Dowager; of the flight of all foreign communities; of the riotous attacks upon our brethren and the wrecking of their stations; we were profoundly ignorant. The muleteer's hint to our captors at Lan-chen Cheo was the nearest approach to information that we had received.

The long descent was over, and we were wending our way amid the verdant rice-fields of Ho-nan. The great Tai-hang barrier was between us and Yu-hsien now; and as I looked back upon its gigantic pile of frowning precipice with fervent thanksgiving in my heart, it seemed to parable the miracle of our escape. Every mountain and hill had been made low; the prey of the terrible had been delivered; for Jehovah, the Rock of our strength and our Refuge, had con- tended with them that contended with us. These reflections gained significance from the fact that at the very time they were in my mind the tragedy of Miss Rice's martyrdom was being enacted but a few miles distant, in the neighbourhood of Tseh-cheo Fu.

An hour or so later we entered a large market town, in the main thoroughfare of which we were halted. The mules were taken out and the litter frame set down, not in an inn, but in the street, inches deep in mud.

Our arrival was the signal for a rush from all sides, and we were at once hemmed in by a crowd of un- certain temper. The escort and driver had betaken themselves to the comfort and quiet of an inn, while we were told that if we wanted food we must go to the south suburb for it, and so left alone in the open to shift for ourselves. It was now that the dreaded words "Ta Tao Huei" grated again upon our ears and shook our hearts. Several of the better disposed in the crowd warned us not to adventure ourselves into the south suburb, "as a detachment of the Ta Tao Huei was there." So, then, the Boxers in Ho-nan was no myth of the muleteer's conjuring, but a fact; and a fact that we might have to reckon with to our cost now and here, on the very threshold of the province we had thought so peaceful. Moreover, in the light of this information it was not difficult to read the reason of the direction given us by the escort. Our abandonment was clearly in the hope that between Boxers and mob we should be done to death.

Faint and weary, we sought shelter from the scorching blaze and the oppressive crush under the "p'eng" of a small bread shop near by, where we hoped to get some necessary food as well. Our first experience of Ho-nan friendliness was not encouraging; we were driven from the premises, the shopkeeper refusing even to sell us a piece of bread. So the ladies and the little ones were forced back to the cramped discomfort of the litter in sheer self-defence, the barrier of the poles supplying them with the only relief they could get from the great pressure.

It proved to be one of the most distressing and anxious times in all our experience. For three full hours we were momently expecting an attack. To leave my dear ones and go in search of food was out of the question. Once separated we should never have been united again in this world. Several thousands were on the street. The roadway in front of us was blocked. Tier on tier, right away back to the shops, they were struggling, a dense mass of men and lads, to get near us. The heat and stench! imagine what it was, with the sun pouring down and any breath of what little air there might have been absolutely shut out! It was fainting work in hunger and thirst, too. I felt sick enough myself, standing up as I was with my head above the crowd. What those in the litter must have suffered I cannot even guess. The continuous working of the fans (such as they were, and worn now with excessive use) was the one thing in the way of natural means that averted catastrophe. I only know the darling children sobbed much with hunger, terror, heat, sores, and utter weariness. Exhausted with it all, and overborne by her great fatigues, my dear wife settled into a kind of swoon where she sat. Head and back being unsupported, she fell heavily over to one side, striking her head violently against one of the uprights to which the poles were lashed. Such was the rest wherewith they caused the weary to rest they to whom that gentle spirit had never spoken any other than words of life and love, to whom she was content to be made all things, yes, even to be made as the filth of the world if by any means she might save some of them. The rude blow that recalled her to the world of consciousness and dread reality only served to elicit a smile, the heavenliness of which was its own index to the mind and thought within. I shall never forget that smile. The very memory of it is a means of grace to me still.

Now and again a hawker of viands or fruits would come our way; but none would sell to us. At last one man was induced to part with a few plums for an exorbitant price, but a bid for a second instalment was refused. Perhaps it was as well for us, ravenous though we were; for they were but half ripe, as is ordinarily the case in China, at least in the north.

As time wore on, the merely uncomfortable element of curiosity gave way to those disquieting signs which our familiarity with Chinese crowds recognized as the precursors of mischief. Noise and jostling were now the order of the hour; and the spirit of something more than rowdiness a spirit of open hostility was beginning to break through it. The opprobrious term "iang kuei-tsi" came ominously to the front, and told of a distinct rise in the tide of feeling. Coarse jests were flung across at us, and in many eyes we read the racial hatred that found vent in muttered curse.

Crushed up against the poles of the litter, I was forced to take refuge within them. But the serious thing was that the poles themselves were creaking dangerously under the pressure. If once the framework gave way, it would be a sure signal to the crowd to complete its demolition and our destruction. A feeling the nearest approach to panic that I had yet experienced came over me as 1 looked earnestly in the direction of the escort's inn. The eye of the soul was lifted up to heaven, and in my distress I called upon the Lord and cried unto my God. Not in vain. Just at the very crisis of our great need the driver appeared with the mules, followed by the escort. The crowd fell back, the animals stood, the litter was hoisted, and we were moving through their midst to- ward Huai-k'ing Pu. Closing in behind us, the mob noisily "song"- ed us to the gate leading to the south suburb — and to the Boxers, whose badge, conspicuous enough, was its own confirmation of the report we had heard. How we ever got through must remain among the multiplied mysteries of our extraordinary escape, and be reckoned among the marvels of our wonder-working God. They demanded of the escort where the "kuei-tsi" were being taken, and for what purpose. The answer probably saved our lives "To the Fu (Huai-k'ing) for execution." Notwithstanding, they urged them to set us down and leave us in their hands; but the muleteer again came unwittingly to the rescue, with the spirited answer, "Too late! We have waited all these hours in the place and you have done nothing; you will have to wait now till we get to the Fu." Whatever they may have thought, they made no demonstration beyond cursing us; but a party of them fell in behind and followed at a distance. (1)

The roads were indescribably awful. Where they were not actually rivers, they were quagmires. Heavy cart and other traffic had churned the softened soil into sticky sloughs, which brought me again and again to the point of despond, as I floundered along here, there, and everywhere. Oozy suction deprived me of my shoe so often that I had (most reluctantly) to discard it altogether; and having no "tai-tsi" to secure my socks above the ankle, nor any time to spare for their rescue and readjustment when syste- matically drawn off by the same delicate process, I found it expedient to plough (or rather slough) my way for the rest of the journey barefoot.

There were times when, by reason of the depth of the waters, I was compelled to take to the pack-saddle. In some parts of the road they widened to the size of a lagoon, from three to four feet deep. It was a peculiar trial to me when this was the case, not so much from the torture of the kia-tsi (though that was bad enough) as from the slowness of my brute. When walking I was able to keep alongside of the litter; but now I had to be separated from my dear ones without knowing when I should be able to overtake them. At last I could stand it no longer; and it happened on this wise. We had come to one of these lagoons the last as it proved, and the worst, both for depth and extent. The litter took the water first, my seng- k'eo and the escort lagging far behind, as usual. By the time we were entering it, the litter was two- thirds of the way across naturally, with two strong mules travelling well. I thrashed the seng-k'eo, urging him all I knew; but his hide might have been tanned leather for all the effect it had. Pointing to the litter I called to the owners of the animal to apply a little of their own gentle persuasion, in the natural belief that if any arts would appeal to asinine susceptibility, theirs would . They, however, were as hopeless to deal with as the other. There was nothing for it, therefore, but to resign one's self to the inevitable, and await the issue quietly. The litter had now reached terra-firma, and was drawing rapidly away. Every minute the distance between us was increasing; and I noted it with a concern that presently became alarm. If once I lost sight of it, I should miss the road they had taken, and what then? Moreover, there came the uncanny suspicion of design in the separation, which grew into the certainty that foul play was in- tended. Thoughts like these, fostered by circumstance and justified by experience, came thick upon me, while my steed stumbled on at his own sweet will. The climax came when, at the deepest part, he gave himself up to the luxury of his bath, and stood in revelling complacency stubbornly immovable. Meantime, the litter was fading into dim uncertainty. With straining eyes I watched until among the trees, a spectral speck, it turned a comer of the road and disappeared.

For the first time in the history of either flight my loved ones were gone from my sight and I from their's. I cried in real distress to God to bring me to them ere mischief befell them by the way, and to show me the road they had followed. I would fain have flung myself into the water there and then, but that I could not know the path to take, or the holes and ditches to avoid. The moment we were in shallow water, I promise you I was off at a dash, with bare feet plunging, sliding, sticking in the mire, regardless of anything and everything save the one thing. At the point where I had seen them turn I found a long stretch of road with but one turning at its extremity, and as I pressed the pursuit at the highest speed I could com- mand, my thankfulness knew no bounds when, at no great distance, the litter showed before me, neither spectral nor a speck, but the large substantial thing I had longed to see. The happiness of the re-union on either side for their anxiety had been scarcely less than my own — was well worth the price paid for it. Not again did I leave them. Yet, indeed, there was no call to repeat the experience; for we were on the outskirts of Huai-k'ing Fu, and in a little more had reached the city gate.

A sorry spectacle we must have presented to the huge crowd that thronged us, as we passed along the street. Our beggarly appearance beggars description. Suffice it to say we looked to their eyes what we were supposed to be, criminals only fit for execution. The sight of our degradation, as legibly stamped upon our mode of conveyance as upon our persons, provoked derisive laughter that followed us the whole way in a continuous roar. One word was upon every lip : "Here come these foreign devils! They are being taken to prison and to death!" My heart failed me as Miss Gates said, "There can be no question, from what they are saying, that we are to die here; for we are not being taken to the yamen at all, but to the common prison." In high indignation I ran to the leader's head to stay further progress, insisting that we should be taken to the yamen and our papers handed in to the prefect. Copious abuse and some roughish hustling were meted out to me for my pains, and as they had matters in their own hands the journey continued as before.

To my intense relief, our goal was not the gaol after all, but the "Hsien" (or sub-prefect's) yamen, into the first or outer courtyard of which we were driven and put down just within the gate. Our arrival had been anticipated and carefully prepared for. Soldiers and runners were in waiting to keep back the mob that pressed in after us. Not only so, but the Ta Lao-ie's palanquin was set there in evident readiness for im- mediate use. Almost before we had time to realize where we were, the cries of the runners to clear the road announced the coming of the Great Man, who hastily took his seat and was lifted to the shoulders of the bearers. The boom of the great gong that preceded him and the shouts of the underlings opened a way for the procession through the dense mass about us, and past us swept his Lordship without deigning to lift his eyes. The next moment we were drawn into the vortex of soldiers and vassals who brought up the rear, and ordered to "follow the chair."

"Follow the chair! " What did it mean? It meant the greatest indignity in the eyes of the Chinese that could be offered to European women. It was an insult of the most flagrant type. That these two ladies should be made to walk the streets, exposed to the gaze of the male populace, told the tale that in its estimation we could not sink lower in the scale of being than we had sunk. Not only so, the insult was aggravated by the fact that it was offered officially. By the Mandarin's own orders it was that they were compelled to take a place intended to brand them with shame, degradation and reproach a place among the menials behind the chair. In the light of his after behaviour towards us, I cannot help hoping that he did it to blind the eyes of the hostile mob to his real intentions, leading them to believe that he was taking us to execution when all the while he was schem- ing for our deliverance. But when I have said that, I have said all that can be said in extenuation. Nothing short of such a motive could justify such a proceeding.

Never shall I forget that walk. If ever we realized what it was to be made a spectacle to men, as the off scouring of all things, it was then. On either side of the street were ranged the city's thousands; around us and on before, the motley horde of yamen henchmen and parasites. Borne by eight stalwart runners, the Great Man's chair hurried on at official pace, heralded by the great gong and the usual frumpery of yamen insignia. To keep up with it was a sheer impossibility, and with not a little anxiety we saw it getting farther and farther away. In their state of exhaustion, however, it was impossible for the ladies not to lag. The tender years too, of the tiny children had to be taken into account, not to mention the layers of mud grease under our feet, the tendency of which was to take us two steps back for every one that we took forward. However, we were expected to do the impossible, and a yamen guard of soldiers made it their business to aid us in the attempt. We kept together as far as we could, but the hurrying, hustling runners about us made it very difficult. Miss Gates was on just a little ahead with Hedley, while I held Hope with one hand, and with the other supported my wife, whose indomitable faith and courage bore her up in an unflinching, uncomplaining endurance that made me marvel at the power of the grace of God.

We must have traversed the city from one end to the other — so interminably long was the way — when we arrived at the place where the Great Man's chair had been set down. It proved to be the "kong-kuan," or official inn, reserved exclusively for yamen use. We were ordered to enter; the doors were shut and locked behind us, and we were taken to a room lofty and comparatively clean, but absolutely destitute of furniture. There was not even so much as a straw mat to sit or lie on nothing but the earth floor. A minute later a couple of chairs were brought in for our use, and another placed in the courtyard fronting the door, whereon his Excellency seated himself, sur- rounded by his retinue. Though considerably under middle height, the dignity of his bearing, supported by the richness of his robes, the pomp and circum- stance of office, and the consciousness of power, carried his inches easily into feet, and made him almost as mighty a potentate in our eyes as he was in his own. We were now ordered into the august presence; but as my wife was too exhausted to stand, she was allowed to remain seated at the door. Our respectful bow was not returned (how should it be? indeed, our presumption was great in not making, and his forbearance greater in not demanding, the "k'eh-teo") nor were his eyes once raised from their fixed and studied downward gaze. As we presented ourselves before him, he rose and remained standing throughout the short interview, in the course of which he asked all about the journey, why we had left our station, and where we were going. On hearing that we were making for Hankow, he remarked, "You are on a fool's errand, for you will never get there"; and with a few instructions to those about him haughtily took his departure.

The comparative kindhness of his manner was so unexpected after what we had hitherto experienced of official treatment, that our hopes rose correspondingly, and our spirits with them. The luxury of a place of refuge from the pressure of rude and hostile crowds, and of leisure (however short) for undisturbed rest, tended in the same direction; and when at length a savoury meal was brought in steaming hot and set before us, it seemed no longer possible to doubt that we had fallen by God's mercy into good hands; and with fervent thanksgiving we blessed His Holy Name.

Having no definite clue, however, to the Mandarin's real intentions, we were not able to divest ourselves entirely of the fears that had by this time become a settled part of our constitution. All along the route it had been dinned into our ears that there was nothing before us but prison and death. As we looked at the place of our abode, we could only acknowledge to ourselves that after all it was a prisoners' cell. Then, too, had not the ofiicial's last word to us been that we should never get to Hankow? And was not this intended to convey, not only that our execution was certain, but that it might even be carried out there? Such thoughts would present themselves; but when an hour or two later the gate was opened to admit a company of soldiers armed with sword and gun, they revived with a certainty that seemed only too well grounded. For aught we knew to the contrary, the intention was to have us privately put to death in the "kong-kuan" during the night; and these were the executioners.

A night passed under apprehensions such as these could hardly be called good in the conventional sense. Yet good it was; for the loving-kindness of our God was manifested in many ways. For instance, the door of our cell was not locked, and we were allowed free access to the courtyard, the gate of which was guarded by sentries. Permission was also granted to take water for washing purposes from the "kang" (or great stone water butt) and two straw mats — filthy enough, but preferable to direct contact with mother earth — were handed in for the use of the women and children. We were glad to catch at every little thing, however shadowy, that could be construed into an evidence of goodwill, and sought to make what return we could to the guard in the way of thanks and courteous attention. In this way we prayed that the occasional word we sought to introduce, as far as they would allow it, on the one theme, might find the readier access to their heart.

My beggar's rag, with the little store of copper cash in it, formed a pillow for the children, and while rummaging for the purpose in a small inner cell leading off our own, I was fortunate in hitting upon two loose bricks, one for my wife to rest her head upon, the other for Miss Gates. A further search brought out a half brick for myself; so we were all supplied with pillows for once. The night was sultry, and outside at the threshold I kept watch under the stars. Oh, the contrast of that still peaceful night with what we had been experiencing, almost without intermission, of racket, rush and riot for days and nights together! Even the fear of death seemed to pass in the unbroken calm that reigned about us.

So the darkness wore away, with no other movement on the part of the guard than an occasional challenge when I got up to ease my aching limbs, or than what was necessary for their own comfort and the ordering of the opium tray. Then the stars paled and slowly slipped from sight. The sky was once more reddening in the east, and by sunrise the court-yard was a scene of animation. Two large three-mule carts were in waiting, into which we were hastily thrust the ladies and little Hope in the first, Hedley and I following; and ere the city was awake, we were rumbling out of the great gate under a guard of eight soldiers with fixed bayonets, officered by the "Shao-ie" himself on horseback, with a couple of mounted troopers to bring up the rear.

Questions to Consider

1. Glover describes his joy at finding two loose bricks to serve as pillows for his wife and Miss Gates. Do you appreciate what God provides for you?

2. What "little things" have you thanked God for providing you? Did you mean it or do you just thank God for "big things"?

CHAPTER TWENTY-ONE

In Weariness and Painfulness

*"He said unto me, My grace is sufficient for thee; for
my strength is made perfect in weakness."*

Now began a series of fresh experiences in the mode of
travel which were destined to tax our strength to the utmost
limit of endurance. For a period of thirteen successive days
we were to be taken on by cart and handbarrow, the suffering
of which can only be described as torture. As proscribed
aliens, with nothing to recommend us to mercy, we were
treated in precisely the same way as the criminal class, and
carried like ordinary felons from prison to prison.

It has been my aim and constant endeavour, in this story of
our escape, to give a simple and natural account of events as
they actually occurred, in the strict impartiality of fact. In so
doing, it has been impossible to avoid setting forth the
undesirable side of the Chinese character; and possibly some
may think that I have given it unnecessary prominence, to the
disparagement of the people themselves and the prejudice of

the missionary cause. The fear, however, if such there be, is more sentimental than reasonable. Nothing can be gained to the cause of Truth by trying to make black appear white. On the other hand, the unveiling of the Truth and the depicting of the heathen as they are in their unenlightened state ought to furnish one of the strongest arguments in favour of their evangelization, to constitute a powerful call to prayer and consecration, and to make our hearts yearn the more over them in the tender mercies of Christ. If the sight of an enlightened nation persecuting the messengers of God, and stoning them that were sent to it, moved the tears of the Lord Jesus, should the record of the same deeds done for lack of light provoke in us anything else than His own compassion in the spirit of His own self-sacrifice?

I may not hesitate, therefore, to say plainly that, in being exposed to the treatment meted out to criminals, we were exposed to much barbarity. No account was taken of sex, years, or physical condition. Woman with child, or strong man; tender infant or mature adult it was all alike to our captors: as little consideration was given to the one as to the other. We were all greatly reduced at this particular time, but especially my dear wife, with the dysentery strong upon her, and the little ones with their wounds and extraordinary fatigues. Yet day after day, for ten days, she and they were called upon to endure an average ten hours of the all but unendurable jolt, bang, swing, crash, of a cross-country springless cart, and that with nothing but the floor board to sit on. With characteristic unselfishness Miss Gates took the worst seat at the far back, thus enabling my wife and little girl to sit forward, where, even if the force of concussion remained the same, at least the swing was not so violently felt. But anyhow and everyhow, it was a case of holding on for one's life. If I narrate a little of my own experience, it will stand for that of the ladies also.

My little boy and I were ordered to the far end of the cart, the body and shafts of which were immediately loaded up with the soldiers of the escort. These took possession of leg space and every other space, often lying curled up or at full length, either smoking or asleep. I was thus forced into a sitting posture with my legs drawn up, Hedley between.

The hands were fully employed in gripping the framework on either side, to forestall the sudden tilt which threatened dislocation at any moment. I remember letting go once, for a second or two, to ease the arms, when a cruel lurch gave me cause for the rest of the day to rue the venture, with a stunning blow to the head, first this side, then that, before I could recover my grip. In an hour or so the cramped position became unbearable, and yet how to alter it was a problem. We had to devise various shifts in utter desperation, and lunge out with the stiffened limb in any direction whatsoever, regardless of the anathemas of the disquieted sleepers blocking us up. The oscillation of the cart was felt in all its force where we were, and the muscles ached again with the severe and continuous strain upon them. Then, too, the unmitigated hardness of the floor seat, the harsh grating of the wheels, and the violent impact of jolt and crash, rasped the nerves and bones at the base of the spine to an exquisite sensitiveness. Some alleviation perhaps over what we might have suffered a day or two earlier was afforded by the softened state of the country roads; but when it came to being rattled over the paved unevennesses of a street or bridge, or the disordered bed of huge stone blocks that lay at the threshold of every city gate, then it was that we tasted real agony. One merit the carts had they were well covered in from the sun's fierce heat. The "p'eng" consisted of a stout thatch of dried rush and straw matting lashed to a strong framework, concave and detachable. Generally, though not invariably, it extended behind far enough to shelter one from the oblique rays of the sun; for there was an opening at our back, which, delightful for ventilation, was also at times dreadful, from the heat it admitted to the nape of the neck.

It will be readily admitted that travelling of such a nature and under such conditions for ten consecutive days, from 7 a.m. to 7 p.m. (sometimes later) was no ordinary test. Indeed, how any woman in my wife's condition could survive such an ordeal (even apart from all that followed after) is a problem that has taxed the wit of doctors. The sustaining power of God, expressly granted, is the only rational answer, as they have honestly recognized.

On leaving Huai-k'ing Fu, we struck due east, our course being directed to the Hsien city of Wu-chi. The roads were largely under water, and it was no uncommon thing for the cart to be axle deep in liquid mud. Often it would tilt over to a dangerous angle, righting itself only as by a miracle. On one occasion at least, we stuck so fast in a bog that, for all the yelling and flogging, our three strong beasts could avail nothing until relieved of our weight.

At noon we were driven into the courtyard of a large village inn. There we were ordered to dismount. The long morning separation made the re-union the chief feature of the halt; in the joy of which pain, weariness, hunger and thirst were for the moment forgotten as we inquired of each other's welfare and compared experiences. We were taken to the commodious guest-room of an inner courtyard (where, however, there was no k'ang) and the gates were shut. Half in doubt as to whether we were in the hands of friends or foes, fearing in hope and hoping in fear, we sat waiting for the next event, which proved to be the entrance of the "Shao-ie." The kindness of his greeting and the courtesy of his manner reassured us at once; and what a lifting it was of what a burden! While we were taking the hand- some meal he ordered for us, he seated himself near the table, smoking his long pipe and chatting in the most affable way. The meal over, he took leave of us with a gracious bow and a gift of 1,500 cash to this extent, at any rate, showing us the consideration of a true gentleman. We did not see him again, as at this point of the journey he returned with his two orderlies, leaving us in charge of the soldiers. Two hours of blessed rest were given us, when to stretch one's self full length on a bit of straw matting was the per- fection of luxury. Then the order to mount; and we were off once more, to the old tune of jolt and swing.

As we neared Wu-chi, the soldiers again fixed bayonets, and, forming up on either side of the carts, took us in as prisoners under arrest. It goes without saying that an immense concourse pursued us to the yamen gates and pressed in after us. The scene baffles all description. I do not know whether I can attempt to give the home reader any idea of it. Perhaps if I try, the account may be taken as a general description of what took place at every city and yamen we passed through.

Picture, then, if you can, the two carts pressing through the city streets as fast as ruts, etc., will allow. The armed escort at once attract notice, and speculation is rife as to who their quarry may be. The news that they have "iang ren" spreads like wildfire; and the first curious few increase to hundreds, and the hundreds swell to thousands ere the goal is reached. I can assure the reader it needed all the grace of God to watch the assembling of the mobs en route and not tremble. Arrived at the yamen gate, we are, as a rule, driven well inside, halted, and ordered to dismount. The vast mob pours in tumultuously and throngs about us, fighting to get the first sight as we make our way to the shafts and from the shafts to the ground. The carts are driven away; the escort, having no further concern with us, go off to report themselves and hand in our papers; and we are left standing alone where we alighted. What objects we look to be sure as we face the hustling multitude! Here at Wu-chi I have a nine days' growth of hair about my face; I stand in a torn, bespattered gown, and in socks caked with mud; and under my arm I hug the rolled-up beggar's rag, purse by day and pillow by night. The ladies' garments are soiled and torn; Miss Gates is shoeless, and stockings worn through; the children's gauze combinations are almost in tatters. They carry in their faces, poor little darlings, the marks of much crying from terror and from pain to which the long wounds from shoulder to elbow bear witness. My dear wife wears only too visibly the look of suffering entailed by her distressing sickness, and all of us the deep impress left by exposure, want and sorrow. No wonder we excite curiosity; but oh, for some to take pity! Aching in every bone with the hard day's ride, and sore with many bruises, we yearn for rest; but instead of rest we have to face the noise and heat of pressing crowds and the always possible imminence of attack. I take little Hope in my arms to keep her from the crush and soothe her fears; and as she clings she hides her eyes and stifles her sobs in my neck. Hedley (plucky little man that he is!) stands by his mother fronting the crowd with sad, wistful face; but never a cry or a murmur leaves his firmly set lips.

Sooner or later soldiers and runners appear on the scene for the regulating of the crowd, which is done as much by the vigorous use of the lungs as of the arms. Now ensues a tumult which is quite indescribable, what with the deafening babel of the soldiers' shouts, the growing excitement of the people, and the resort to the bamboo flail to keep them back. Sometimes we are kept standing thus in the open for a con- siderable time; at others we are taken straight to the common prison, and either lodged in a cell or in the guard-room adjoining, there to await the Mandarin's pleasure. Distracted with the noise and fearful of attack, we hail our prison quarters as a place of refuge. And yet even here we are not safe from molestation especially if the gaol prove to be at the entrance to the yamen, or anywhere else than within an inner enclosure of its own, when good-bye to all hope of rest and quiet until darkness falls and the hour for closing the big gates is come.

It was at Wu-chi that we made our first acquaintance with a bona-fide Chinese prison. We were taken to a small courtyard soon after arrival, without any idea on our part as to the place we were going to and told to seat ourselves on the narrowest of narrow benches against the outside wall. It cut too painfully, and we preferred to stand. A survey of our surroundings quickly told its own horrible tale, and the truth was brought home to me in all its dread reality that we were classed as very criminals, and were to suffer as such. I shall never forget how my heart sank at the discovery, or when for the first time I heard immediately behind the clank of chains, and saw within touch the poor degraded looking creatures who wore them crowding to peer at us through the wooden bars of their prison door. Were we then after all only delivered from Shan-si to die in Ho-nan? for to be taken to prison was surely the preliminary to being taken to death. It was out of the depths truly that I cried, "Lord, hear my voice"; for hope sickened in the knowledge that we were actually in the yamen prison, and that this was an official act. "Gracious is the Lord and merciful." A time, long in coming, came at last when a messenger entered with a squad of runners, and led us out across the first courtyard into the second, the gates of which were closed after us. Here we were given a small room to ourselves, so far as occupation went. Not visitation, however; for from the minute we entered, we were besieged by groups of yamen officials, gentlemen, and employes who were considerate enough to show real interest and kindly sympathy with us, and inconsiderate enough to stay till midnight. Stiff, bruised, and aching all over, too weary for words, we scarcely knew how to meet the innumerable questions with which we were plied most of them trivial and childish to a degree, and repeated over and over with every fresh batch of comers.

Among our earliest visitors was the Mandarin himself. With becoming awe, the effect of our last experience, we prepared at the announcement of his approach to receive him. Runners cleared the way. A chair was set, and a moment later we were face to face with the Great Man. A mere boy to look at, tall, spare, with an indolent stoop from the shoulders, he was in all respects, save in the matter of dress, a direct contrast to his colleague of Huai-k'ing. Dignity he had none; the lack of it was supplied by a spurious make-up of autocratic swagger which, for peevish impotency, was as humbling an exhibition of moral infirmity as could well be seen. As soon as he was seated, he addressed himself to us as to prisoners in loud, bullying tones, the offensiveness of which was possibly more apparent than real, while a retainer handed him his long tobacco pipe. He remained seated throughout the audience, only rising to stamp his foot and shout at the unheeding crowd of suitors that clamoured at the door, when their lawless irreverence inconveniently broke bounds. With all his mannerism he was a friend to us, whether in his heart he wished us well or not; and when he rose to leave, we genuinely felt the thanks we gave him for his kindness towards us. Indeed, the fact that he had granted us an audience at all was no small favour, as we were to realize yet more fully in the painful experiences to come.

It was also at Wu-chi that we gleaned our first tidings of the outside world and of the fearful trend of things in China itself. We were told that all the great Powers were at war with the Middle Kingdom; that the foreigners had fled in confusion even from Hankow and Shanghai; and that there was not one of them left in the country. How much of this was to be believed it was impossible to say; but the bare fact that it was thus commonly reported among the people was a severe menace to our hope of getting through in peace and safety, and moreover it explained in some measure the prefect's enigmatical warning at Huai- k'ing Fu on learning our destination, "You are on a fool's errand; for you will never get there."

The fear, however, that the rumour had a distinct basis of fact to rest upon was distressingly increased by the tidings now made known to us for the first time of the awful tragedy at Pao-ting Fu. We were told that the whole foreign community in that city had been massacred — the women with great barbarity, their breasts having been cut off, and themselves thereafter hanged over the city wall. We were also warned that to go on towards Hankow by the ordinary route (via Nan Yang Fu) was attended with the greatest risk; that several stations had been rioted; and that in certain districts en route no foreigner could hope to pass through unmolested. We were advised that our only chance of getting safely to the coast lay in taking the course due west into Shen-si, and then striking south to Tong-king, through Si- ch'uen and Kuei-cheo. The futility of attempting such a journey was so apparent on the face of it that it had only to be mentioned to be dismissed; and we had to fall back on the risk and decide to continue as we had begun.

Our decision seemed to call out much genuine sympathy; for all agreed that we could never get through alive. Seeing the kindly feeling manifested, my wife turned the occasion to practical account, and put in an earnest plea for cast-off clothing for the children. We were touched at the response it met with; for not long after, several garments were brought in, sent by the Secretary's "t'ai-t'ai" (lady) and forthwith the little darlings were arrayed in yamen pants and tunic. My wife was affected to tears, and could scarcely speak her gratitude. I never look at these garments now without a vivid realization of that scene, and a renewal of the thanksgiving that went up on the spot to God.

Hope and Hedley in their prison garments.

There seemed to be a real spirit of inquiry towards the truth of God in Christ; and precious opportunities were given, through the many questions pressed upon us, of preaching unto them Jesus. Miss Gates especially was greatly helped in speaking, and one cannot but hope that the seed then sown was, to some at least, unto life eternal.

When all had at length withdrawn we had leisure to reflect on the significance of the news we had heard. A tale of war, riot and massacre was not calculated to raise our spirits or to lead us to think that we were likely to be any better off in Ho-nan than in Shan-si. The gloom of the prospect was deepening rather than lightening. How soon might not we be called to go the way of our martyred brethren and sisters in Chih-li? For to-morrow would see us at the Yellow River, the fords of which we had heard were held by the Ta Tao Huei; and how could we hope to cross unchallenged? Nevertheless, we thought upon God; and in thankful remembrance of all the marvellous way He had led us hitherto, we committed the keeping of our souls to Him. Then stretching our- selves on the bare brick k'ang, only glad that it was not a cell in yonder prison courtyard, we gave our- selves up to the untold blessedness of quiet aloneness, and were soon asleep.

The following morning (Sunday, July 16), the carts were ready at an early hour to take us on another stage. The route chosen as likely to prove less hostile was via Cheng-cheo, Hu-cheo and Sin-yang Cheo. Breakfast was given us along with a little store of road money, and withal some kindly advice about Hope's hair! The Secretary produced a pair of scissors of antique pattern, and suggested that we should make her look as much like a native child as possible, to avoid attraction. It went to my wife's heart to do it, but she saw the wisdom of the advice and bravely cut off the cherished locks.

And now we were bound for the Yellow River and the Hsien city of Yung-tsi on the other side. I do not know why, but the thought of safety seemed, in spite of everything, to connect itself with getting safely to the other side, and I longed intensely to see the barrier of its waters separating between us and terror. So the irrepressible hope and the inexpressible longing were again uppermost, in the mercy of God, and kept me stayed on Him in an expectation that I know was from Him.

Our soldier escort, however, was anything but satisfactory. Six in number, powerful looking and evil eyed, they crowded us up in the cart, and let us know right well that we had better take care how we behaved ourselves. These were the men who when I sought to speak to them of the grace of God turned on me fiercely with an order to desist, saying, "Stop that talk; don't you know that the Emperor has made it a state crime to preach the Jesus doctrine? Your Jesus has brought trouble enough to China; but China will have no more of Him now for ever." Those guarding the ladies occupied themselves with reading aloud our official papers, from which it appeared that the Wu-chi Mandarin had, with all his kindness, done nothing to relieve the misery of our condition offi- cially. No "uen-shu" was given us, to replace the criminal's "lu-p'iao." Whether it was in his power to do this or not I do not know; but judging from the strong independent action of some humane and noble-minded governors through whose hands foreigners passed, it seemed to be largely a question of the individual himself. However, the fact remains that neither as regards the mode of travel nor the billet assigned us at the end of the day's journey, was any difference made, or to be hoped for, over that accorded to the ordinary criminal. The soldiers commented with jocular satisfaction on the clause in the Lu-an paper relating to our dismissal from China, which they took to be an order for our official execution; an impression which had nothing to counteract it in the Wu-chi despatch, and which, therefore, bore its own fruit in their conduct towards us.

Not far from the Yellow River we were halted at a quiet wayside station, where we were mercifully free for once from crowd-inquisition and its horrors. The incident of our halt there, however, has survived in my memory not on this account, but because of a narrow escape we had from death at the hands of the escort. We did not appreciate at the time how near it had been; but in the light of after knowledge we felt that the Hand of God alone had held our soul in life. While we were eating, two of the soldiers entered and sat down before us.

"A few li more and we shall be at the River," they said. "There are great dangers there for you foreigners, and we can't undertake to get you safely across unless you pay us for our trouble."

The dismay such a demand struck into us may be imagined, for we had to keep a jealous watch upon our tiny store of cash, as the margin for daily living was none too large, and at any yamen (as, indeed, on one occasion we proved) even the criminal's rate of allowance stated in our papers 30 cash per head a day was liable to be withheld. However, without betraying our inner feelings, we replied good-humouredly, "Pay you for your trouble, good sirs? Why, it has nothing to do with us, as you know. This is a yamen matter; we are being forwarded by his Excellency of Wu-chi, and he has made himself responsible for all payments by the way, your own included."

"What the Lao-ie gives us won't nearly pay us for the risk we run. We must have so many hundred cash more per man or we can't do it."

Seeing that their manner was becoming dangerous, I said to the ladies that perhaps it would be wise to meet them half way, and strike a bargain for a certain sum; for to give them what they actually demanded would have more than exhausted the exchequer. How- ever, I was outvoted, and in deference to Miss Gates' wide experience in things Chinese, gave way to her strong conviction that to yield the position by so much as a hair's breadth would be fatal, encouraging them not only to increase their demand, but also to rob us of all that we had, under threat. So we gave a positive refusal to grant them a single cash. Time was given us to reflect upon our mad decision, and they left the room, to re-enter it shortly before the start in company with the rest of their comrades.

"Have you settled what you are going to give us?"

"We have told you once. We have but little more than the necessary food money for ourselves by the way, and the matter of your taking us across the River is not ours, but the Lao-ie's."

Abuse followed freely as they gave full vent to their rage, and when this failed to make the due impression they turned to threat. "Who but we can take you across in safety? Pay us the money we ask, or we will make off with the cart and leave you to find your way to Yung-tsi as best you can."

Their looks were terrible enough for anything, and made one inwardly tremble; but to retreat from the position now would be to run a greater hazard. To keep a firm, unflinching front with our eyes upon God was the only thing to do with these bullies; and we did it, without realizing the full gravity of what we were exposing ourselves to. Finding that we were immovable, they went out with the threat to abandon us on their lips and the longing to kill us outright in their eyes; and it is certain that nothing but the restraining Hand of God kept them from both one and the other. The rest of the journey to the River's bank was a period of much inward fear and crying to God; for every yard of the road we were liable to be set down and left to ourselves, if not (as appeared afterwards) to be actually set upon and despatched.

But the mercy of God brought us through; and with what mingled fear and joy we saw at length the turbid waves of the famous Huang Ho before us it is impossible to tell. The longing with which I looked across the broad mile of flood to the south bank, and prayed to be there! For we had now reached the assigned limit of escape. At Lan-chen Cheo it was affirmed that, even if we succeeded in getting so far, we could get no farther; and had not the escort just been warning us to the same effect? It was no idle rumour either; for subsequently, on reaching Hankow, we found a belief current, "on the best authority," that we had all been cut to pieces at the Yellow River as the result of an Imperial order to close the fords against all foreigners; and further hope of ever seeing us alive had consequently been abandoned.

The spot to which we were taken was a comparatively quiet one not one of the more important fords (like that, for instance, of Yu Men K'eo); or else the long wait at the riverside might have been attended by serious consequences. Possibly, as being out of the ordinary beat, it may not have been thought necessary to watch so unlikely a crossing. Anyhow, no guard of Imperial Boxers came forward to challenge us, and but few were there to take notice of us at all.

And yet how we got across God alone knows. Another attempt was made on the banks of the river to levy blackmail, and when they found us still im- movable, they sat down to discuss what course to take. For hours our lives hung in the balance. I believe we were as near death then as ever we had been hitherto, and a good deal nearer than we had any idea of at the time. It was not merely a matter of the soldiers, either. The ferrymen had to be taken into the reckoning. With the deepest concern we saw the supposed negotiations to take us over fall through. At any other time one would have thought nothing of it, accepting such delay as part of the ordinary experience of everyday travel in China; but every- thing was out of joint now times, conditions, nerves, everything. With an Imperial death-warrant Out against us, under circumstances of flight from a relentless pursuer, enemies on every side of us, our very escort threatening us, it was not to be expected that we could watch the dilatory processes of driving even the usual bargain with the usual equanimity much less where the bargain involved issues of life and death, and where moments were precious. For it amounted to nothing short of this on the one bank death, on the other life. And the frenzied hubbub of the bargainers had subsided in a sullen refusal to take us to the life side!

It was another opportunity for proving the power of God to keep him in perfect peace whose mind is stayed on Him. Our trust was in Him not in the escort nor in the boatmen, but in Him Whose it is to turn the heart whithersoever He will for the accomplishment of His purposes; and again we waited for our God.

The soldiers' irresolution as to what in the circumstances they had better do, kill or leave us, gave the ferrymen time to reconsider the advisability of securing a fare while they had a chance, and on the principle that half a loaf is better than none, they made a fresh advance. Whether the escort saw in it a welcome escape from an uncomfortable dilemma I cannot, of course, say. I only know that we saw in a satisfactory conclusion of the bargain the inter- vening Hand of our delivering God, as truly as did Israel of old when they went through the flood on foot; and there did we rejoice in Him. Planks were forthwith laid to the boat, and the carts rolled on board; the six mules were huddled into the well in the bows (not without some inconvenient demonstrations of passive resistance); the moorings were slipped, the sail hoisted, and we were being borne swiftly down the current of the mighty River from death to life.

Questions to Consider

1. Glover says that his description of the "undesirable side of the Chinese character" was not meant to disparage the Chinese but to point out the need for their evangelization. Do you think his story makes that point?

2. Applying the above idea to the present, do we avoid sharing "facts" about other cultures so that we don't appear to be bigoted or judgemental even though those "facts" should motivate us to share the gospel with those cultures?

CHAPTER TWENTY-TWO

From Prison to Prison

"But thanks be unto God which always leadeth us in triumph in Christ."

The crossing, which occupied some three hours, was effected without any noteworthy incident. There was nothing attractive about the monotonous dead-level of the banks on either side, nor could one exactly say that with two carts and six mules on board, plus escort and crew, the accommodation was all that could be desired. Yet the bliss of that sail on the bosom of the Huang Ho was beyond anything I have known, in past care-less days of pleasure on home waters.

The luxury of unconscious movement after the agony of the springless cart; the relaxation of spirit in the knowledge that, with another dreaded barrier past, and progress towards the goal steadily maintained, the chances of death were diminishing; and above all, the deep sweet peace of God, in presence of a fresh manifestation of His glorious power in our behalf; combined to lend a zest that constituted it the most memorable experience of its kind I have ever enjoyed.

We were not taken immediately to the opposite bank, but to a point at some considerable distance down, either for privacy, to ensure our greater safety, or as a more convenient landing-place for the route chosen. Beyond a traveller's booth or two, the deep cart-ruts from the water's edge, and the casual groups of riverside loafers waiting for a job, one would never have known it for a ford at all. As the boat drew in and touched bottom, truly it seemed to me, in spite of all we had heard of ugly rumour and gloomy forecast, that we had reached the farther shore of the Red Sea. "With His own right hand, and with His holy arm had He gotten Himself the victory;" and in the sight of it, the wilderness and the enemies on before could be calmly faced. As we set foot on "the other side," to which we had so often prayed and longed to be brought, in the will of God, it seemed too good to be true; and the only fitting language of the heart, in reviewing the way by which we had been led hither, was, "The Lord is my strength and song, and He is become my salvation."

An uncomfortable delay occurred, just at the moment when all was in readiness to resume the cart journey, due to a noisy demonstration by the boatmen. With the soldiers at their back, they came down upon us for "tsiu-ts'ien" (wine-money) a traveller's bonus or gratuity which custom has converted into an unwritten law, and which is practically demanded as a right. Strictly speaking, it was the escort's place to make it over to them, not ours; for we were Government prisoners, and were being taken on at Government expense. However, that was nothing to them. Having failed to pick our pockets directly, they would do it indirectly; for their moral support of the claim could never be so disinterested as to have no eye to the main chance. Happily, to give way now, without losing face, or forfeiting the principle for which we had before contended, was as possible as it was expedient. "Wine-money," at least, was not blackmail, and really in the spirit of a thank-offering, not grudgingly or of necessity, I handed them what I could out of sheer gratitude at finding oneself with a whole skin on the other side. It was reassuring to find that the bounty was received with every token of satisfaction; and for the remainder of the journey to Yung-tsi, we were left in peace.

Owing to the fact that we were unable to make any diary records, I can now do no more than present the reader with a general sketch of our journeyings through Ho-nan for the next eleven days, until we reached the city of Sin-yang Cheo, on the confines of the province of Hu-peh. During that period, we travelled on an average 90 H (30 miles) a day, or a distance of between 300 and 400 miles, in the course of which we passed through the yamen of ten cities (including Yung-tsi) in the following order:

CART
July 15. Yung-tsi Hsien
July 16. Cheng-cheo
July 17. Sin-cheng Hsien
July 18. Hu-cheo
July 19. Yin-ling Hsien

July 20. Yen-ch'eng Hsien
July 21. Si-p'ing Hsien
July 22. Sui-p'ing Hsien
July 23. (On the road).

BARROW
July 24. K'ioh-shan Hsien.
July 25. (On the road).
July 26. Sin-yang Cheo.

An uninteresting list of odd-sounding names; but how many a picture does it conjure up before my mind! How many a variation does it strike from the chords of memory, of joy and sorrow, hope and depression, comfort and disappointment! Against each of those names must be written the word "prison"; and between each successive name and the next must be read the sufferings of prisoners en route to prison.

We had now reached the period of fiercest heat, and henceforth until the end of our journeyings we had to face the "dog days" of the abnormally hot summer. Yet, severe as was the ordeal, I have often thanked God that our flight was "not in the winter." Nothing more distressing can I imagine than a condition of things of the kind we had to endure, under the rigours of excessive cold. Stripped as we were of even the necessaries of life (let alone the comforts) with nothing but a thin calico garment next the skin, I do not see how we could have survived it. And yet, in face of what we did survive, I fear to say even this much; for the seasons are God's; and, if

His will be so, He can work for him that waiteth for Him not less effectually in cold than in heat.

At every yamen the rumours we had heard at Wu- chi were confirmed, so that (as I have already said) we were kept in a state of perpetual uncertainty as to what was awaiting us on before. The continual expect- tation of attack by the way, with the possibility of execution at the hands of the next Mandarin, created a nervous tension which nothing but communion with God could relieve. When we came within sight of the city whither we were bound, I cried in my heart, "O God, carry us out of it in peace, if it be Thy will"; and when we left it, in the new joy of a fresh experience of answered prayer, it was still to pray, in view of the next city ahead, "my God, for Thy glory go before; and carry us in in peace, even as heretofore." For when we left a yamen, we never knew what might befall us on the street ere we reached the gate of exit; and when we entered a city gate, with the certainty of a following mob, riot might assail us even before we reached the yamen precincts. In covering the distance, too, between city and city, what eventualities might not occur in the meeting of an idol procession, the encountering of theatricals, or the lighting upon a fair; not to mention the always possible display of anti- foreign feeling at any time, in any town or hamlet we passed through. So, whether it were hamlet, town, city, or yamen, we prayed our way in and we prayed it out.

Generally speaking, it was a time of hanging in simple faith upon God, apart from any special realization of His nearness. But there were occasions when the consciousness of the Divine environing was such that I knew it as certainly as

Elisha in Dothan or Paul in Corinth. At those rare and blessed times, in the very midst of excited mobs, every particle of fear vanished, and I realized nothing but the serenity of an absolute security, the conviction of which I would seek to impart to my little son, saying, "We have nothing to fear, darling boy. These people have no power to hurt us, for the Lord God has covered us with His wing. Our real guard is, not these Chinese soldiers, but God's bright angels; and if he were to open our eyes, as He did the eyes of Elisha's servant, we should see just the same sight as he saw horses and chariots of fire round about us."

At the close of our long day's weary ride, we were usually lodged either in the guard room or in a cell immediately adjoining that occupied by convicts. The former was, as a rule, only divided off from the common prison by a barrier of strong wooden bars, within which the chained criminals were caged like beasts. The clanking of their fetters gave indication of their whereabouts before the eye had become sufficiently accustomed to the perpetual gloom to detect it; and then how sad and revolting the sight that revealed itself! a sight the horror of which never grew less, familiar as we became with it. Thank God, we were spared the fate, meted out to some of our brethren, of being thrust in among them. Even as it was, the near neighbourhood of such a place was enough to sicken one; though indeed the heart went out to them poor darkened souls, fast bound in the misery and iron of a more terrible captivity than that which was seen!

One such guard room stands out before me with peculiar distinctness. I remember the utter weariness and bodily distress of our condition when we were driven into the huge yamen courtyard, and the more than usual difficulty we had to face in the swarming thousands that hedged us in. It was one of those occasions to which I have referred when the runners and soldiers failed to make any impression on the mob until the bamboo was brought into play; for we were left where we were set down, until definite orders from the Lao-ie had been received. We were then hustled to the guard room and locked in until dark. It was, I think, the strangest room I was ever in for old-world curiosity. In the centre of the room, facing the entrance, was an elaborate structure of ornamental wood, carved in the rudest and most grotesque style of the most pronounced Chinese type, its tawdry monsters and pagodas thick in immemorial dust and curtained with cobwebs. The design was ludicrously childish, and looked like a huge toy transplanted from some barbaric nursery. Doubtless it had a religious significance, as occupying the place of (or possibly enshrining) the usual votive tablet. From the low ceiling, slung on nails, were rows of the mushroom-shaped, red-tasseled hats worn by the yamen folk, and the filthy walls were hung with a medley of pre-historic arms, cudgels, uniforms and accoutrements. At the farther end of the room from where we had been ordered to lie was the strong barrier, separating from the prison, from behind the bars of which peered the eerie faces of the victims of crime. They talked and laughed freely with the gaoler on duty over the latest addition to their numbers in the persons of the "foreign devils," with their eyes intent upon us. The arrival of meal- time created a diversion in favour of their stomachs, when the food was pushed in through a sliding panel and taken greedily, amid much rattling of chains, as though it were the one event of the day. Lying on rush mats, or lounging on benches round the room, half naked, the twelve or fifteen men comprising the guard smoked their opium and tobacco, while they indulged in the coarse and boisterous hilarity common to their class. In our state of exhaustion, the noise was distracting and the stench insufferable; while so vitiated was the whole moral atmosphere that we could not but pray to be delivered from having to pass the night in it. An earnest representation, on the ground of my wife's critical state of health, met with better success than I had dared to hope for; and a runner was at last des- patched to negotiate an interview for us with one of the secretaries, with a view to getting a change of quarters. In the tender mercy of God, he returned with the marvellous news that "the Chang-fang" (Bursar?) "would see us"; and under his guidance Miss Gates and I sallied forth by lantern light to the inter- view. Nothing could have been outwardly kinder than the reception accorded us. Our request was readily complied with; and though the change was still to prison quarters in another part of the courtyard, and the cell allotted to us a dismantled building with the roof half off and strewn with debris, yet we had the unspeakable comfort of being alone, in quietness and fresh air; and before that, the minor inconveniences disappeared.

On this occasion our abode, though part of the prison buildings and adjacent to the convict cells, was detached from them, so that we enjoyed the rare luxury of real privacy. So much so indeed, that I was not aware that we were in ward at all, until a little incident revealed it. Our door having been left open, and finding therefore that we were free to go in and out at our own sweet will, I indulged my liberty to the extent of making a little tour of inspection. A narrow passage from the door led to a small quadrangle where, in a line with our own tiny room, I found myself before a long low building. In the darkness I did not notice that the door was fitted with the unmistakable bars, and I stood there trying curiously to pierce the secrets of the gloom within, when they were revealed, with a shock that made me recoil, by the clank of chains. At the same moment a figure rose from a bench close by and confronted me with a surly challenge, and the order to get back to my own quarters. I realized then that we were actually in the yamen prison and under surveillance. This was disquieting, to say the least, as tending to create the dread that the kindly reception given us was only official "hsu-kia," veiling other motives and sinister designs.

We were not always so fortunate in our accommodation. Indeed, I remember this cramping crumbling cabin as the most wholesome of its kind in our experience. Once we were locked for several hours into a dark and noisome hole, some ten feet by six, with the narrowest of arrow slits in the thick brick wall, opening off a small courtyard two sides of which were prison cages filled with victims. It was only the "t'ai-t'ai's" interest in the children that under God was the means of saving us from the otherwise certain misery of a night there. The usual thing was a small dark filthy room, destitute of furniture in any shape or form, plentiful in vermin, and reeking with miasma. One scarcely dared to look at the floor before lying down. The offensive odour, that could not be disguised, told its own story; and we could only ask for grace to endure it.

I gladly turn from such a subject, distressful still, even in the memory of it. Our prison experiences were not all darkness. Gleams of light from time to time broke through to cheer us, tokens always of the merciful kindness of Him Who had never left us, and Whose word was pledged never to forsake us. Three times the children were sent for by one and another Mandarin at their wives' request, and treated with great kindness. On one of these occasions. Miss Gates was allowed to accompany them to the official apartments; on the other two they were summoned alone. There was no help for it — the order was imperative; and though our hearts sank at the thought, we were obliged to submit. I remember how my wife's eyes filled, and how I felt myself, as we watched the two babes, in sweet obedience to our wish, tearfully but without remonstrance walk the length of the court- yard hand in hand under the runner's charge, and then disappear within the inner enclosure. For how did we know that we should not be put to death, and they retained, to be adopted and brought up in the yamen? In point of fact, at one of the yamens we passed through, so charmed were the ladies with the "iang ua-tsi" (foreign babes) that the idea of adoption was not only entertained, but the proposal actually made, the Mandarin offering to buy them of us, in the assurance that, under such conditions of poverty, we could never be proof against the temptation of so handsome a bid! I need not say their reappearance was hailed with intense relief and thanksgiving; and that, not merely on the score of their safe restoration to us, but because of the tokens for good which they brought with them, in the shape of choice confectionery and strings of cash. Our heads were safe, we felt, for that night at least, and we could lay them down in peace. The recollection of one other such occasion lingers pleasantly in my memory, when, however, the order of proceeding was reversed, and instead of the children visiting the yamen, the yamen came to visit the children. We were actually honoured with a visit in our prison quarters from the "t'ai-t'ai" and her family, accom- panied by several ladies of her suite. It was a great event for us; and, notice having been given beforehand, we had time to make such preparations as the circumstances would admit. In due course they arrived without pomp or fuss of any kind, just walking (or rather hobbling) in, in a simple natural way, and taking the chairs placed for them in the tiny courtyard. The rich hues of their embroidered silks and the bright coloured garments of the children contrasted strangely with our own forlorn appearance and squalid surroundings; but everything gave way before the satisfaction of seeing real live foreign babies, and the outward demonstrations of friendly interest were lively and voluble to a degree. The family consisted of three dear little girls, the eldest about ten, whose manners were as engaging as their looks, and gave one the impression of their having received the nearest thing to a careful training conceivable to China. When the shy reserve began to thaw, and the first feelings of rather fearful curiosity to give way before the discovery that the little strangers were flesh and blood like herself, it was pretty to see the eldest child take them by the hand and prattle to them in her own vernacular. The many days of terror, pain, and privation, had left their mark upon our darlings; and the merry laugh and dancing smile habitual to them before had now faded quite away. Only a settled sadness in the wan little face was left to tell its own tale of what they had passed through so sad and so settled that it seemed as though they could never laugh again. The little girl's parting gift of sweetmeats did just succeed in recovering the faintest reminiscence of a smile, as the sight of "goodies" lit up the listless features for one brief moment, and they bowed their thanks in native fashion. So kindly was this good lady disposed towards us that later on she sent the children a further gift of money and— most welcome of all all — "pi-tsi" (or wadded quilt) to sleep on. The Lord remember it to her!

This was not the only "cup of cold water" given us during these eleven days, to call out praise to God and prayer for the givers. Another "t'ai-t'ai," also after a visit from the children, sent a "pi-tsi" as a small offermg to their mother a gift which touched us the more that some such provision had become a matter of really vital importance to my wife, and had been made a subject of definite prayer. Now and again one and another article of clothing would come in for the little ones, until we had quite a bundle of goods (tiny enough, truly, but still a bundle) which we could call our own. Perhaps the most serviceable end it answered, whether "pi-tsi" or bundle, was to be sat upon; and oh, the unspeakable comfort of having something between bone and board in the awful cart and barrow rides something soft, and (in the case of the cart) something slightly higher than the level of one's feet!

One burning day we were set down in the late after- noon at the yamen of our destination, and, after the usual exciting preliminaries, taken to the guard room. The crowd grew to such dimensions, and became so hopelessly unmanageable in their feverish anxiety to get near us, that at length the guard ordered me outside, if perhaps a good long stare at me might allay their suspicions and quiet their feelings. A chair was set in the midst of this seething mass of latent riot; and there I sat for something like a couple of hours in benign loneliness, striving to convey the impression of innocence by look and manner where speech was denied me. What was my dismay when a man came pressing through the dense crowd, elbowed his way to where I was sitting, and, addressing me as "sheng fu " (holy father), prostrated himself before me and made the "k'eh t'eo" by striking the forehead thrice upon the ground. The man was of course a Roman Catholic; and I knew well that if the suspicion once gained ground that we were his co-religionists, certain riot and death were before us. I instantly rose, therefore, and, dragging him to his feet, told him, with much warmth and in a voice intended for all the bystanders to hear, that such an act was an offence to me; that the Je-su Kiao (Protestant Church) and the T'ien Chu Kiao (Roman Catholio Church) were two separate and distinct churches; that the one had no "lai-uang" (intercourse) with the other; and that as I belonged to the Je-su Kiao, I could have nothing to do with him. However, he persisted in having his say to the effect that he was himself a refugee, the church to which he belonged having been broken up by the Boxers; and that hearing of the arrival of a priest(!) in the city, he had come to bring me the sad tidings and to warn me that we could never hope to get through. I told the poor fellow I was sincerely sorry for him in his distress, and commended him to the mercy of God; but anything beyond this would have been utterly misconstrued. It was not the time to show feeling appreciative of his professed sympathy with myself, especially when he dropped on his knees again and produced as his credentials a Roman prayer book with a coloured picture slipped inside of his patron saint "St. Joseph!" I had to be loud in my Protestant protestations, and stern in my determination to know nothing of him and his ilk; and I begged him to begone. This vigorous action revealed what had been working in the mind of the people. They had suspected us of being Romanists; and now that the suspicion was removed by my open repudiation of the T'ien Chu Kiac, the tide of feeling turned, and my "Job's comforter" was hustled off with more haste than ceremony to the outskirts of the crowd, when he made the best of his way out and I saw him no more.

From that time their lively demonstrations died away, and ere long we were left in comparative quiet. A considerable number still visited us out of pure curios- ity in the guard room; among whom was one old woman, who evinced a really touching sympathy for us. She sat on and on talking with Miss Gates and drinking in the words of eternal life, as if they were to her in very truth "living waters"; and when at last she had most reluctantly to go, having noticed that the " kiao-si's" little rush fan was worn literally to shreds, she presented her with her own a gift which at such a time was valued, not only as a precious boon in itself, but yet more as a gracious token of unsuspected love.

The treatment dealt out to us by the Mandarins of these various cities was, speaking generally, of such a character as to leave the impression that, whether for or against us, they were anxious one and all to be rid of us and to shunt the awkward business of extreme measures, entailed by our unfortunate arrival, on to the next man. It was clearly a case of wishing us farther and washing their hands of as much of the responsibility as they conveniently could. For this reason we were invariably refused an audience with one notable exception which I may here relate.

A grave period of suspense awaited us at Yung-tsi, where the question of no "uen-shu" almost decided the Lao-ie to send us back across the River. Other counsels prevailed, however; and for reasons known only to himself and God, he deemed it expedient to pass us on to his next door neighbour of Cheng-cheo. Possibly he knew the temper of the man and judged that the method he was certain to employ would be a shorter and easier solution than his own, of the problem, "What to do with the foreign devils?" Accordingly to Cheng-cheo we were sent.

Arrived at the city, enormous crowds thronged us to the yamen, the courtyard of which was soon a sight to behold. We were dismounted about the centre of the great square, and left as usual to shift for ourselves. The natural instinct of self preservation led us to seek refuge as near the gates of the second courtyard as we could: for access there would (we argued) be the more readily granted if we were found to be close at hand in the dire event of trouble. The gates were approached from a broad platform, which in its turn was reached by a flight of some dozen long stone steps. To a position at the base of these steps we made the best of our poor way.

It being early afternoon, the sun's power was still excessive, and with the pressure and growing restlessness of the great multitudes the heat was distressing. Presently the gate opened, and the "men-shang" (or Mandarin's deputy), holding our papers in his hand, stepped forward to the edge of the platform and ordered us to stand before him. So there on the topmost step we stood, behind us a troubled sea of excitability, and before us a face to make one tremble. We were then put through an examination much as follows, Miss Gates being the chief speaker :

"What country do you foreign devils come from?"

"Your Excellency's Little children are from Great England."

"And how far off may Great England be?"

"Thirty thousand 'li' of water " (i.e. 10,000 miles by sea).

"Ai-ia! You have not come all that distance to the Middle Kingdom for nothing. What are you here for?

"We are here because we have been sent here by the one living and true God, the Creator and Saviour of all men, to preach the glad news of His salvation for all men, through the forgiveness of their sins."

"To be sure. You are of the T'ien Chu Kiao " (the Roman Catholic religion).

"No we have nothing whatever to do with the T'ien Chu Kiao. We are of the Je-su Kiao. The two religions are separate and distinct."

"Je-su Kiao? Je-su Kiao?" (with a scowl). "But what else have you come to this country for, besides preaching?"

"For nothing else."

"Don't tell me you are not here to make money out of us. What's your 'mai-mai'?" (trade).

"We have no 'mai-mai' Our sole work is to persuade men to repent and turn to God from idols, by believing in Jesus His Son, who died for them and rose again from the dead."

"And pray, how long have you been in the country preaching this doctrine?"

Miss Gates answered for herself, "Fourteen years; and I for myself and family, "Three years."

Fixing his eyes on my queue, he sneered, " You only three years, and grown all that hair? That's too good! Where have you been residing in China?"

"In the province of Shan-si, at the prefectural city of Lu-an."

"In Shan-si Lu-an Fu, eh? And where are you going now?"

"We are going back for a time to our own land, and are on our way to Han-kow."

"Oh yes, of course," he sneered again; "skulking out of the country. And for what reason, I should like to know?"

"It is not by our own wish that we are going. Your Excellency knows well that we have no choice in the matter, owing to the disturbances created by the Ta Tao Huei."

Such a reference to the Patriotic League of Boxers brought out the latent fury. Pointing to the papers that quivered in his hand and glaring the passion with which he shook, he thundered, "I'll tell you what you are. You are a parcel of runaways, and you shall be dealt with accordingly."

This was an evident allusion to Yu-hsien's order that all foreigners resident in Shan-si were to be forwarded direct to him at the provincial capital of T'ai-yuen Fu, in accordance with the Imperial decree issued for our extermination; and harmonized with the report in circulation that the fords of the Yellow River were to be closed against fugitives from that province.

The ominous manner of the man and his yet more ominous utterance could not fail to arouse the gravest apprehension for our safety. It seemed only too evident that we were in the hands of a Boxer official of the Yu-hsien type; and if the order for our destruction were not carried out there, it would only be to give the Shan-si murderer the satisfaction of doing the deed himself, seeing that we belonged to his jurisdiction. The "runaways" were to be sent back, or the "men- shang's" words had no meaning.

He had scarcely finished speaking when who should present himself at the gate but the Ta Lao-ie himself. And now was enacted one of the most extraordinary and withal most shameful scenes in all our varied experience of either. In the fever of his passion, he had not allowed himself time even to robe; and he hurried on to the platform bare-headed and fighting his way into a soiled gown. Official etiquette could be dispensed with where the "iang kuei-tsi" were in question. Ordinary decorum even was thrown away on such scum. And so we were treated with the contempt we deserved, a contempt that came back upon himself (poor wretched old man!) in sincere pity that he should make himself thus vile in the eyes of his people.

From the moment of his appearance, the Mandarin's mouth was filled with cursing and bitterness, launched against us with all the vehemence of frenzy. Pacing the platform like one possessed, he stormed and raved and raved and stormed, hurling invective and anathema with an exhaustless energy that could only be of the devil. At length, wheeling suddenly upon me he said, (or rather shrieked), into my face:

"You 'devils' ought to have your heads off, every one of you do you hear? Do you know that there is an Imperial Edict out for your destruction? You may thank your lucky stars that I don't behead you here and now: indeed, it is only by the greatest stretch of mercy that I spare you."

As he spoke, he suited the action to the word, and with the edge of his hand chopped and sawed my neck so violently that

I felt the blow for hours afterwards. Then, having delivered himself thus far, he disappeared within the gate.

I had not been able to follow fully and connectedly the gist of his remarks, but had already concluded from the manner of their delivery that they boded nothing else than our execution. When, however, the practical demonstration of his meaning was given, by the very action of beheadal, all room for doubt was taken away, and turning to the ladies I said:

"There is to be no miscarriage of the death sentence
this time. He means to cut off our heads without a
shadow of a doubt."

Imagine my relief when Miss Gates was able to re- assure me by giving the exact tenor of his words as quoted above, and the meaning of his action as inter- preted in their light! But really I do not know which was the greater the sense of relief or of amazement that came over me. The virulence of his hate against us was such as to exceed anything we had yet experienced, in the way of official malevolence openly expressed. To believe it possible that, animated by such feelings and with every facility at his disposal for gratifying them in the way most agreeable to himself, he should yet hesitate to put us to death, was out of the question on any mere natural hypothesis. I cannot sufficiently emphasize the miraculous nature of our escape on this occasion. The following elements in the situation will serve to illustrate it in some degree.

To begin with, there was the violent antipathy of the Mandarin to the foreigner, as such. Then, the Imperial Edict ordering our destruction was in full force at this time, and was fully known to him. For, a week later, when the Saunders-Cooper party arrived at Cheng-cheo, they were treated to a repetition of much the same splenetic conduct on the part of the old Lao-ie, who, however, informed them that in exercising the prerogative of mercy, he was able to do so only and solely in virtue of a counter-edict from the Throne, issued but a few hours before their arrival, whereby the previous edict of extermination was annulled, and all foreigners were to be afforded safe conduct to the coast.(1) The question then naturally arises How came it that we, who were covered at the time of our arrival by no such safeguard, should have been let off? The more I think of it, the more inexplicable does it seem, and the more marvellous.

The "counter-edict" referred to would seem to have been the one that was issued by telegram, the original text of which only the more urgently enforced the decree of extermination. The two officials, however. who were charged with its transmission, with daring courage altered the fatal word "shah" (kill) into the word "pao" (protect), and the revised form in which it was actually issued, instead of reading (as the Empress Dowager intended it should), "All foreigners are to be killed without fail. If they withdraw (to the coast) they are none the less certainly to be killed" — ran thus: "All foreigners are to be protected without fail. If they withdraw (to the coast) they are none the less certainly to be protected." For this heroic act, both officials were seized and put to death with cruel torture.

Another extraordinary factor against our escape at this time was the powerful incitement offered to the people by word and deed to be instant in requiring our destruction if not actually to rise up and compass it themselves. Thousands in the vast area behind us were eager witnesses of the whole scene, and the blood- thirsty intentions of their chief could not be mis-read by them. The ravings of his fury, even if they were not heard by all, could be seen by all; and when they culminated in the acted suggestion of murder, it was enough to inflame them to the point of murder themselves. If ever a mob would have been justified in giving full vent to their anti-foreign feeling, it would have been the mob then gathered within the yamen precints of Cheng-cheo. And why they did not can never be explained on any principle of natural causes. I think there can be no question that the old Mandarin, in taking the line he did, had this very object in view of stirring up the people to demand our immediate execution, that the ultimate responsibility might (in the event of a future inquiry) be referred to the uncontrollable action of the multitude. Yet they made no attack upon us, nor even a demonstration against us. Those who know the Chinese will be able to estimate the phenomenon at its true value.

Thus God wrought for us at Cheng-cheo. It was a notable miracle, not only by reason of the fact that we were not put to death there, but also that neither were we sent back (as seemed the inevitable alternative) to Shan-si. Nay, more. In the short interval that we spent there — for small carts were brought and we were packed off to the next "hsien" with as little delay as possible- God touched the heart of the savage "men-shang" with something of compassion for the children; and when we left that terrible enclosure, we were the richer by a money gift of a thousand cash (made to them in sums of 600 each), and how vastly richer in the experience of the mighty love and keeping power of our God! We could say as literally, in our measure, as Israel said of old, that not only had He brought us forth, but that He had "brought us forth also with silver and gold."

The treatment we received at the next yamen (Sin-clieng Hsien) was a gracious contrast to the terrors of Cheng-cheo. The Mandarin himself, it is true, refused to see us; but his chief secretary was exceedingly kind. On examining our papers, he had found that there was no regular "uen-shu," and at once sent for us to inquire into the matter. It was a dreadful moment when he turned to me with, "There is no 'uen-shu' here. How is this? "The natural sequel would have been, "I have no alternative but to send you back; for I have no authority to forward you;" and my heart stood still as I waited for the next word after our ex- planations had been made. For some minutes he conferred with his colleagues, and then said, "I will do the best I can for you;" the result being a document as nearly equivalent to the coveted passport as it was possible to frame. The unaffected graciousness of his manner was in harmony with the kindness of this official act, and one could not but realize how truly noble the Chinese magnate is, when seen to advantage, as in this case. Whatever merit his memorandum possessed, it certainly seemed to lay the "uen-shu" difficulty once for aU. Not that it could so settle the matter, I suppose, as to make it impossible for successive Mandarins to do other than send us forward; but the fact remains that we heard no more of it, and were sent forward in every case without any known demur.

Why we were not sent back from K'ioh-shan Hsien (or something worse)can only be explained to my mind by the fact that the supposed "edict of protection," mentioned above, had just come to hand, much to the Mandarin's disgust, if one may judge from his behaviour. In my dear wife's increasingly suffering condition, I sought an audience, with a view to getting some amelioration of our prison hardships, only to meet with an insulting refusal. When the hour of departure came, we found that the journey was to be continued by barrow, the cart being considered too luxurious a mode of conveyance for such vile stuff; and thence- forth we travelled under conditions to which even the cart was comfort. Not only so, but we were sent off without so much as the prison allowance for food being made us for the road 30 cash per head the only instance where we were so deprived.

Barrow travelling under ordinary conditions can, I believe, be made, not only tolerable, but actually agreeable. Where you are in sound health, and can command your barrowmen, furnish your barrows, and make your own dispositions, going when you please and halting where you please, all well and good. But where you have no choice in the matter, either as to barrows, men, time, place, physical condition, or any- thing else well, try it and see. I can scarcely wish you a worse fate than barrow journeying after the manner of Chinese criminals.

With a record of eighteen days of sufferings such as I have related behind us, our fitness for this kind of travel may be imagined. The barrow is driven by two men, one pushing behind, the other pulling in front. We occupy a narrow board, one on either side of the single central wheel, which is protected by a wooden encasement, dividing us. Our back is to the direction in which we are going, and we have to arrange for the accommodation of our legs as best we can; only it must on no account be in such a way as to disturb the balance of the machine, or we shall hear of it again, if not in the way of an ugly spill, yet certainly in the way of ugly words from either Jehu. Possibly the barrow may be fitted with the semblance of a "p'eng" — that is, a single strip of straw matting above us, tied to a flimsy rod of bent bamboo. If so, we are fortunate. But we are still more fortunate if the matting does not gape in seams or part from the strings. The great merit, however, of our barrow is the sweet music it discourses in the ears of its drivers — wheel-melodies from out the box in the centre, to which the creaking of an ungreased cart wheel would be as Mendelssohn to a hurdy-gurdy. No orthodox barrowman would ever dream of running a silent barrow. The hideous screech that shreds the nerves is the hall mark of his line. He would as soon be without his professional creak as the coster without his cry. One slight alleviation is possible to the agony of ruthless jolt and crash in the shape of a thick hempen tyre, which can be fitted to the wheel when the nature of the road is such as to require it. But alas for us! when we entreat this kindness of them, our barrowmen invariably find that the nature of the road does not require it.

So we journey on, under the burning sun. At intervals of so many 'li', wayside booths are erected for the refreshment of travellers, generally a mere shanty of mud and stubble, occasionally a more substantial building of "t'u-p'ei" (sun-dried bricks); but always in either case a structure of thatch, however slender, before it, with tables, benches, and ever grateful shade. To pause here for a short five minutes, moisten the parched lips with a sip of water, or a slice of melon, and throw one's self on the ground in utter weariness to ease the aching stiffness, is the one thing longed for and the next event looked forward to. How many times have I seen my poor wife and Miss Gates just drop from the barrow where it stopped and lay themselves down right there! The picture rises before me as I write of these two dear sufferers lying thus under a burning sun full stretch in the dust, for lack of other resting room, too weary and worn for words.

When, on arrival at our destination, we had at length been installed in our prison quarters, we would give our thoughts of course to the relief of our immediate needs. If a runner could be readily found for a "tip" to supply them at once, we were happy indeed. Often enough we had to wait some hours before food was brought to us, depending on the chance kindness of the guard for a cup of " k'ai-shui " (hot drinking water) in the meantime. Water in anything like sufficient quantity for purposes of ablution was a luxury to be dreamed of, perhaps, but never enjoyed. If, after the children had been washed, we contrived to get the small hand bowl replenished for our three selves, we looked upon it as a mercy of no small degree. Many a time have we washed in turn, all five of us, in the same water, and barely two pints of it at that. Occasionally we have longed in vain for water at all, and simply had to go without. The dog days, too!

In her tender care of the little ones my wife was as characteristically thorough as in her own home. Her strong sense of parental duty, combined with the devotion of a truly wonderful mother-love, led her to fulfil these nursery ministries with her own hands almost to the last that is, until her strength was absolutely gone. The fact that she became, towards the end of the flight, unequal to the task was a more alarming symptom to me of the real exhaustion of her state than any other. Often and often did we entreat her to allow one of us to take her place while she rested; but the grateful smile that accompanied the refusal, as she avowed herself quite equal to her own loved work, was always to be taken as final. The "sheo-kin" (or coarse calico square) that served to shelter their head by day was the "Turkish glove"; and the towel my one and only gown, of which I divested myself for the purpose. As far as it was possible to do so, she kept their hair decent with the use of the wooden comb, and with infinite pains cleansed their clothes from vermin. To her extreme care I attribute, under God, the really remarkable healing of their sun wounds. In answer to definite prayer, the raw blisters, which at one time showed ugly signs of suppuration, dried and cicatrised most satisfactorily; and by the time we reached Sin-yang Cheo, there was scarcely a trace of them to be seen. But more than this, I have not the slightest doubt that her devotion saved their lives. When food was difficult to get and scarcely to be had, I have known her frequently to give her own portion to them at a time when nourishment, however meagre, was to her a vital necessity. Her jealousy to secure them their proper rest, in the day time as well as by night, watched ceaselessly to that end; and never did she lay herself down until she was satisfied that they were as comfortable as she could make them.

One thing we had occasion to be devoutly thankful for. We were never once put in irons. This is note- worthy, as it must ever be borne in mind that until we reached the city of K'ioh-shan Hsien, the edict for our destruction was in full force, and our prison treatment at every yamen spoke to the fact. Once only were we warned that at the next city we should be chained, since the "Hsien" was notorious for dealing thus with his prisoners. We laid our trouble before God, willing, if it were for His glory, to suffer hardship even unto bonds; and on arrival, while we scarcely dared to look for any other than his usual treatment at the hard official's hands, we found an abundant answer to our prayers, not only in the fact that we were spared the threatened suffering of chains, but that we ex-perienced a measure of leniency beyond all expectation.

Another gracious fact I may also note here. By the route we followed, south of the Yellow River, we saw nothing more of the Ta Tao Huei. Pro-Boxers were rife enough in towns and cities; but the Boxer proper, with his distinctive badge and bearing, was nowhere in evidence. I also remarked that the use of the offensive term "iang kuei-tsi" (foreign devils), as applied to ourselves, became the exception rather than the rule, nothing harsher than the term "iang ren" (foreigners) taking its place. This was a greater relief to the mind than it is at all possible to convey to the home reader. The ominous hiss of the former expression affected the nerves until it became a positive terror, suggestive as it always was of the spirit of active hatred which might easily turn to murder; while in places where the milder "iang ren" was in vogue one usually found that such fears might be laid aside.

Indeed, the country folk were, on the whole, quiet and inoffensive, and gave no cause for serious alarm. How far this attitude would have been maintained had we made a prolonged stay among them is a question. Experience showed only too plainly that, as a rule, a couple of hours or so in any place was long enough. There were times when we had to hurry through a village or market town in instant fear of the threatening crowds that hooted us. Twice only were we allowed to sleep on the road, when the stages proved to be extra long; and then we were not dismounted, in the one case, till midnight, when all would be quiet and our arrival unobserved ; while in the other, having been overtaken by rain, we were securely lodged in a "kong-kuan" (or official inn) with a strong escort at the gate.

The staple food on which we subsisted was rice — "kan-fan" (dry rice) and "hsi-fan" (wet rice). Some- times we were able to vary it with raw eggs and a preparation of bean-curd, which looked and tasted not unlike junket, and was of a delicious coolness. For delicacies water-melons and an occasional cucumber about exhaust the list. The usual drink was an infusion of leaves (either beech or elm, as far as I could judge) of a pale tea brown colour, and dignified by the name of "ch'a" (tea). When served hot it was not disagreeable, but lukewarm it was sickening. Thirst, however, never panders to the palate, and we eagerly took with thanksgiving whatever came to hand. Sometimes we could get neither "ch'a" nor "k'ai-shui," when we were glad to drink from the well or the water-butt, regardless of the rules of hygiene. On one occasion, I remember, at a wayside shanty, where we had halted for a few minutes, we called for "ch'a" in almost an agony of thirst. The soldiers and barrowmen, however, were draining the last drop of the slender supply, and nothing was left but water from the butt. The first draught fell to my wife, and the next to the children; but what was my dismay, when my turn came, to find it simply putrid! So thirsty was my wife that she had not noticed it! Death was in that pot to a certainty, and I could only pray God to keep us from the natural effects of such a potion. In course of time, the want of variety of food, along with the unappetizing character of the supply, almost nauseated one, and made eating a real penance. The dry rice was too dry, and the wet rice too wet; and even the "ts'ai" and the "ts'u" (vegetable and vinegar) failed to make it relishable. One happy day I found a man at a wayside booth selling a drink I had never heard of before, which he called "t'ien tsiu" "wine of heaven." Fearing that it might bear some suspicious relation to the ordinary Chinese "tsiu" — a spirit much like brandy — I hesitated to taste it; but on being assured by Miss Gates, who knew it of old, that it was an unfermented drink corresponding very much to our lemonade, my teetotal scruples were at rest, and I invested in eight cash worth. Oh, the luxury of that draught! "Wine of heaven" indeed it was to me and to us all a most gracious gift from the hand of our Father in heaven. I never think of that chance (?) find without giving thanks again to God for what was in very truth a signal mercy.

The treatment we experienced at the hands of the soldiers of the escort was not invariably harsh. Any- thing like real kindness was exceptional; but a negative attitude of not unkindly indifference was by no means uncommon. Even a rough geniality would betray itself on occasion towards the little ones, with whom they would play and joke as we jolted along, when a weary smile would come back to the children's eyes, as though they were too strange to it and too tired for it now. Two dear fellows gave us their "sheo-kin" to protect our heads, whereby we were each provided for in that way; and we seldom appealed to them in vain when we found difficulty in catering for our- selves on the road. There were times, indeed, when we sincerely regretted parting with one escort for another, especially if the change would not bear comparison. Many a time I have thanked God for the way those soldiers did their duty by us. One illustration must suffice. We came to a large village market, on entering which it became at once apparent that mischief was brewing. The people swarmed about the barrows with curses and threats, and had the guard wavered for a moment it would have gone hard with us. They hedged us in, however a little bodyguard of eight amid thronging hundreds ready to charge at the first suspicion of attack: and so we traversed the long stony street, expecting every moment to be engulfed, ourselves and our defenders. The mob pressed us to the gate, and then prepared to stone us; whereupon the escort turned and charged, and the crowd broke and disappeared.

Thus, amid all our varying trials and perils, God proved Himself to be still our God, faithful and true. And thus, with Him for refuge and strength, we passed on through the length of beautiful and fearful Ho-nan, until we came in His safe keeping to the border city of Sin-yang Cheo, on the confines of the province of Hu-peh.

Questions to Consider

1. The two Chinese officials who changed the orders from "kill" to "protect" saved the lives of many. "For this heroic act, both officials were seized and put to death with cruel torture." Had you been in such a position as those two officials, would you have changed the orders in order to save innocent people?

CHAPTER TWENTY-THREE

Christ's Hospital

"O my God, my soul is cast down within me.
Why art thou cast down, O my soul ?
and why art thou disquieted within me?
Hope thou in God, for I shall yet praise Him,
Who is the health of my countenance, and my God."
(Ps. xlii. 6, 11)

Our arrival at Sin-yang Cheo introduced a phase of
experience materially different in several important particulars
from that which we had hitherto known. The whole period of
our second flight falls naturally at this point into two distinct
parts; for not only did the date of our arrival divide it all but
exactly (Thursday, July 26, completing the third week), but
the character of the almost three weeks of captivity that
remained to us was largely changed. So altered were the
circumstances that the two periods can hardly be compared.
Each contained its own full measure of suffering; and each
witnessed, in its own degree, the marvellous workings of God.

As we jolted through the streets and were trundled into the great yamen enclosure thronged with the usual multitude of unknown quantity, the same fear and trembling was upon us as heretofore the same anxious inward questioning, Is it for death? the same cry to God, "Carry us out of this yamen and city again in peace for the glory of Thy Name." We were set down just within the gate, and left as at other times face to face with the swarming mob.

The condition to which we were by this time reduced can be imagined rather than described. I remember how the ladies and the little ones looked, as we stood there by the guard room, with the deafening roar around us of soldiers keeping off the pressing crowds; and I knew how they *felt* — just as I did, strengthless, spiritless, all but hopeless, in the growing consciousness that it was impossible to hold out much longer.

Presently two yamen gentlemen in faultless silks made their way through the crowd with the help of runners, and stood before us. Addressing me politely the younger of the two said; "What is your country? Are you English?"

I could scarcely believe my ears; the question was asked in my own tongue! No one can imagine the joy that filled us at the sound, and the hope that welled up in the heart strong and free again at its inspiration. I almost forgot that I was a Chinaman and a prisoner withal, and under the impulse of a strange emotion, was eager to seize his hand; but prudence prevailed, and with the orthodox native bow I said:

"Oh, sir, do you speak English? We are indeed from England, and we trust you to help us in our misery."

"Please come this way," he replied "follow me;" and through the midst of the wondering multitude we passed within the gates of the second enclosure, and beyond this again to an inner and smaller court- yard. Here were gathered a goodly group of the lesser officials connected with the yamen, who gave us a reception that fairly broke me down. The liveliest sympathy was evinced, which took the practical form of ministering to our needs forthwith. The food that was set before us included foreign biscuits, sweet- meats and loaf sugar. A barber was called, and for the first time for three weeks a razor passed over my face and head, and a comb through my queue. The luxury of it shall I ever forget! When I came back, my wife scarcely knew me, as her greeting testified, "How delightfully clean you look, but oh how thin and altered!"

The usual preliminaries over (of much questioning and so forth) we were taken to our appointed quarters. Not the prison nor the guard room, thank God; but a small temple in the second enclosure. It stood in a courtyard of its own, just within the gate, and occupied the north side of the tiny square. The room on the east was assigned to the guard; a couple of disused rooms ran along the south side; while the west was formed by a high wall and entrance gate. One grateful feature of the little quadrangle was the fair-sized leafy tree in the centre, which proved to be in truth a shadow from the heat in the burning days we spent there; but we were not long in making a discovery far otherwise than grateful in the existence of a more than usually foul cesspool or Chinese latrine, close under the open framework of our abode.

The temple itself was a room measuring (as nearly as I can judge) about twenty-two feet by ten. Facing the entrance was the shrine a recess containing a large figure of Buddha seated in contemplation, with many doll disciples about him adoringly on either side. Dingy drapery, hung with cobwebbed dirt, helped to create the dim religious light that made it mystery to the worshipper. Before it stood the grimy incense table with two or three bronze bowls filled full with grey ashes and half-smouldered sticks, that repre- sented countless prayers and vows, as cold and dead as the figure to whom they were made. Beside the table at either end, and facing each other, stood two colossal satellites armed with half-moon prongs, guard- ing their god. They were of devil design, one painted red and the other black, with horns and bolting eyes quite horrible and fearful in their realism. Even the fact that we were well accustomed to such sights did not altogether prevent a certain eerie feeling coming over one at times, in presence of these hideous evidences of Satanic power, especially at nightfall; and but for the overshadowing of God's presence, it would often have been terrifying. Symbols stand for facts; and only too consciously awful to the soul were the unseen realities to which the grim monstrosities before us bore perpetual witness. Beyond the incense table, the room was absolutely destitute of furniture. The floor, of course, was of earth, uneven and unswept. The long lattice work of the window-frames on either side of the door was innocent of paper, save for sundry dirty shreds and strips. For this we were not sorry, as it was our only source of light and ventilation.

One other feature calls for notice. In the wall, on this side the table and on that, were two tiny cellar-holes, for which we had reason to be thankful later on.

Such was the abode to which we were committed. A princely place compared with many we had been in; but the chief charm about it lay for us in its seclusion. Not only was it in the second and more private enclosure, but it was shut off from this again within a courtyard of its own; and by the Mandarin's orders the gate was to be kept shut, and no one outside the yamen admitted without special permission.

I cannot convey to the reader the untold sense of relief with which we took in the new conditions of our captivity. It was rest we yearned for quietness and rest. And now God was giving it to us in a way we had scarcely dared to dream of. Alone and undisturbed, we were free to use to the full the sweet liberty of rest.

Even in these exceptional circumstances, however, one can only use the term in a comparative sense. No accommodation was made for our comfort, not even to the extent of a stool to sit on. Our chair was the ground, and our bed, mother earth. The hard unevennesses chafed our aching limbs, and gave but restless sleep to pillowless heads.

The second day we were informed that the Lao-ie had decided to detain us on account of the passing through of troops ordered to Peking to oppose the advance of the allies. Anxious as we were to press on to the end of so distressful a journey, we yet realized the mercy of God in the order, more especially in regard to my wife, whose condition was now precariously weak; and in the knowledge that we were at least in kindly hands and free from molestation, we settled to our new circumstances with something of thankful acquiescence.

Of the eight days of our detention here, five were days of almost unrelieved monotony. The guard would have none of us, so far as any attempt at inter- course was concerned; and, but for an occasional visit from our English-speaking friend or his deputy, we were left to ourselves. But indeed, we were not loth to have it thus. Our whole being craved for aloneness, and to leave us to ourselves was the truest consideration.

Each day had certain occupations in ordered regularity. We were too weary for much exertion; but in the absence of books or writing materials wherewith to beguile the hours, we found it expedient to devise ways of our own, for the children's sake especially. The day was begun and ended with the usual exercises of prayer and praise. After breakfast, we set about "spring cleaning" our temple-house (not before it wanted it) a lengthy process that stood us in good stead. A broken birch brush, found in the cellar-hole, did transforming work in the busy hands of the de- lighted little ones, and proved a veritable God-send. Much time was given conscientiously to lying down; for days of travel were yet before us, and this was our God-given opportunity of recuperation. The toilet was always a lengthy process, with but a single hand- bowl and a single comb between us all; as was also the uncomfortable, but necessary, daily operation of cleansing the garments from vermin. The remainder of the time was mostly given to singing with the children, telling them stories, or making them toy "chiao-wo-ri" (litters) from fragments of wood and withie strips found in the yard.

From day to day, some little token or other of kindly remembrance was sent from the Mandarin. One time it was a small bottle of ginger-wine for the ladies; another, a bottle of lemonade; another, about a tea-cupful of ground coffee. These were to us, I need hardly say, luxuries of the first order so rare, in fact, that we were loth to partake! The coffee was eked out a finger-pinch at a time, dropped into our break- fast cup of "k'ai-shui" (boiling water); while the opening of the lemonade bottle was quite an event, a sort of festal occasion reserved for a specially hot day. The Mandarin's kindness found its climax, however, in what was to us perhaps the most appreciable form it could take. The third day, a large parcel was sent round, the contents of which were found to be five sets of brand new blue "pu" (or cafico) garments, a set apiece. No words can tell what such a gift meant to us, or our thankfulness upon its receipt. The squalor of prison life, the rough usage of the mob, and the wear and tear of such knockabout travel as we had been subjected to, had left their own mark behind, and their own impression upon the compassionate heart of our benefactor. So now at last the first time for just upon a month we elders had a change of raiment. The Lord give mercy to the house of that good Lao-ie; for he oft refreshed us.

Two other incidents of those days are written on my memory. The one was the Sunday morning service we held in our temple prison the first and only occasion during our flight on which we were able to worship without distraction. The sweet sense of Sabbath rest and of all the goodness and mercy that had followed us until now, made it a memorable hour. Hymn books, prayer books, Bibles, we had none; but a happier hour of heart fellowship with God we never enjoyed. I believe each of us could say that. The word specially given me to speak upon was Hebrews x. 19-23 the believer's "boldness" in the blood of Jesus and with great joy did we draw water from that well of salvation the greater, possibly, that we were privileged literally "before the gods to sing praise unto Him," under the very shadow of Buddha and his demon guard.

The other incident I have counted worthy of record seems naturally to follow on. In the course of that day, the Lao-ie sent his tiny boy (about four years old) with a couple of maids to worship the temple god. When, however, he was told to make the k'eh-t'eo, he absolutely refused. Every means was tried to induce him to do it; but threat and cajole were alike unavailing. Even force was attempted; but the strenuous resistance offered by the sturdy youngster carried the day, and his attendants took him off with the wondering exclamation that they "could not tell what had come to the child; he had never been known to behave so before." They knew not that the Lord was there.

The following day, July 30, was to be a memorable one for us. In the course of the morning news was brought in that a large party of foreigners was expected, and that they were to share our quarters. No information was forthcoming that could serve as a clue to their identity. Our flight had been taken in complete ignorance of the movements of others who were in similar peril; and we could only assume that the fears anticipated by Mr. E. J. Cooper in his last letter to me had been realized, and that the party in question was none other than the Lu-ch'eng refugees.

The thought of seeing these dear friends completely lifted us out of ourselves, and created a keen expectation. How eagerly we watched and made ready for them! The room was carefully swept again and put in order, and we arrayed ourselves, one and all, in our new garments to do them honour. These scant preparations were scarcely completed when the rumble of carts was heard, the little courtyard gate was flung open by runners, and the arrival of foreigners announced. All eagerness to welcome them, we hurried out.

Shall I ever forget the sight? Slowly and painfully they were descending from the carts, a company of twelve — three men, four women and five children. As one by one they emerged from under the p'eng, they appeared in their rags, emaciation, and utter woe-begone-ness, more like apparitions than beings of flesh and blood. We had not been mistaken in our surmise. It was the Lu-ch'eng P'ing-iao party, recognizable still, though so pitiably changed. Mrs. Cooper was the first to come forward. My dear wife ran to her, and with a tender embrace led her gently in. She just lifted her eyes and smiled wearily as she greeted me in these only words, "Oh, how nice to see somebody clean!" Next came her husband, his arms around a litter of loose dirty straw, as much as they could contain; then the Rev. A. R. Saunders and Mr. Jennings in like manner. These were followed by the ladies — Mrs. Saunders, Miss Huston and Miss Guthrie, leading or carrying the children, though scarcely able to support their own weight.

Truly it was "a time to weep." They passed within the enclosure to their temple quarters; and stretching themselves on the ground, as we had done five days before, gave thanks to God for the reviving of His grace in the rest provided after weeks of torture. But oh, the sadness of that sight! The earth-floor of our room was covered, every yard of it, with sick and wounded. In the corner, to the left as one entered and beneath the lattice-work, lay dear Mrs. Cooper on a shake-down of straw, her torn " san-tsi " revealing gangrened sun-wounds about the breasts, and with ulcerous sores where the cruel "kia-tsi" had galled her limbs. Added to this were the pains of dysentery. Opposite her, by the incense table, was stretched Miss Huston, with broken jaw, a gaping scalp wound that laid bare the brain, flesh wounds in either fore- arm deep to the bone, and her whole body a mass of contusions the work of the Boxers. Next her was Mrs. Saunders, terribly reduced by dysentery; and near the door Miss Guthrie, apparently in the last stage of the same disease. The intervening space was taken up by the children, who in their painful distress looked the personification of the misery to which their moans and sobs bore continual witness. Poor little dears! they were one and all in the throes of dysentery; and not only so, but in the agony of undressed sun-wounds. In this respect, Jessie Saunders and Edith Cooper perhaps suffered the most. Their arms, from the shoulder to the elbow, were gangrened sores, alive with maggots.

Two of that fugitive party "were not." Baby Isabel Saunders had succumbed to the hardships of the flight; and Miss Rice had been murdered outright by the Boxers of Tseh-cheo.

Little by little we gleaned, with fresh wonder and amazement, the details of their escape details that came out only to emphasize the conviction that they, not less than we, had been brought forth by a definite act of Almighty purpose and power. The narration of fact after fact was once more the revelation of miracle after miracle; and as we compared notes, we agreed in ascribing the glory of our common deliverance to Him Who alone doeth wondrous things. A concise and deeply instructive record of their journeyings and awful perils has been already issued.(1) I will only, therefore, refer to the single incident of their flight which bears more particularly upon my own story, viz., the sufferings of Miss Huston and the martyrdom of Miss Rice.

The details of the tragedy were supplied to Miss Gates without reserve by Miss Huston herself, and may be briefly summarized as follows. Arrived at a large village called San-chia-tien (where only three months before, Dr. Hewett and I had preached the Word to crowding, but not too friendly, audiences, and where we were all but refused a lodging for the night), the two ladies, in their excessive weariness, became separated from the rest of their party, who were being driven before a Boxer mob. Finding themselves isolated and realizing the hopelessness of getting through, they sat down by the roadside to await the end. They were immediately surrounded and exposed (as we ourselves had so often been) to the excited execrations of the mob, whose fury soon passed from words to deeds. Insults of the grossest kind were heaped upon them, the worst indignities being offered to Miss Rice. They were then set upon with the terrible cry, "Ta! Shah!" "Beat and kill them!" and under the rain of blows Miss Huston lost consciousness not, however, before a heavy springless cart had been deliberately driven over her body to break the spine. When she recovered, it was to find that her face had been plastered over with clay, in the belief that she was dead, and so in lieu of burial. Her first thought was for her sister, and creeping to her side as best she could, she removed the plastered mud from her face also, and watched for signs of life until satisfied that God had taken her. All through that night she kept watch by the body, keeping off the dogs and waiting for her own expected end, when with morning light a yamen troop arrived to bury the dead and take on the living to the next city. The story of the circumstances under which Miss Huston eventually re-joined her party, as related by Mr. Saunders, is amongst the most remarkable of that remarkable period, and is its own confirmation of the miraculous nature of their (not less than of our own) escape. Her survival of such an experience, not only physically, but mentally, was to us who could appreciate to the full what it involved an amazing act of Divine keeping. Even as it was, her expression, especially in repose, wore a haunted, hunted look, revealing all too painfully the nature of the scenes that were photographed upon the mind within. She spoke but little to any, save her intimate, Miss Gates, with whom she had been closely associated in the work of past happy days. Indeed, we none of us talked much together. Sickness, sorrow, and utter weariness bound our spirits and laid a hush upon them.

With our numbers swollen thus from five to seven- teen, and under such insanitary conditions, our small room soon became more like a pest-house than a hospital. Medical resources we had none. Without, under the fierce heat of the dog days, the latrine just beneath the window became a foetid mass of reeking corruption; while within, wounds and bruises and putrifying sores fouled the atmosphere and sickened the senses. Add to this that the aforesaid latrine was the only accommodation available for such an abnormal state of things as nine out of the seventeen afflicted with dysentery; and the reader can imagine the straits to which we were quickly reduced.

The next day Miss Gates succeeded in securing an antiseptic of some Chinese sort, and set to work forth- with to cleanse the wounds with a cold solution. The process, in the case of the dear children, was distressing, who shrieked under the agony of "being scalded with boiling water" so they expressed the sensation. Jessie Saunders suffered most. When the hour came round for her arm to be dressed, in spite of the utmost tenderness in the treatment, she was convulsed with terror at the bare thought, and the shrinking endurance with which she submitted to the ordeal was touching to witness.

All this wrought severely upon nerves already sorely tried. There was no exemption by day or night. Each with his own had a full sufficiency of work. The nature of the children's malady alone called for incessant attention, now with one and now with another; while their moans and cries of pain put sleep out of the question. And yet dear wee souls! behind it all was the suffering patience and self-forgetfulness of maturer years. I remember particularly little Jessie's concern for her mother, as at night she would beg her to change places with her on the hard earth floor, be- cause she was "sure her own bed was the more comfortable!"

Performing the toilet (euphemism for a smudge with a wet "sheo-kin"), dressing the wounds, washing the infants' clothes, and cooking for the sick, were now among the chief items of the daily round; and we gave ourselves to our various employments with such cheer- fulness as the grace of God supplied. Privacy was impossible, save such as was afforded by the two small cellar-holes already referred to; and these were thankfully utilized, pitch dark though they were, as dressing-rooms by the ladies. The sense of utter strengthlessness was very great; and under the intense heat and oppression of the offensive atmosphere, it became increasingly so. I see Mr. Cooper still, the ghost of his former self, wearily washing out the soiled garments of his two children, and thereafter stretching himself at his wife's side, all but exhausted, to fan the flies from her open wounds.

The day following their arrival (July 31) was my little son's birthday. Five years old that most sad day, surrounded truly with love, but also with how much of sorrow and pain! Instead of a children's party, with toys and games and birthday cake, the dear little ones sat each in their places on the floor, looking across at one another, as if they were utter strangers, speechless, listless and wistfully sad. Sighs took the place of laughter, and groans of song. We tried our best to put a birthday complexion on the hours; but it fell very flat, and the expression in the dear boy's sorrowful eyes seemed only to say, "Don't mock me."

Several visits of inquiry were made by the Lao-ie's representatives, and various tokens of goodwill sent in, in the shape of clothing for, the newly arrived party, and gifts of food and money. Occasional groups of city gentlemen, too, were allowed admittance, when they would stand at the threshold holding their noses or inhaling perfumes, while they interrogated us. A not uncommon idea prevails among the Chinese that foreigners are offensively unclean in their persons, and only to be approached on sufferance in the above way. Certainly the condition in which these gentlemen found us now was not calculated to disabuse them of the popular notion, or weaken their prejudice. The only wonder to me was that they could endure it as they did.

From day to day we eagerly inquired as to the prospects of getting on. It was evident that to remain much longer in the place under such pestilential conditions would involve a crisis not less serious, certainly, than anything we were likely to incur on the road; and we entreated to be sent forward at the earliest opportunity. Hopes for "to-morrow" were held out only to be dashed, until the heart grew sick with waiting. The road (it was said) was not yet clear of troops; and the Lao-ie refused to take any risk with us; but "we will see to-morrow." And so it went on; and so also went on the poisonous germs fructifying in our vitals. With the expected result. My two children presently developed large boils and dysentery; with which latter complaint I also was attacked, bringing the number of victims up to twelve, out of a total of seventeen.

Miserable as our condition actually was, and desperate as it was becoming, we were yet sustained by the unfailing consciousness that God was for us. He Who had brought us from the gates of death and had kept us hitherto was able to save to the uttermost, and to hold our soul in life, if it were for His glory. A helpful evidence of this was given in the case of Miss Guthrie. Her prostration under the dysentery was such that it was clear she had not long to live. In this conviction, she called upon me to "pray over" her "the prayer of faith," under the persuasion, borne in upon her by the Spirit of God, that upon her complying with this condition, the Lord would raise her up (James v.). Most thankfully did I respond to my dying sister's request, and from that time she received strength to recover. The sickness was not immediately arrested; but His strength was so perfected in her weakness that its hold upon her relaxed, until it pleased Him to bring her in due course under careful medical nursing.

Many of the most precious lessons of my life were learnt in this "Christ's Hospital" at Sin-yang Cheo. Under suffering of the most distressing kind, where bodily anguish was reinforced by haunting memories of a harrowing flight, where even ordinary comforts were wholly wanting, and where no assuagement of any sort or kind was forthcoming, not one single syllable of murmur or complaint fell at any time from the lips of any. Even the children, amid the tears and cries forced from them by unaccustomed pain, never said one word that could be construed into distrust of the love of God, or a questioning of His way with them.

The all-enduring, uncomplaining patience of the ladies was wonderful to witness a tangible and irre- futable evidence of the transforming power of Divine grace. Through the long hours of the long weary days, in the sultry heat, Mrs. Cooper lay on the vermin-ridden floor, the prey of myriad flies that fed upon her wounds, as, with nothing easier to rest upon than a scant litter of straw, ulcers and dysentery drained her life. Yet never a groan or even a sigh escaped her; and when one spoke to her, only the lighting up of a gentle smile, and a word of thanksgiving to God for His love to her was introduced with the answer she returned. So was it with each one of them, until one saw a new meaning in the words, "The noble army of martyrs praise Thee."

I thank God, too, for the lessons He taught me through the spirit of brotherly love that prevailed in our midst. The ministry of mutual cleansing in the lowly "washing of one another's feet" was most graciously exemplified and beautiful to see. No man sought his own, but each his neighbour's good. The self-denial of the dear brethren Saunders, Cooper and Jennings, as they gave themselves wholly to the work of ministering to all, was in the very spirit of Christ's sacrifice. To Miss Gates, who alone of the ladies was free from actual sickness, fell the major share of the nursing; and how faithfully, zealously and self-forget-fully she discharged, in all her own utter weariness, the onerous duties love imposed upon her, I can never tell. A tender-heartedness, the outcome of meek submission to the known will of God, which was recog- nized at all times to be "good, perfect and accept-able," breathed through all our relations with one another, infusing into them withal a certain cheerfulness that killed irritability in the germ. Even there, amid so much that tended to wretchedness, we were given "beauty for ashes, the oil of joy for mourning, the garment of praise for the spirit of heaviness;" for His right hand had holden us up, and His gentleness had made us great. To Him be glory for ever. Amen.

Questions to Consider

1. After listing the "news" of so many other missionary deaths, Glover asks "What do we choose to complain about?" It's a good question. As we consider what is important in life and in eternity, what do we complain about? Those complaints will reveal a great deal about our hearts and our priorities.

CHAPTER TWENTY-FOUR

From the Cross to the Crown

*"These are they which came out of great tribulation,
and have washed their robes, and made them white in
the blood of the Lamb. Therefore are they before the
Throne of God."*

The long-wished-for day dawned at length, and on the morning of Friday, August 3, just at the moment when things showed at their worst and hopes were down to zero the welcome news came in that the road was clear of troops, and we were to be sent on forthwith. Oh, the joy of it! For this was the ninth day of our own, and the fourth of the Lu-ch'eng P'ing-iao party's detention here; and anything was preferable, if the will of God were so, to a continuance of conditions which were consciously sapping the springs of life.

It was, however, something more than a surprise it was a disappointment creating the keenest distress to find that nothing easier than barrows had been provided for our transit.

It would appear that the good Lao-ie's intention had been to give chairs for the stronger and bamboo stretchers for the weaker amongst us. But his benevolence had been frustrated by the passage of the Wu-ch'ang troops through the city, the officers having commandeered every chair and lounge, and requisitioned every professional bearer. Stretchers could be easily knocked up, but bearers not so easily. Hence it came to pass that two and no more could be placed at our disposal, and accordingly the available two were allotted to Mrs. Cooper and Mrs. Saunders. For the rest of the party, whatever the degree of prostration or pain, nothing remained but the horror of jolt and screech, joined to the hardness of a knife-board.

Thankful as we were to be once more on the move and working steadily towards the goal, the memory of the Lord's great goodness in having provided such a place of repair as the yamen temple we were just leaving, was very sensibly upon us. The kindness, too, of the Lao-ie and others on the place made us feel the going forth again to the dread uncertainties of the road more than we otherwise should have done; and it was not therefore with wholly unmixed feelings that we bade farewell to place and people

It was here at Sin-yang Cheo that I felt it desirable to part with those singular tokens of God's mercy to me the beggar's coat of rags, and P'ao-ri's trousers. Being now decently habited, there was no further call to keep the garments for necessary use; and associated as they were with events too painful for the mind to dwell upon, I could not bear the sight of them. I have often regretted since that I found no way to retain them as memorials of that most marvellous time; but in any case it was out of the question, as they were hopelessly riddled with vermin, and fit only for the fire. So wrapping them reverently together, I left them in the black cellar-hole attached to our own quarters, not less thankful to my God for the original permission to have them than for the present permission to have done with them.

How strange it seemed, after nine days' seclusion, to pass out again to the bustle of the great yamen square! Here were the stretchers at the door, on bamboo frames that looked the essence of comfort with their yielding flexibility and awning overhead; and here, too, were the barrows some six of them cruelly naked, and only with the usual shoddy apology for p'eng. Beyond what we were able to do for ourselves, no effort was made to lighten the discomfort of the ride before us. No clean straw was obtainable, and that that had been in use during the period of detention was not fit to be carried out. Nevertheless, being put to the shift, it had to be done;. and out of the legs of a discarded pair of trousers the Misses Gates and Huston succeeded in producing a highly original but eminently serviceable bolster. Of the two wadded quilts that had been given us, as already stated, I reserved one for my wife and children, wrapping it fourfold beneath them. This was all we could manage; for with the large addition to our party the little bundle of children's clothing, that had served for cushion heretofore, had disappeared before more urgent needs. All was soon in readiness for the road. The stretchers with their invalid freight, swinging easily from the shoulders of their stalwart bearers, passed on before; to be followed in due succession by the long file of screeching wheels and dislocating boards, an armed escort of some dozen soldiers attending.

The record of that day's journey runs on all fours with what has already been given of similar experiences, and needs not to be repeated. It was just the old conditions over again broiling heat, broken p'eng, sorry food and surly barrowmen, with the same accompaniments as before of jolt and bang, aching limbs and anxious looking lest evil should break out in open violence. In the present circumstances, however, as compared with the former, there was an advance upon the suffering entailed by such a mode of travel; for dysentery was upon us all myself and children as well as my wife, whose condition was now the more enfeebled by its long and unabated con- tinuance. The excruciating pain of the thud, thud, where the barrow dropped one ruthlessly the other side of a deep rut, or ran relentlessly over a series of stone paving blocks, was too dreadful for words. My short experience of it (two days) was long enough to make me marvel how my wife had strength to endure it, under dysenteric weakness, day after day for several weeks, and without a murmur. Once only, as I sat beside her, on the last day of such agony, did I hear a deep groan escape the compressed lips, when we crashed over the more than ordinarily cruel way at the entrance to the city of Ying-shan.

Unable to cover the distance between the two cities in one day, we were compelled to take the risk of spending the night on the road, and at sunset were halted at a village called T'an-kin-ho. Half the party, including ourselves, were driven into a large barrowshed: the rest, including the Saunders family, were taken to an inn higher up the street.

In the mercy of God, our arrival seemed to excite nothing beyond the ordinary curiosity. Crowds as usual hung about us; but no word indicative of active hostile feeling came from them. Covered by the escort, we were allowed to make our dispositions for the night in peace; and spreading the quilt where a convenient space admitted between the barrows, we lay down to rest.

We had not yet succeeded in getting to sleep when, about ten o'clock, the startling news was brought down from the inn that Jessie was dead! Prostrate as we knew her to have been, even to the extent of having to share her mother's stretcher, there was nothing to call for immediate apprehension, so that the tidings came with something of a shock. The more so, that it was the first appearance of death in our midst, and solemnly suggestive, where most were sick, that it would not be the last. Moreover, there could not but arise a nameless dread in connection with such an event occurring on the road, where it might easily work on the superstitious fears of the people to our cost. The occasion, therefore, was one that called for special grace, wisdom, and prayer, for the bereaved parents first, and for the entire party.

As soon as the news was brought, I went out to look for the inn. The night was still and the street quite quiet. An unwonted hush seemed to be on the place; and where I had thought to find much people and excitement, there was only the silent street before me. No need to ask which was the inn:

I knew it by the sight that shortly met my eyes. There in the roadway opposite the door, whither (according to the superstitious custom of the people) the landlord had had the dying child carried out, lay darling little Jessie on a rush mat. The moon fell upon her upturned face, revealing its lovely features in all the calm of placid sleep, amid a tangled wealth of golden ringlets. With one arm out, she looked as though she had just thrown herself down in utter weariness, and was now at rest in a most sweet and tranquil slumber. Beautiful indeed it was to see; but oh, the pathos of it! Set in an aureole of golden hair, the pale sweet face of the child- martyr looked, in the moon's soft light, as the face of an angel; for the scarce cold clay, though wearing still the impress of her stem discipline of sorrow, was luminously fair, as if reflecting the very radiance of the glory into which her spirit had even now entered. Beside her, supported by Miss Gates, sat the stricken mother, in calm resignation to the will of Him who was calling her for His Name's sake to part with her eldest, as but a little while since He had asked her youngest.

It was not for me to intrude upon the sacredness of such grief, and with but one word of Christian sympathy, I withdrew. The arrangements for the funeral were, in the mercy of God, made quickly and without any such contretemps as the state of the times led one to fear. The officer in command of the escort gave most valuable assistance, and the parents had the comfort of feeling that, in spite of the urgency of the hour and the peculiarity of circumstance, everything was done decently and in order. The little grave was dug on a hill outside the village gate, and at sunrise, coffined in a box, sweet Jessie was laid to rest by her sorrowing father in the land of her short life's affliction, "until the Day break and the shadows flee away."

In spite of the precautions taken by the Mandarin at Sin-yang Cheo, we were not, after all, to escape the dreaded peril of encountering soldiers on the march. The news that we were likely to fall in with them ere we could reach our destination was disquieting to a degree, and led us to unite in special prayer for protection and deliverance. Our only chance of escaping them lay in the possibility of reaching Ying-shan Hsien before they did; and our escort accordingly called an early start.

The experience of that day was not an enviable one. Under the burning heat, from the power of which the flimsy p'eng but ill sufficed to shield us, we were hurried over all sorts and conditions of roads, without regard to the effect upon ourselves. It was almost as much as one's life was worth to crave a short halt from our merciless drivers, and we could only pray for grace to possess our souls in patience. The intervals at which we were rested were longer than heretofore; but of course there was a reason for it, to the urgency of which we were fully alive so much so indeed, that we feared to stop as much as we dreaded to go on.

As the morning advanced it became certain that we could not evade a collision with the Wu-ch'ang soldiery. According to report, the vanguard of five battalions had already passed through Ying-shan, and must by this time be in our near neighbourhood; so, as we had to dismount for a hilly steep, Messrs. Saunders, Cooper and I found a convenient opportunity for committing our respective parties into the hand of God, praying as we walked.

Towards noon we were halted at a wayside booth for the mid-day "ta-chien," and while we were discussing the meagre bowl of "wet rice," the soldiers came. Banners, flags, rifles, spears, tridents and half-moon prongs, preceded by a long string of barrows laden with arms, ammunition and accoutrements, told of their approach, and a few minutes later we were in their midst. It was a strange experience, and another notable instance of the intervention of God on our behalf. When they found who we were, a great com- motion ensued, and the determination to put us to death was freely expressed. "The Imperial Army and the Loyal Boxers were one" (they said) "and under the same orders from the Throne to exterminate the foreign devils. They were on their way now to drive them into the Yellow Sea; but there was no need to wait till they got to the Capital before tasting foreign blood they could begin here."

As the men poured in the excitement grew, until it seemed likely to overpass the bounds of discipline. Our escort stood loyally by us; and doubtless the officers recognized that, being under official surveillance, we should be dealt with in due course according to the terms of the Edict of extermination, in which case their interference would be undesirable. Anyhow, they did their utmost to avert bloodshed. No sooner had the men swallowed their bowl of "hsi-fan" than they were formed up and marched off, with a smartness that surprised me amid what seemed to be only babel and chaos. Even so, however, they were with the greatest difficulty restrained from falling on us. One company all but mutinied, in their rage against us; and how we escaped death is known only to God, our Shield and our Deliverer. Miss Huston was roughly handled, while Miss Gates beside her was dragged from her seat by the hair. Our barrow, too, was surrounded, and a spear levelled at little Hope. I believe that, under God, a catastrophe then was only averted by the staunch attitude of a young soldier of the escort, whose calm and ready answers to the fierce suspicious questionings of his interrogators certainly turned them aside.

The most painful experience in this way was that of the two invalids, Mrs. E. J. Cooper and Mrs. Saunders. Owing to the fact that their stretchers were borne of four, it was impossible for us to keep up with them; for the bearers refused to adapt their pace to ours. Thus it happened that they were far ahead and alone when the soldier-crisis came. Not only so, but as soon as the column was sighted, the bearers set their burden down, and bolted.

The ladies were soon discovered to be "foreign devils," and as such adjudged to death. As they lay in all the prostration of sickness, with closed eyes, fearing to look upon the cruel faces about them, they were prodded with the butt end of musket and spear, when they heard the men say, "They are not worth the killing; for they will be dead of their sickness in an hour or two;" and so found themselves presently alone and alive.

The rest of the journey to Ying-shan was marked for me by two distressful features the cruelty of the barrowmen, and the terror that now settled upon our darling Hope.

The road became so shocking that at a certain halting place I sought the help of the escort in negotiating a chair for my wife, which I had noticed in the street on entering. The bargain was satisfactorily arranged; but when the time came to go on, the chair was not forthcoming. One by one, I watched the barrows move off, and the escort with them, until our barrow alone remained. I waited, but no chair came. I became uneasy; and the old nameless fears, springing from an acute sense of isolation, returned in force upon me. Still there was no sign of the chair, though emphatic assurances were given us continually that it "would be here directly." At last, the vision of further detachments of the Wu-ch'ang battalions swarming in upon us and cutting off our escape led us to abandon the thought of the chair and finish as we had begun.

Our decision was met with abusive remonstrance from the barrowmen, and a deliberate refusal to take us on. It was clear they were partial, for sufficient reasons of their own, to the chair scheme; and nothing I could say would induce them to budge. At my wits' end, I could only cry to God; for the rage of these men was promoting an ugly feeling against us in the place, and every moment was of consequence. The quiet determination not to quit our seats on the barrow told at last; and with the warning that we should have cause to rue our choice, they caught on to the handles and ran us passionately out.

Truly that last barrow ride was a fitting climax to the nineteen days we had endured of such like travel. A paved way of unusual length, formed of huge, rough- hewn slabs of stone, with here and there a steep ascent up which we had to toil on foot under the searching sun-blaze, was found to be our portion this time; and the malice of our drivers had full scope for play. Instead of running the barrow into the smooth of the well-worn wheel track at the side, they deliberately took us over the raw blocks, that the thud and crash of our painful progress might be its own justification of the truth of their warning. My wife bore it with a heroism that never uttered groan or murmur. It was only when the barrow halted, or when we dismounted to walk the hills, that the real effect upon her was apparent. Bent double with weakness and pain, her limbs refused to support her weight; and I had almost to lift her along, as she fell forward in her staggering gait.

As for little Hope, her nerve power seemed to be quite gone. She sobbed continuously now, and when-ever the barrow stopped, even for a momentary halt, her terror knew no bounds. Piteously and imploringly she clung to me with the cry, "Go on, go on! they are coming to kill us!" and any attempt to reassure her was only met by a fresh paroxysm of screaming, stamping fright.

Thus we came at length to Ying-shan, whether for good or evil we could not tell. The anguish of that last barrow ride over the paving blocks before the gate and the cobbles on the street was "the last straw" in the long series of such journeys, and suited to the inner suffering that all came back as the city crowds swarmed once more about us. I remember distinctly the feeling of nervous strain, well nigh insupportable, over the growth of the silent multitude that pressed right on to us; when, as we turned up the narrow street that led to the yamen, a gentleman made his way through, and placed himself beside us with the greeting, "Ping'-an!" In a moment the dreadful tension relaxed and my heart was at rest; for I recognized in the Christian salutation of "Peace!" the Spirit of the God of peace; and I knew that we were in friendly hands.

A few minutes more, and we were at the yamen gates. There, for the first time in all our experience, and naturally to our amazement, was the Mandarin himself, with other lesser officials, ready to receive us, and still more amazing to welcome me, as I alighted, with a cordial English hand-shake! With a few kindly words of pity and reassurance, he led us to the ante-room of his own private apartments, where a lounge and several easy chairs of foreign make were placed at our disposal. The gentleman whose salutation had so revived my spirit reappeared, and entered into close conversation with his Excellency a further confirmation that things were working for our good. Light refreshments in the shape of tea and foreign biscuits were brought in, and a bottle of wine opened for my dear wife, who had swooned away from the ejects of the barrow ride. Eventually, special quarters were assigned us in a small orphanage lower down the street, where we were sheltered from the curious behind a heavy gate, securely barred.

Here for six days of unspeakable weariness we endured a further detention by reason of the passage of more troops, and with it a repetition (if in somewhat milder form) of the painful conditions under which we suffered at Sin-yang Cheo. The gate admitted to a repository stored with official chairs, opening on to a small courtyard, at the farther end of which was a wing of the orphanage. In the repository lay Mrs. Saunders, Mrs. Cooper and ourselves; the two small rooms on the far side of the courtyard being occupied by the rest of the party.

It was here that we saw exemplified from day to day the living power of the Word and Spirit of Christ to change and beautify a heathen soul. The gentleman referred to above, who gave me the first gleam of comfort in the salutation of "Peace," proved to be the evangelist in charge of the London Missionary Society's work in Ying-shan; and a nobler instance of lowly, self-sacrificing service, after the mind and pattern of Christ, than Lo Sien-seng's ministry to us from the first hour of arrival, I have never witnessed. Having brought us to the privacy of our quarters, he "laid aside his garments," and, to the entire neglect of his own wants, ministered to our necessities. No task was too menial for him, none too disagreeable. Patiently and tenderly, in the sympathy and compassion of his Lord, he went from one to the other, making himself least of all and servant of all, unweariedly from early morning till late at night. His record is on high and, as I rejoice to know, his reward also; for the debt under which his so great love laid us could be fully recompensed of God alone.

How to drag through the weary hours in these most dreary quarters we scarcely knew. Each day, the prospect was held out of getting away on the morrow; and when the morrow came, it was still, "To-morrow." The terrible straits to which we were reduced by the nature of the prevailing sickness intensified the desire to be gone; while the consciousness of ever increasing weakness robbed one of the power to bear up against the strain of hope deferred, until it seemed only too probable that even now the greater part would not reach Hankow alive. Mr. Jennings was seized with dysentery, and in Mrs. Saunders' case the malady had reached so acute a stage that she called me for special prayer, as in a dying condition. My dear wife also appeared to be sinking.

On the afternoon of the third day (August 6), Mrs. E. J. Cooper was called to exchange the martyr's cross for the victor's crown. In the same beautiful patience that had signalized the whole period of her sufferings, she lay with nothing specially to indicate that the end was at hand. When her husband had prayed with her as usual in the morning, she had remarked, "I think I shall not die; for my life is yet strong in me," and so lay quietly as before, until about two o'clock she became faint, entreating for "Air, air!" We carried her below the steps to the vestibule, open to the sky, where she continued awhile in quiet consciousness, her husband beside her. Shortly afterwards, as we were standing together in silent prayer, she uttered with a clear strong emphasis the words, "Rest, rest, rest!" and with one gentle sigh was gone. It was deeply affecting to hear from the lips of my weeping brother, as he closed the eyes of his beloved dead, the chastened utterance, "The Lord gave, and the Lord hath taken away: blessed be the Name of the Lord;" and as we knelt on that most hallowed spot, I learned how possible it is "in all these things" to be "more than conquerors through Him that loved us."

Mr. Cooper's own words, in a letter written to his mother from Hankow, August 18, form a striking testimony to the same effect:

"You will have learned by cable that dear Maggie has fallen asleep in Jesus. I may as well tell you the worst first. She died at Ying-shan, about 100 miles from Hankow, on August 6, after a month's pain and suffering for Christ.

"Billow after billow has gone over me. Home gone, not one memento of dear Maggie even, penniless, wife and child gone to glory, Edith lying very sick with diarrhoea, and your son weak and exhausted to a degree, though otherwise well. I have been at the point of death more than once on the road. In one village, after a heavy stoning with brickbats, they put ropes under me and dragged me along the ground, that I might not die in the village itself.

"And now you know the worst, mother, I want to tell you that the cross of Christ, that exceeding glory of the Father's love, has brought continual comfort to my heart, so that not one murmur has broken the peace within.

"If God spared not His own Son, all is love; but now we see through a glass darkly, but then face to face. Although wounded and suffering, Maggie said to me, 'If the Lord spares us, I should like to go back to Lu-ch'eng, if possible.' Devoted soul! Denied by her Master of doing the work so near to her heart, she never turned in purpose and desire to win some of the Chinese for Christ, The Lord has accepted her desire' and honoured her in her death for Him." (1)

Thus Mrs. Cooper passed to her eternal rest and reward. The body was placed in a Chinese coffin the same evening, and remained with us till our departure three days later, the Mandarin having courteously arranged for its removal to Hankow for interment.

On the morning of August 10, we took a thankful farewell of our most sad abode albeit lght had arisen to us in the darkness, carrying our thought beyond the light affliction to the far more exceeding weight of glory. Chairs now took the place of barrows, and for the first time we were shown mercy in respect of the mode of travel. Lo Sien-seng accompanied us, in the resolve not to leave us until he had fulfilled his ministry in bringing us to Hankow itself.

We halted for the night at the city of Teh-ngan Fu. As the brown battlements came in sight, the vision of mob and prison rose instinctively before me, and it was no small relief to find that our course deflected to a hill outside the walls, crowned by the Examination Hall. Here we were lodged and tended, to our comfort, by a native doctor of the Wesleyan Mission.

Thence the following morning (August 11) we pursued our way to Yun-meng Hsien. The eager freshness of the early morning air, the singular beauty of the scene bathed in the glory of dawn, and the joyous sense of freedom after the long fortnight of distressful detention,revived my spirit greatly. The dysentery, too, was stayed, and strength began in measure to return.

Yun-meng was reached about three in the afternoon. Our coming had been anticipated and three rooms allotted us in the Examination Hall, whither we were carried direct without touching the yamen. No provision was made for our comfort other than that afforded by a few boards to lie on.

The excitement aroused by our arrival was as great as at any previous time in our experience, and the manifestation of it little short of alarming. Ever increasing crowds swarmed up to the gate beyond which we lay, and were forced back by the yamen guard amid deafening noise. So persistent, however, were they in the resolve to get to us that the soldiers closed the gate; whereupon it was stormed by the mob and carried, in spite of barricades.

Such was the scene all tumult, uproar and confusion from which another of the martyrs of Jesus passed to heaven's perfect peace. While waiting on my wife, Miss Huston came across to me from the room opposite and said, "Oh, Mr. Glover, will you pray for me? I feel so strangely ill." I took her back and besought the Lord to strengthen her to the journey's end, for His own glory Miss Gates uniting with me in the prayer. An hour or so later, she called to me again to re-bandage the huge gaping wound in her left arm, when she appeared distraught and somewhat excited in manner. Comfortable words, however, from the Word of God's grace revived and soothed her troubled spirit; and I returned without apprehension to my sick family. Towards evening, I was summoned once more, and for the last time, by Mr. Saunders in the words, "Miss Huston is dying; will you come?" Our sister was lying on the bare board of a trestle bed, with closed eyes and evidently unconscious, breathing stertorously. Seeing that the end could not be delayed, we commended her spirit into the hand of the Lord Jesus; and about the time of the going down of the sun, without word or struggle she finished her course. The prayer she had asked was answered in a fuller, deeper sense than we had prayed it. "For His own glory" He had "strengthened her," not in the outward but in the inner man; and "to the journey's end," not of an earthly goal but of a heavenly.

Here again, as at Ying-shan, the kindness of the Mandarin made matters easy. When the event became known, the curious crowd withdrew, and the last sad dispositions were made without distraction. The request that the remains might accompany us to Hankow was readily complied with; and by dawn of the following day all was in readiness for the road.

Sunday, August 12, will for ever be a memorable day to me, as introducing the last stage of the strangest and weariest of overland journeys I am perhaps ever likely to know. The goal truly was well within sight now; but one hardly dared to believe it, so chronic had the disposition become to discredit the hope that had so often been mocked. Besides, reduced as most of us were by the long stress of conflict, should we last out the three hundred and odd "11" that yet remained? Reports varied as to the distance yet to be covered. We were led to conjecture that some four days at least still remained to us; and how to endure we knew not.

More than once that day I thought my dear wife was dying. Owing to the fact that her bearers travelled faster than mine, I was unable to be with her, except when a longer halt admitted of my coming up with her chair. On one of these occasions, I was startled to find her sitting back in her seat, to all appearance dead. The shock was so great that I, found Mr. Saunders and said, "I do believe my wife is dead. Please come at once." We moistened her lips with a little wine given by the Mandarin, at which she revived, in the mercy of God, and opened the half-closed eyes.

In sweltering heat we reached Hsiao-kan Hsien, and amid thronging crowds were taken to a large temple and set down to await the Lao-ie's pleasure. A couple of hours later, we were told to re-enter our chairs, for that we were to be taken to the premises of the London Missionary Society. The glad surprise of such tidings can scarcely be imagined; for we had no idea that the truths of Christianity were even known here, much less that the city was a centre of aggressive Christian work. It seems that as soon as the news of our arrival reached them, the native Church members, on their own initiative (for all foreigners had left), went at once to the Lao-ie to beg leave to take us to the Mission quarters and care for us themselves.

Of the reception they accorded us I can never think without emotion. It was in very truth a foretaste of the love of heaven. From the oppressive noise and heat of excitable crowds, we found ourselves suddenly transplanted into a little paradise of peace and rest; for the sweetest garden, with shaded lawn and bright flowering beds, was there behind the buildings, where not a sound from the world without intruded to mar the sense of perfect quietude. Every attention was given to our wants. The sick and wounded were first carefully tended by the medical assistant in charge of the dispensary; after which we were introduced to what appeared in our eyes a veritable banquet. No such fare as was now set before us had passed our lips for many weeks. Fish, fowl, and potatoes were the staple delicacies, with preserved meat and fruit. But most acceptable of all was the milk supply. Several large biscuit tins had been converted into cans, and filled to the brim with a Nestle solution too delicious for words. I fear we must have appeared in the eyes of our benefactors much like Saul's host when they "flew upon the spoil," so ravenous were we in the presence of palatable food; but our rapacity seemed only to create the liveliest satisfaction, as the best evidence we could afford their benevolence of our grateful appreciation. Another sumptuous meal was provided ere we left that evening, the interval being spent in the luxury of the greensward couch, beneath the garden trees.

At nightfall, we bade farewell, in a quiet service of thanksgiving, to this Christlike band of native brethren, and were soon threading the tortuous lantern-lit streets to the river-side. To our intense relief, the remainder of the journey was to be by water; and how can I express the pure delight with which I exchanged even the chair for the boat! I say "even"; for though the chair was bliss itself compared with cart or barrow, yet it was by no means bliss unalloyed per se: for the conveyances supplied to most of us were the rudest and commonest of their kind, my own being in so dilapidated a state that it afforded no shelter from the sun; and the narrow strip of wood mis-named "seat" having twice given way under me, the nicest (that is, pain-fullest) sitting was required to hold my ground at all.

Up to the last we were to be kept in fear for in the long interval before the boats cast off we were recognized, and a crowd of men and lads came down to the water's edge in a spirit that was anything but friendly, some of them even wading in to insult us where we lay under the p'eng. Then, as the boatmen poled us out, the old dreadful yell went up of curses for the "iang kuei-tsi "; and running parallel with the boats, they pelted us till we were out of reach.

It was an altogether new and wonderful experience to feel that we were travelling, and yet with no conscious sense of it. With fervent gratitude to God we laid us down, but how to rest we found not. The heat under the low "p'eng," as we tried to pack five of us into the well of the boat, was exhausting to a degree. So prostrate indeed was my wife, that I feared she could not last out the night. It was only by constant fanning, and feeding her every two or three hours with an egg beaten up with a little Chinese wine, that the vital spark was, under God, kept in.

So insufferable was the heat that about midnight I went outside for a reviving draught of air. How still it was! Not a sound save the gentle plash of the boatman's oar, and the gurgle of the water as it parted at the prow. We had started, so far as I saw, three passenger boats in all; but now there was a fourth, silently gliding past in the moonlight with a solemn freight of holy dead; for two huge coffins were mounted on it, containing the bodies of our martyr sisters.

Thus we made our sorrowful way through the long weariness of the night and the burning heat of the next day, shadowed to the last by the presence of death. My dear wife herself lay as if dying, and our little son was prostrate with what proved to be the beginning of an all but fatal illness.

The sun was westering, when the boats drew toward the large "ma-t'eo" that was to prove the haven where we would be. I certainly was not prepared for the news that Hankow was before us, until we threaded the maze of river craft, and stayed. Could it be possible that the impossible was actually realized? Had God done the mighty work of bringing us up from the gates of death, and of turning our thousand miles of peril into His thousand miles of miracle? We had to confess it, for the fact was there; and with hearts bowed in adoration, we gave thanks to Him that liveth for ever and ever, the only wise *God, our Saviour.*

* * *

One last test of suffering still awaited us. Owing to the dilatoriness of the Tao-t'ai, we were not taken off the boat till the next day; and what it meant to us, in our dire extremity, to have to pass another night of unrelieved misery, when life itself (for some of us at least) hung in the balance, I can never tell. How longingly we watched and watched for the chairs that never came! — until, in the recognition that our heavenly Father knew, we yielded our hearts to be kept in the patience of Christ, and wished for the day. But I never think of that last night without suffering; for I scarcely dared to hope that either my wife or little son would live to leave the boat.

The long, long darkness passed to the dawn when the shadow of death was to be turned into the morning; and in due course the chairs appeared. The emotions of that hour were too deep for tears. We stood to receive the dear friends who came to our succour as in a dream, scarcely knowing whether we were in the body or out of the body. Mr. Lewis Jones, of the China Inland Mission, accompanied by Dr. Gillison (London Missionary Society) and Dr. Hall (Methodist Episcopal) rendered us the most loving and sympathetic service. Baskets full of foods, medicines and cordials were brought, and the sick immediately tended and prescribed for. In much trepidation by reason of his delinquency the Tao-t'ai himself came down to receive us, and to forward the business in hand, until the last chair had disappeared for the last ten of our long three thousand "li."

It is not too much to say that something of a sensation was created in Hankow by the news that a party of Shan-si refugees had arrived. The common belief, founded upon a reliable report, was that, while a certain number had succeeded in escaping out of the Province, yet none had lived to cross the Yellow River: all had been slaughtered at the fords. When the veteran missionary, Dr. Griffith John, saw us, he exclaimed, "Do my eyes deceive me? Am I looking upon men, or spirits? Truly I see you as the dead raised to life again; for we had long since abandoned all thought of ever seeing you alive."

On reaching the Home of the China Inland Mission, I realized, to an extent I had not before, how severe had been the strain imposed by ten weeks of daily dying. The consciousness that we were really safe at last and among our own people brought an experience altogether unique. There was one definite moment when my heart was suddenly lightened of a mighty load, which rolled from off me as distinctly as if a literal weight had been loosed from my back. The strangeness of the feeling I can neither describe nor forget; but it was a revelation to myself of the burden under which my spirit had been bowed, and of the real heaviness of the yoke to which it had long become accustomed.

Together with this experience came another not less noteworthy. The atmosphere of peace and love into which we were now introduced, as compared with that of habitual riot and murderous hate, formed a contrast to which no words can give expression. It was the nearest thing to heaven I have ever known, in the comfortable sense of rest, of the environment of love, and of the wiping away of tears.

I do not at all know how to speak of the loving kindnesses and tender mercies with which God crowned us at the hands of the many dear friends who now ministered to our necessities. Every conceivable attention was shown us, not only by the missionary brotherhood, but by the European community generally. Our Consul, Mr. Eraser, and the acting American Consul, Mr. F. Brown (a dear personal friend of my own) were foremost in the practical expression of their sympathy; while from Dr. Griffith John, the patriarch of foreign Missions in Hankow, we received the tenderest welcome in the Lord.

The day following we took farewell of our beloved brother and benefactor, Lo Sien-seng, who, having discharged his gracious ministry to us, was now re- turning to the work at Ying-shan. A small subscription from amongst ourselves was handed him by Mr. Saunders, in token of our love, esteem and gratitude; and, commended to God and to the Word of His grace, he departed, in the same lowly, unassuming spirit, as counting his services not worthy even of mention.

The critical condition of the greater number of our party taxed the strength of the small medical and nursing staff to the utmost. Doctors Gillison and Hall worked strenuously in the great heat, never taking their clothes off for days together; while the nurses (the two Misses Fleming, and the two Misses Smith of Kuei-k'i, in Kiang-si Province) toiled unremittingly in day and night shifts, both in the children's ward and with the adults. Miss Gates was the only one who, after a few days' rest, was pronounced fit to go on to Shanghai; but no sooner had she started than she succumbed to a terrible reaction, and for several weeks was laid aside with critical nervous prostration. (2)

On the afternoon of the day we arrived (August 14) the bodies of our sisters, Mrs. E. J. Cooper and Miss Huston, were laid to rest in the Cemetery, when the solemn service was most impressively conducted by Dr. Griffith John, in the presence of a large and repre- sentative following from the Settlement. Though scarcely able to walk, Mr. Cooper was strengthened to attend and to discharge, as chief mourner, the last offices of Christian faith and love. Yet even now his cup of sorrow was not full; for, a week later, he was to pass that way again, in the calling of his infant Brainerd to join the martyr host.

In the early morning hours of the fourth day after our arrival (August 18), my wife gave birth to a living child. So narrowly did she escape the sorrows of delivery under flight; and so graciously did the mercy of God provide that, instead of the hardship of a prison at such a time, she should enjoy the comforts of a home. The fact that the little one breathed was regarded by the doctors as no less a miracle than that the mother should have lived to bring her into the world. Doctors Gillison and Parry did not hesitate to pronounce it the most extraordinary case of physical endurance they had ever known or heard of, and affirmed that, antecedently, they could never have believed it possible that a woman with child could have survived such sufferings, and her offspring with her. Deeply sensible that it was "by the power of God" alone that either were "kept" to the end, we gave our little daughter to the Lord under the name of "Faith," whereby to enshrine the memory of His great goodness, and to give Him the honour due to His Name.

With the burden of suffering now rolled off, but in extreme prostration, my dear wife gave herself up to the quiet content of the hour, thankfully resting in the careful love and tenderness with which God's mercy had here surrounded her. Through the skill and extraordinary attention of Dr. Parry (Si-ch'uan Province) she slowly rallied, until the hope of ultimate recovery became well nigh assured.

Meantime, Hedley was lying at the point of death with sun-fever. For several days his life was despaired of, and it seemed probable that his mother would never see him again. The trial to her of being shut off by necessity from ministering to him in his extremity was very keen; but it was borne with the same gentle fortitude that had characterized her all through, and the same submissive committal of her boy into the hand of God. When the crisis was over, and the dear child on the way to convalescence, it was seen that he was reduced to a mere skeleton. Little Hope, too, had passed through a critical illness. "Oh, shall I ever forget when we got here!" her mother wrote; "she had fever, and could do nothing but scream, frightened of everything." But the love of God spared us the deep sorrow of losing either; and in their full recovery we could not but recognize another act of His wonder-working power.

With the rallying of my wife, the progress of my two elder children, and the satisfactory condition of the new-born infant, my heart was greatly comforted and lifted up. But about the sixth day, the babe turned from its food, and in spite of every attempt refused to be coaxed either to the bottle or the breast. For a while she lingered thus, and on August 28 ten days after birth breathed out her little life into the hands of the Saviour for Whose sake it was laid down.

The funeral service was conducted the next day by Dr. Griffith John in the garden, under the open window of my dear wife's room. She chose the hynm herself, beginning, "Hark, hark the song the ransomed sing," with the refrain a favourite theme of hers:

Glory to Him Who loved us, And washed us in His blood, Who cleansed our souls from guilt and sin By that pure, living flood.(3)

The tiny coffin was afterwards carried to the river by two dear brethren of our Mission, Mr. Bruce (of Hu- Nan)(4) and Mr. Tull (of Shen-si), and we took it by boat to the Cemetery, where I left my darling baby sleeping beside the other martyrs of our band, "till He come."

The spirit of my dear wife's resignation to the will of God in the removal of a cherished hope was beautiful to witness. With her eyes ever God-ward, she dwelt, not upon her own loss but upon her precious child's gain; and though on my return I knew she had been weeping, yet her countenance was lighted with a heavenly smile as she said, "My sorrow in her loss is eclipsed by the joy that my lamb is beyond all suffering now in her Saviour's bosom." In a letter written a few days later, I find her expressing herself thus pathetically, with something of a prophetic reference to her own end:

"To me, our little Faith's entrance into life was wonderful. It seemed an earnest of my entrance in, as He had received her, so He would me; and I could only rejoice, and do still. She is in His arms, and her blessedness is so great, who could want her back? Dear Mrs. Cooper and her little one of two years, dear Miss Huston, and little Faith, all lie here together till the resurrection morning."

A fortnight later, her progress and that of the children was so far satisfactory that Dr. Parry saw no difficulty in our accompanying him to Shanghai, whither he had been called professionally. Accordingly, on Tuesday, September 11, we took farewell of the place that had been to us "none other than the house of God and the gate of heaven." No tenderer memories could circle round any spot on earth for us than those that centred in Hankow; as my dear one afterwards said to me, when recalling the blessings with which God blessed us there, "I can never think of it in any other light than that of home. For there He gave us our little Faith; and there, too, has He not given us 'a possession of a burying place'?"

We travelled to Shanghai in the greatest comfort, a first class passage having been secured for us by the loving self-denial of two dear fellow-workers in Shan-si, Mr. and Mrs. Dugald Lawson of Yu-wu, who (with others) were on the quay to greet us on our arrival the following Friday morning. A short drive brought us to the China Inland Mission Home, where a most affectionate welcome awaited us from Mr. and Mrs. Hoste, Mr. Stevenson, Bishop Cassels, Mr. Alexander Grant, Mr. Montagu Beauchamp, the Rev. F. A. Steven, and many other beloved and honoured friends.

Shanghai at this time was full of missionaries of every denomination, gathered from every part of China, large numbers of whom, unknown to us in the flesh, took the opportunity of expressing a sympathy as generous as it was practical. Gifts of clothing and money came in freely, until our need was more than supplied. But above all, prayer was made by them without ceasing for our restoration. My dear wife's case excited peculiar interest and called forth much intercession, special meetings being convened, as the graver symptoms developed, to plead with God in her behalf.

For the first few days, her progress was well maintained, and she was allowed to see the children and a few of her more intimate friends. On September 19, however, a serious relapse took place. Peritonitis set in, and, on the 22nd, the conviction was borne in upon me while reading the evening portion in "Daily Light" that she would not be given back to me.

Through five more weeks of suffering, she continued to bear witness to the sufficient grace of God, in a most calm and gentle patience that spoke Christ to those about her. Two texts were ever before her eyes one, on the wall, "Certainly I will be with thee;" the other, pinned to the screen beside her, "In Whom we have redemption, through His blood." Upon these "true sayings of God" her soul was stayed, and by them strengthened to endure, in the weariness of utter weakness, the sharpness of protracted pain, or the onslaught of the more dreadful and more dreaded Tempter.

The living power of the Word of God over her, to revive, refresh and subdue, was remarkable. There was always an instantaneous response to it, as to the Voice of "Him that speaketh from heaven." On one occasion of delirious distress, the single word, whispered in her ear, "They overcame by the blood of the Lamb," recovered her to instant peace and joy.

On another, when she was casting about for the reason why God withheld healing from her after so much importunate prayer, her soul found immediate rest and comfort in the answer, "It is written that the God of hope will 'fill us with all joy and peace, not in understanding, but 'in believing'" (Rom. xv. 13).

As it had been a peculiar refreshment to her to receive the visits of her beloved sisters of "The Christians' Mission," Ningpo, so was it a peculiar trial when those visits were withdrawn. But the Divine wisdom and love were never questioned. Her faith only made it the occasion for a fresh subjecting of her own desires to the ruling of the Spirit, and her soul for a more realized hanging upon God. Tenderly her Shepherd fed her; for He was with her; His rod and His staff they comforted her. She spoke but little, lying for the most part in the silence of enduring weakness; but when she did, it was only to evidence the grace of God that was keeping her mind stayed on Him, and in glad submission to His will, whether for life or death. The hope that she would be raised up in answer to prayer, to testify to the delivering mercy of God, was strong in her; yet as the knowledge was borne in that it was by death rather than life that she was now to glorify Him, she yielded herself into His hand unreservedly, in the prayer, "Let Thy will, Father, be done perfectly in me, that Thy Name may be glorified." From that time, she ceased to pray the definite request, as aforetime, that she might live and not die." I have no prayer given me," she would say, "except that all His will may be done in me."

To the prayerful attention and assiduous devotion of her doctor (Dr. F. Judd) and also of her nurses (Mrs. F. A. Steven, Miss Batty, Miss Lucy C. Smith, and Miss Carmichael) the prolongation of her life was undoubtedly due. Their loving sympathy and tender solicitude touched her deeply, and frequently called forth the fervent gratitude of her heart in thanksgiving to God.

As she was able to bear it, I would read and pray with her, when her soul would magnify the Lord and her spirit rejoice in God her Saviour. Not infrequently she would offer prayer herself — prayer that brought one sensibly into the Holiest of all, and before the very Face of God. It was a source of distress to her when, through excessive weakness, the mind was no longer able to fix itself definitely upon the things of God, or the memory to retain the Word of God. Her rest in Christ was, however, deep and unbroken in spite of it. Ill her own words: "It is a trial deeper than I can express to find that I cannot remember any pass- ages of Scripture, that I cannot think, that at times I cannot even pray. I only know this, that I have been redeemed with the precious blood of Christ, — that is all." To which I replied, "Yes, darling, that is all, and all is in that. It is everything, and it is enough. He needs no more, neither do you." And the answering look of satisfaction testified that it was indeed enough.

The last day (October 24) was marked by much spiritual conflict. At intervals she would exclaim, "Is not the Lord of life standing in the midst?" "Help, help! O Lord, help me!" "Where is it written, 'I will uphold thee with the right hand of

My righteousness?'" "Pray, pray, pray!" Then the words
would come with earnest emphasis;

Peace, perfect peace, in this dark world of sin!
The blood of Jesus whispers peace within.

and then, with a note of triumph, the hymn-refrain :

Glory, glory to the Lamb
Who was slain on Mount Calvary!
Hallelujah! Hallelujah! Hallelujah! Amen.

Towards evening, she drew me down to give me what
were evidently meant to be her last messages; but I was only
able to catch clearly so much as this:

"I want all to know He has given me perfect peace, and has
shown me how fully His grace is sufficient."

For some time after that, she lay in apparent unconsciousness, when, as I repeated the hymn:

Jesus, Lover of my soul!

she suddenly took it up in a strong clear voice, at the
words:

Leave, ah! leave me not alone,
Still support and comfort me.

At 10 p.m. I read the evening portion in "Daily Light " and prayed with her, as usual. She herself followed on in a most fervent and beautiful prayer; after which she begged me, with her customary thoughtfulness, to retire to the rest so needful to me. There was nothing specially to arouse apprehension; and to spare her anxiety on my account, I consented.

About 3.45 a.m. (October 25) I was roused by Nurse Carmichael and told to come instantly. Dear Hedley beside me was already awake, and singing quietly to himself; and the burden of his song was this:

O that will be joyful,
When we meet to part no more.

My beloved was lying in apparent unconsciousness, her left hand under her cheek in the accustomed attitude of sleep, and evidently free from pain. Taking her right hand, I gently breathed a few comfortable scriptures into her ear; but she gave no sign that she had heard. So, seeing that the moments were but few now, I knelt to commend her spirit into the hand of the Lord Jesus; and as I ceased, with no other movement than of one deeper breath, at 4 a.m. she was "with Christ." The last verse she heard consciously and followed fervently in our reading six hours before, was this:

"O God, Thou art my God; early will I seek Thee;
my soul thirsteth for Thee, my flesh longeth for Thee
in a dry and thirsty land where no water is."

And over all the unspeakable sorrow was the heavenly consolation that the deepest longings of her soul were satisfied now; for God Himself was with her, her God, and had wiped away all tears from her eyes.

***

The next day, October 26, I laid her to rest in theOld Cemetery. The precious dust was committed to the grave by our dear friend Bishop Cassels, after a most solemn preliminary service in the Hall of the China Inland Mission, where he spoke to a large audience from the words, "Father, the hour is come."

Affectionate tributes were also paid to her memory by Mr. Dugald Lawson, who had been closely connected with us in our station work, and by Doctors Parry and Judd, to whose devoted services she owed so much. At the Cemetery itself was assembled the largest company (it was said) that had ever gathered there, the deep sympathy felt making itself apparent in the visible emotion of many. The sun went down as the coffin was lowered, and, amid the fast falling shadows, the hymn was raised the very one with which she had been wont to sing her own children to sleep:

Sun of my soul, Thou Saviour dear!
It is not night if Thou be near.

The darkness that hung about the grave of my be- loved Flora, as I left her sleeping there, was but the darkness of an hour; "for yet a little while how little! how little! and He that shall come will come, and will not tarry." The knowledge of her present felicity "with Him," "in Whose Presence is fulness of joy," and the certainty of "that blessed hope" in the near future of together being "forever with the Lord," brought the light of the resurrection glory of God in Christ into the place of the darkness of death, and turned my sorrow into joy, through Him that loved us.

My precious wife had not lived her short life of eight and twenty years in vain. Of none could it be said more truly than of her that she "overcame by the blood of the Lamb and by the word of her testimony, and she loved not her life unto the death." Whether she lived, she lived unto the Lord; and whether she died, she died unto the Lord: and to her was given the signal honour of being counted worthy of a place among the martyrs of Jesus, as the last of the "noble army" of 1900 to pass from the cross to the crown.

"What shall we then say to these things?" Let the following words suffice for answer, from the last letter but one my wife was permitted to write;

C.I.M., Hankow, Sept. 10, 1900.
My own darling Father, Mother, and Sister,

I feel to-day I can send you a little word. It seems difficult to write, not only because of bodily weakness, but also there is so much, and words can never express all that is in one's heart. It is truly wonderful that we are here to-day, the living to praise God. I am sure your hearts with ours are bowed in deep praise and gratitude to God for His marvellous loving kindnesses to us so unworthy, in answer to the much prayer of His children. So few as yet have escaped from that dark dark Province [of Shan-si]; and again and again the question comes to me, why are we here in safety and comfort, and many are still suffering and have died there? And then, too, darling parents, His wonderful love to us on the road, keeping us from being beaten or stoned, and we look at our loved friends from Lu-ch'eng and P'ing-iao beaten, stoned; and dear Miss Rice and Miss Huston more than this. I cannot write of it now, and *it is better to dwell on the glory side.* Their blessedness is great, "of whom the world was not worthy "; and I love to think of my sweet baby Faith with these His honoured servants and dear Mrs. Cooper. . . . *My heart is daily praising God for the blessed experience He has given us,"partakers of the sufferings of Christ";* destitute and forsaken it seemed almost as if by God; and yet He proved to our fainting hearts that He was for us. Oh, it is all praise. . . . The suffering on the road is forgotten now. It seemed as if I must die. I think a few days more would have been enough . . . The Lord will guide about our home-going, and prepare us and you for His will. We cannot say yet what the Mission will decide, and then *my heart longs to return to Lu-an as soon as possible.* Yet we will wait the Lord's decision. Fondest love, my darling parents and Katie, from

Your very loving
FLORA

What then did she say to these things?

(1) "It is better to dwell on the glory side."

(2) "My heart is daily praising God for the blessed experience He has given us. Oh, it is all praise."

(3) "My heart longs to return to Lu-an as soon as possible."

Who would not wish to possess the secret of the Lord as this devoted servant of Jesus Christ possessed it?

— (1) the power that lifts the soul above all suffering and death to "the glory side," "only seeing glory when face to face with death";

— (2) the grace that gives, under peculiar trial, "the garment of praise for the spirit of heaviness"; and

— (3) the love that is ready only and always "to bless them that curse us, to do good to them that hate us, and to pray for them which despitefully use us and persecute us," only and always to "spend and to be spent "for the Son of God, "Who loved me and gave Himself for me."

Dear reader, suffer one word as I bid you farewell. Do you possess this secret? It may be yours even as it was hers; for "He died for all that they which live should not henceforth live unto themselves but unto Him which died for them and rose again." Delivered by His death from my own self-life, I am set free to live" the life that is life indeed"; for then "Christ liveth in me," and from my heart I rejoice to Say, "Henceforth to me to live is Christ. And Thou art worthy; for Thou wast slain and hast redeemed me to God by Thy blood."

Questions to Consider

1. After losing her newly born daughter, Mrs. Glover said, "My sorrow in her loss is eclipsed by the joy that my lamb is beyond all suffering now in her Saviour's bosom." How do you view death?

2. As you consider this story, would you be willing to suffer if it meant God was glorified?

The grave of Mrs. Flora Glover in Shanghai

COVENANT WITH GOD.

I TAKE

God the Father to be my God (1 Thess. i. 9).
Jesus Christ to be my Saviour (Acts v. 31).
The Holy Ghost to be my Sanctifier
(1 Pet. i. 2).
The Word of God to be my Rule
(2 Tim. iii. 16, 17).
The People of God to be my People (Ruth i. 16)

I GIVE

Myself—all I am, and all I have—to the Lord
(Rom. xiv. 7, 8).
And I do this **Deliberately** (Josh. xxi. 15).
Sincerely (2 Cor. i. 12).
Freely (Psalm cx. 3).
And For Ever (Rom. viii. 35—39).

Here I give my all to Thee,
Talents, time, and earthly store;
Soul and body—Thine to be,
ONLY THINE, FOR EVERMORE.

Name. *Flora C. Kelly*

Address *11 Harold Terrace, Dover.*

Prayer. *Dec. 28. 91.*

"Oh my Father, I dedicate myself afresh to Thee.
I desire to place myself and to-day's undertakings in
Thy hand, enable me to suffer hardships with Thee as
a good soldier, and to remember that "on service no
soldier entangleth himself in the affairs of this life that
he may please Him who hath enrolled him as a soldier."
In my daily work and occupation make me to serve in
the Spirit, bring my inclinations and desires under His
control and renewal, enable me to give up all that is
wrong and to offer up to Thy use and service my spirit,
soul and body. Sanctify me wholly and preserve me
blameless. Give me an increasing spirit of prayer, that
all may be begun, continued and ended in Thee.—For
Jesus Christ's sake. Amen.

TAKEN FROM MRS. GLOVER'S BIBLE, IN
HER SISTER'S POSSESSION.

One year later.
Hedley, Rev. A.E. Glover, Hope
holding a picture of her mother, Flora

REDUCED FACSIMILE OF MEMORIAL BRASS WHICH, BY THE PRIVATE SUBSCRIP-
TIONS OF FELLOW-WORKERS, IS BEING PLACED IN THE C.I.M. HEAD-
QUARTERS AT SHANGHAI IN MEMORY OF ALL THE C.I.M. MARTYRS.

END NOTES

Chapter 1 A Cloud Out of the Sea

From an address by Mr. Stevenson (C.I.M.) and the unveiling of the Memorial Tablet of the Martyrs of the China Inland Mission, Shanghai, Befruary 21st, 1902.

[2]"That so many parties, travelling under the conditions which have been imperfectly hinted at, should have passed through hundreds of miles of hostile territory, being seen by hundreds of thousands, and in the aggregate by millions, of enemies, many of whom were eager for their death, and yet have escaped to tell their story, is a moral miracle to be accounded for only by the recognition of the restraining hand of God." -- Dr. Arthur Smith (in *China in Convulsion, vol. ii. p. 619*).

[3] That this in itself a term of odium and reproach would possibly be questiond by some. The point was settled in my own mind during our flight. The distinction made between "iang ren" and "iang kuei-tai" was very marked; the latter being invariably employed by the Boxers in Shan-si, and the pro-Boxers in Ho-nan; the former invariably in friendly Hu-peh.

[4]"*In Deaths Oft*" by C.H.S. Green (Morgan & Scott).

[5] *China from Within.* By Stanley P. Smith, M.A., pp. 19 and 20.

[6] *Fire and Sword in Shan-si.* By Dr. E.H. Edwards, pp. 58 and 59.

Chapter 2 The Cloud Upon Our Horizon

Chapter 3 The Darkness Deepens

Chapter 4 The Breaking of the Storm

Chapter 5 Into the Valley of the Shadow

Chapter 6 Out of the Depths

(1) On July 1, the Deputy- Director of our mission, Mr. William Cooper, together with Mr. Bagnall, our District Superintendent, Mrs. Bagnall, and their little daughter Gladys, were beheaded just outside the South Gate of the city.

(2) As a matter of history, an edict went forth the next day, July 2, from Peking, ordering the expulsion of all foreigners and the persecution of Christians ; while four days previous (June 28) an order had been issued from the Throne to all Viceroys and Governors to support the Boxer Rising.

Chapter 7 Flee! Flee!

(1) One of the little band waiting to greet us on this occasion, Mr. Feng (the most devoted and consistent, perhaps, of them all, though stone deaf) died subsequently from injuries received at the hands of the Boxers.

(2) The Rev. A. R. Saunders, Mrs. Saiinders, and their four children, Jessie, George, Nellie and Isabel ; Miss Guthrie and Mr. A. Jennings.

Chapter 8 The Tenth Day of the Sixth Moon

(1) The "cash" of the Chinese currency is usually valued at the fortieth part of a penny. When, however, it is considered that 120 cash constitutes a good day's wage for an able-bodied labourer, it will be seen that a sum of 10,000 cash would represent to a Chinaman something nearer £10,of our money than £1.

Chapter 9 Condemned

Chapter 10 The Sorrows of Death

Chapter 11 The Great Conflict of Suffering

(1) In saying this, I am only extolling the grace of God, apart from which I should have known nothing but the spirit of resentment and revenge, as the incident of the seizure of my wife's wedding ring related above sufficiently shows.

Chapter 12 A Hairbreadth Escape

Chapter 13 In the Mount with God

Chapter 14 Arrest and Treachery

(1) An official passport, guaranteeing the traveller safe-conduct from one magistracy to another, until his destination is reach

Chapter 15 With the Rain Processionists

Chapter 16 A Night to Be Remembered

Chapter 17 Travelling to Execution

Chapter 18 Left to the Mob

Chapter 19 The Death-Plot of Lan-Chen-Cheo

(1)The literal translation of this is: —

Praise, praise the Lord Jesus,
Who gave His life for the world,
And Who rose again from the dead.
Praise be to Jesus, the Lord of grace! —

a translator's version of the familiar chorus

"Glory, glory to the Lamb,
Who was slain on Mount Calvaryl
Hallelujah! Hallelujah! Hallelujah! Amen."

(2) Isaiah xli. 10. Rotherham's translation of A.V. "Be not dismayed; for I am thy God."

Chapter 20 New Perils in Ho-Nan

(1) I learned subsequently at Shanghai from a fellow-worker in those parts that this particular town (the name of which I have forgotten) is notoriously antiforeign, and he expressed his amazement at the fact that we had, in the peculiar circumstances, come out alive.

Chapter 21 In Weariness and Painfullness

Chapter 22 From Prison to Prison

(1) See *A God of Deliverances*, by the Rev. A. R. Saunders (Morgan & Scott)

Chapter 23 Christ's Hospital

(1) "*A God of Deliverances*" by the Bev. A. R. Saunders (Morgan & Scott).

Chapter 24 From the Cross to the Crown

(1) See Martyred Missionaries of the China Inland Mission pp. 79, 80 (Morgan A Scott).

(2) In spite of her extraordinary sufferings, and in the full experimental knowledge of all that was involved. Miss Gates expressed the earnest wish, not only to return to the work to which she had consecrated her life, but also to be sent again to the very place where she had been so cruelly ill-treated. Accordingly, after a necessary furlough, she went back in the autumn of 1902 to her old station, Lu-an Fu in Shan-si Province. She is still labouring in the same Province (at Pa-k'eo T'ang-shan) for them that despitefully used her and persecuted her. I may add that the same is true of every one of the survivors of that terrible time. All (I believe, without exception) have returned to the field, until it would seem that I only am left, the medical verdict having, for the time being, gone against me, in the will of God.

(3) Sacred Songs and Solos, No. 598.

(4) Mr. Bruce was himself martyred two years later, together with his colleague i\lr. Lowis, at Ch'en Cheo, Hu-nan, August 15, 1902.

A Thousand Miles of Miracle in China by Rev. A. E. Glover
is in the public domain and is available for free download
from several sources.

This annotated version by Clint Morey includes
photographs and questions to consider
while reading the book.
It is hoped this would make it more useful
for small group studies.

If you found this book helpful please consider
giving it a review on Amazon.com.

Made in the USA
Columbia, SC
11 April 2021